KEEPERS OF THE SEA

KEEPERS OF THE SEA

A History of the Yachts and
Tenders of Trinity House

by

RICHARD WOODMAN

TERENCE DALTON LIMITED
LAVENHAM   .   SUFFOLK
1983

Published by
TERENCE DALTON LIMITED

ISBN 0 86138 018 5

Text photoset in 11/12 pt. Garamond

Printed in Great Britain at
The Lavenham Press Limited, Lavenham, Suffolk

Contents

For my father

Keep then the sea abought in specialle,
Which of England is the towne walle;
As though England were lykened to a cite
And the walle enviroun were the sea.
Keep then the sea that is the walle of England,
And then is England kepte by Goddes hande.
Anon, fifteenth century.

Author's Acknowledgements

IT would be cavalier of me not to apologise to the many colleagues and ship-mates whose exploits do not occur in the closing chapters of this book. Space simply did not permit a complete record of these and I hope I am forgiven.

My especial thanks are due to Captain Sir Miles Wingate and the Board of Trinity House for their permission to delve in the Corporation's archives and reproduce a number of their paintings. Gratitude must also go to members of the Trinity House staff, George Stamp for his hospitality and help, Miss F. M. Gillespie, Archivist, Eric Greenhalf for his photography and Nick Cutmore and Paul Ridgway for their unfailing confidence in the project. To the many people with whom I have corresponded or whom I have interviewed go my thanks. They are too numerous to mention in full and I hope they will forgive the omission. However Captains Goodman, Thompson, Catesby, Meyrick, Burnell, Tarrant and Dove, Mr W. R. Foley, former Surveyor to the Corporation and ex-Chief Engineer of *Patricia*, and the late "Tim" Kendall-Carpenter have proved invaluable sources of recollection and information. A special word of thanks must go to Archie Smith, sole survivor of *Argus*, who put up with my painful probing with stoic patience, and to Neil Hollander of Adventure Film Productions. Finally my wife should not be forgotten, for she has borne the greatest burden of all.

The following publishers receive grateful acknowledgement for permission to reproduce quotations from their works: The Oxford University Press, The Illustrated London News, Thomas Nelson and Son, Longmans Green and Son, Lloyds List. My thanks also go to the Cruising Association.

Foreword

by

Captain Sir Miles Wingate, K.C.V.O., Deputy Master of Trinity House

THROUGHOUT the history of Trinity House, the lighthouse tenders have played a vital role in the Service both in wartime and in peace, from the early days of Trinity Yachts to the present-day sophisticated vessels. Whilst much has been written about the Trinity House Service in general, the story of the lighthouse tenders has been somewhat neglected. Therefore the appearance of this book is most welcome.

Commander Woodman, a serving Trinity House Deck Officer, has researched his subject well and has displayed remarkable erudition to this quite considerable subject; bringing authenticity and first-hand experience to the work.

I found the account and anecdotes of the Service in the latter part of the book covering the post-war years of particular interest.

Introduction

THE history of lighthouse tenders is naturally bound up with that of lighthouses themselves, and the pedigree of these strange structures dates back to antiquity. The pharos of Alexandria was one of the wonders of the ancient world. So too was the Colossus of Rhodes, a giant whose feet bestrode the entrance to Rhodes harbour and in whose hand an enormous torch bore a cresset to guide mariners.

At the mouth of the Tiber the Roman port of Ostia boasted a pharos, and in the shadow of the eagles of the Caesars fire towers were constructed at several places in the Empire. Indeed the Romans may take credit for founding what is recognised as the oldest working lighthouse, that at La Corunna in northern Spain, built in the second century A.D.

The historian Strabo mentions another Spanish lighthouse at Caepio as "Completely surrounded by water on all sides." This, it would appear, is the first mention of an isolated tower. Most of the ancient pharoses were land-based and accessible to men with pack animals or cartloads of wood. Strabo's lighthouse excepted, therefore, the logistical problems posed in supplying offshore structures are, by comparison with the towers themselves, of recent origin.

Vessels employed in the service of replenishing and maintaining lighthouses, lightvessels and buoys are relatively obscure ships, attending to their duties without fuss or publicity. Indeed even the professional mariner may be uncertain of their existence and the public as a whole has been more readily acquainted with the parvenu oil rig tender than with the vessels of the lighthouse services. Yet the material wealth of Great Britain and Eire is largely based upon sea transport which in turn is, even in this electronic age, still dependent upon lighthouses, buoys and beacons as much as on the local knowledge of pilots.

To the steady stream of mercantile trade navigating the waters of the Narrow Seas must be added the thousands of European yachtsmen and women, most of whom benefit from these services at no cost to themselves.

For a great maritime nation to be ignorant of the small but essential part played by these vessels seemed a matter for correction. For the role played by these ships at moments of national crisis and in the day-to-day affairs of trade is vital. They, and the men who manned them, deserve a better memorial than oblivion and it is with this in mind that I have endeavoured to show their contribution to our past and present.

All opinions, unless otherwise stated, are my own, and reflect no policy of the Corporation of Trinity House.

Richard Woodman
Harwich, 1982

CHAPTER ONE

Trinity House and the Origins of Lighthouses

"Why the name of Trinity House is given to these societies of
mariners hath been wondered at by many and indeed the name
hath given occasion to sundry profane jests in common discourse
and even in Parliament."

Samuel Pepys

THE first builders of lighthouses in Britain were the Romans. The idea of
kindling beacon fires on headlands or high places is undoubtedly much
older, but the interest of the Romans in our islands necessitated them undertaking the navigation of the unpredictable Oceanus Germanicus and for this
they required certain aids. Despite the well-known descent of Julius Caesar upon
the coast of Kent in 55 B.C., it was actually 43 A.D. before Claudius annexed
Britain to the Empire. The importance of communications, well understood by
the Roman military authorities, soon resulted in the building of fire towers at
Boulogne and Dover, where the shortest sea crossing was to be found.

There is also evidence that a tower was constructed at West Mersea in Essex
to lead the imperial galleys to Camulodunum, or Colchester, once the largest
Roman city in Britain. Whether or not the pharos was destroyed by Boudica
and her warriors is uncertain, but after the suppression of the Iceni revolt
Colchester never recovered its supremacy in the province.

The destruction of Romano-British civilisation in the fifth and sixth
centuries draws a veil over such matters, but the curious may observe what
remains of the Roman pharos at Dover, within the ramparts of the castle.

The administrative authorities for lighthouses and buoyage in the United
Kingdom and Eire are today three in number. Of these Trinity House is the
senior. The other two are the Commissioners for Irish Lights based at Dublin
and the Commissioners for Northern Lighthouses based at Edinburgh. Trinity
House provides and maintains the majority of lighthouses, buoys, beacons and
lightvessels on the English and Welsh coasts, the Northern Lights those of
Scotland and the Isle of Man, and the Irish Lights are responsible for the whole
geographical coast of Ireland.

Certain ports maintain their own navigational aids within their limits but,
with the exception of naval ports, they are inspected regularly by officials of
Trinity House who retain the statutory responsibility to Parliament for securing
the maintenance in good order of all aids to navigation in the United Kingdom.

The Trinity House Yacht approaching the River
Humber for an inspection of the Spurn
Lighthouse, 17th April, 1777. This is a detail of a
painting by Francis Holman.   *Trinity House*

In addition to being the senior of the three principal authorities, Trinity House is the most ancient, having been incorporated by Royal Charter by Henry VIII in 1514. However it claims an older lineage and Trinity Houses were known to have existed in other ports, principally Leith, Newcastle-upon-Tyne and Kingston-upon-Hull. Possessing an older charter than the London establishment, the Hull Trinity House still exists, some of its board sitting on the licensing authority for Humber Pilots, and administering charitable funds. That at Newcastle, tucked away in a warren of chares* off the Town Quay, continues to maintain a handful of buoys on the Northumbrian coast.

These curiously named "Trinity" Houses appear to have been conceived originally as guilds for the protection of shipping in hazardous waters. They developed in influence with the growth of trade and the technical improvements in navigational aids. In common with all medieval institutions, they had a strong religious bias which remains to this day. As will be seen, their prime motive in a lawless age seems to have been one dedicated to the protection of property and trade rather than a philanthropic desire to erect lighthouses and seamarks. Although this may have been laudable in the sixteenth century, it brought a certain amount of opprobrium on the heads of the Elder Brethren during the eighteenth and early nineteenth centuries. The religious connections probably stem from two sources. The deep medieval involvement with the Church resulted in all guilds seeking a degree of ecclesiastical protection, and in addition the great monastic houses frequently maintained lights and, if poets are to be believed, buoys. The legend of the Inchcape rock and the Abbot of Aberbrothock is of uncertain origin, but hermits and anchorites did maintain rudimentary lights.

References exist to lighthouses at Winchelsea in 1261, on the Ecrehou reef in the Channel Islands in 1309, at St Catherine's (Isle of Wight) in 1314 and at Spurn Head in 1427. A chapel still stands at Ilfracombe from which, until recent times, a light was shown for local boats.

It has been suggested that these religio-maritime houses were founded in the reign of King Alfred, in which case Trinity House can claim coeval descent with the Royal Navy. But, as with the Royal Navy, there is little real substance in this. One is on surer ground when claiming descent from the Church in the semi-secular person of Stephen Langton, Archbishop of Canterbury and Chancellor of England. The see of Canterbury had acquired the attainted Harold Godwinson's dubious rights over areas of the Kent coast, derived some revenues from shipping and sought to curb the pillage of wrecks.

Royal interest in nautical matters was further aroused in 1120 when the heir to Henry I, Prince William, was drowned in the loss of the White Ship. The vessel was crossing to England from Normandy in calm seas, contrary to the interpretations of Victorian artists, when, during the night, through an excess of wine and the neglect of her pilot, she struck a rock and sank. This may have led

---

* narrow lanes, a name peculiar to Newcastle.

Richard I to incorporate the maritime Laws of Oleron, from his Dukedom of Aquitaine, into the laws of England. They conferred *carte-blanche* on the master of any ship to summarily behead a pilot who failed in his duty!

However, neither the development of naval architecture nor the political atmosphere of the country permitted the establishment of any kind of regular maritime body for several centuries. It was only after the Tudor dynasty had brought a measure of stability to a united England and Wales unknown since the *Pax Romana* that the country began her climb to maritime supremacy. Contemporaneously ship design had improved so that trans-oceanic voyages were possible and war at sea had changed from the concept of sea-going castles with the advent of cannon and the broadside.

By the reign of Henry VIII the king's majesty was concerned with the defence of a united realm. There was no standing navy at this time, seaports, especially the Cinque Ports, providing ships in time of national emergency. By the end of his reign, however, Henry had created a Royal Navy of some fifty ships and in 1514 he regularised the affairs of Trinity House by incorporation.

Two years prior to the granting of the charter the guild of Trinity House had been well enough established to have been thoroughly reorganised by the then master, Thomas Spert. And in the person of Spert we have an idea of the close links that then existed between Trinity House and the King's navy, for he was a courtier and in turn master of the Royal ships *Mary Rose* and later the magnificent *Henri Grace Á Dieu*. To say he was master is not to claim for him the chief command, which would have been the prerogative of a favoured nobleman. Spert was in fact the ''Sailing Master'', or chief navigator, and had to man, organise, load and stow the ship and handle it tactically under the strategic direction of the gentlemen-at-arms. He was, to paraphrase Drake, a ''mariner'' rather than a ''gentleman'', although he attained nobility by knighthood in 1529. He died in 1541 and lies buried in St Dunstan's, Stepney.

The Henrician charter was the result of several petitions to the king. These stated that a number of young men ''unwilling to take the labour and adventure of learning the shipmen's craft on the high seas'' were engaged in unskilful pilotage on the Thames. It was also emphasised that there were dangers in allowing foreigners, particularly ''Scots, Flemings and Frenchmen'', to learn ''the secrets of the King's streams.''

On 20th May, 1514, the charter was granted ''to our trewe and faithfull subjects, shipmen and mariners of this our Realm of England'' to ''begyn of new and erecte and establish a Guild or Brotherhood of themselves or other persons *as well men as women*, (author's italics) whatsoever they be . . . ''

Management was vested in the hands of a Master, four Wardens, and eight Assistants entitled ''The Master, Wardens and Assistants of the Guild or Fraternity of the most glorious and blessed Trinity and St Clement in the parish church of Deptford Strond in the county of Kent.''

The original charter was destroyed by fire, but that of James I (1604) raised the number of Assistants to 31 and named them "Elder Brethren". Over the centuries this number has been reduced to ten salaried and working Board members, with a number of notable honorary Brethren such as the late Earl Mountbatten of Burma and Sir Winston Churchill.

In the Jacobean charter there is provision for other members of the guild to be called "Younger Brethren". These remain, about 300 of them being masters in the Merchant Navy or officers in the Royal Navy. They are permitted certain voting rights and Board members are elected from their numbers.

Although it was found necessary for certain officers of the Ballast Department to be made Younger Brethren in the 18th century, the inclusion of members of the Lighthouse Service is a recent occurrence.

The transactions of the Corporation in these early days are vague. It seems the business of conducting or piloting ships, or at least examining those who did so, was early undertaken. From Spert's time until their eventual disappearance in 1867 Trinity House examined and passed the Sailing Masters and Mates who were the Royal Navy's navigating branch. This involvement with the embryonic navy is worthy of digression.

In 1585 Thomas Spert's successor, William Borough, wrote to Lord Henry Seymour, commanding the Cinque Port ships, that a fleet of 30 or 40 good ships would be sent to assist him from Flushing. A chart of the Thames and Medway was included. Whether this fleet was raised at Trinity House's expense is not clear.

Three years later, with the descent of the Spanish Armada imminent, Robert Salmon, then master, wrote to Lord Burghley that there were "30 sail of merchant ships which might be fitted within four days to join the Lord Admiral." Again it is not known whether the Brethren acted as agents or actually fitted the vessels for war, but the early involvement of the Corporation in belligerent operations is interesting and was to persist up to our own times.

Salmon was himself ordered to sea during the Armada scare. Lord Henry Seymour commanded the inshore squadron off the Flemish coast, watching the Duke of Parma's army. Seymour instructed Salmon to proceed with his galley to guard the mouth of the Thames.

Galley was a generic term and indicates a substantial craft employed on an important service, for Salmon's task must have been to guard Seymour's communications and prevent him being cut off on a lee shore. As Salmon proceeded on this duty in his official capacity, whether or not his craft was owned or chartered by the Corporation is irrelevant; it is the first recorded vessel managed by Trinity House.

The long struggle with Spain left England with a clear vision of maritime possibility and her fiery sons were not slow to appreciate their opportunities. The "Arte and Mysterie" of navigation was a science that developed steadily until it stumbled on the longitude problem. This expansion in nautical activity soon revealed the need for the establishing of seamarks, and with maritime guilds already in existence a committee of management was to hand.

In 1566 an Act of Elizabeth had empowered Trinity House to erect seamarks at the expense of the Elder Brethren. By the close of Queen Bess's reign demand was exceeding supply and the main stumbling block was finance. Curiously, in solving this problem the Crown unwittingly enriched the Corporation well beyond the expectation of either party. No one in the late 16th century could forsee the rise in London's trade two hundred years later, but on 11th June, 1594, Lord Howard of Effingham, Lord High Admiral, surrendered his perquisites of ballastage to the Corporation. Having been transferred to Trinity House, this monopoly continued until 1893 when steam ships, iron hulls and water ballast had reduced it to an uneconomic minimum and it was discontinued.

The monies derived from this transaction were urgently needed. On 5th January, 1606, 31st May, 1607, and 31st May, 1609, Orders in Council were directed to the Corporation to erect lighthouses in the neighbourhood of Lowestoft and Caister. Here on the Caister, Scroby and Holm Sands there was annually great loss of life.

Additional finance was raised for the maintenance of these seamarks by levying a tax of 12d per 100 tons on all ships sailing from the ports of Newcastle, Yarmouth, Hull, Boston and Lynn. These sums were to be collected by the "customers", that is the custom house officers, and to be sent to Trinity House to "support the buoys and beacons between Leistoff and Winterton." Three years later in 1609 a further injunction was despatched to Newcastle to levy 4d per passage on all colliers voyaging to London. Thus was established the principal of Light Dues, in which the lighthouse authority raises its own revenue at source, and the practice continues today, customs officials deducting these monies from the port dues paid by all ships using British ports.

The allusion to buoys indicates that they were in use at this time, although present records show the earliest stations as being established some eighty years later. However, there is no reason to doubt the assertion. More frustrating is the total lack of information regarding their servicing, but it is safe to assume it was undertaken locally in the same manner as the later introduction of lightvessels.

Interestingly enough, Trinity House did not rush to establish seamarks. Early proposals to erect lights on the Goodwins were rejected by the Brethren not on the grounds of impossibility but for the reason that it would result in mariners neglecting to take pilots.

No less a person than Samuel Pepys supported such a narrow view. Usually an ardent advocate of improvements, Pepys was both Secretary to the Admiralty Commissioners and Master of Trinity House. In a memorandum to James, Duke of York (afterwards James II), he advised against the erection of lighthouses as they were "a burden upon trade". It was to be an oft-repeated argument and one is tempted to wonder if Pepys had ulterior motives. Since he often eulogises the cuisine at Trinity House one is apt to be left with the impression that the Brethren were more preoccupied with gastronomic activities than they should have been, but to be fair, this is not the case. The Elder Brethren provided the government with a ready-made body of nautical consultants and, even before the reforms of Pepys, had been asked for advice on a number of matters. They had recommended the siting amidships of cookrooms in H.M. ships (1618) and in 1621 were asked by the Navy Commissioners for a suitable location for a boom across the Medway. This indicates their involvement with marine

Lowestoft Highlight, erected during the Mastership of Samuel Pepys, as it appeared about 1870.
R. Malster

surveying, for which they probably had their own pinnace. In the same year they tried to compel the East India Company to pay their seaman a proper rate and in 1625 recommended an increase for naval ratings which, with little improvement, was to stand until 1797. Two years later they were asked for their observations as to the correct freeboard for the lowest tier of guns in a three-decked warship. At the same time they were also surveying all ships based on the Thames as to suitability for naval service. Finally in 1632 they were consulted on the naval requirements for a proposed expedition against the Algerine corsairs.

The Corporation's finances were now very secure, for in 1631 they subscribed £1,300 for an attempt to discover the North West Passage and in 1635 were promoting the conservation of oak trees for shipbuilding.

Another facet of their work which regrettably still exists is first recorded in 1636 when the Brethren, or their agents, actively salvaged wrecks. This ancient and prescriptive right probably devolved from the responsibilities or perquisites of the Lord High Admiral. It remains to this day; any total wreck becomes the property of the controlling lighthouse authority for the purpose of marking or dispersing as a danger to navigation.

But the shadow of civil war was falling over the country, and it is often asserted that Trinity House was dissolved by Parliament during the Common-wealth and Protectorate. An Act to this effect was passed in 1647, and with its strong court connections and those with the Royal Dockyard at Deptford (and presumably the touchy subject of Ship Money), this is scarcely surprising. However, the implementation of the Act can only have been partial, for in 1650 the House "provided" transports for Cromwell's Dunbar campaign. Again in 1652 we learn of the Lord Protector himself going to Trinity House to ask advice as to a suitable man to command the State Ship *Resolution*. In the same year Trinity House provided fire ships to the Navy Commissioners and carried out surveys of rope cables.

The return of a Stuart Prince to the English throne saw the beginning of the modern lighthouse service. Paradoxically it saw also the introduction of a practice that retarded the growth of that service. This was the patent system and the granting to private persons of the right to erect lighthouses and collect dues for personal profit.

Charles II was hard put to oblige his friends, and the penniless monarch had obligations to many local adherents who had squandered their fortunes in his service. He shrewdly exploited several expedients for discharging these debts, one of which was to grant patents to selected individuals for the building of lighthouses. The owner had the right to levy dues on passing ships, if he could, and, although it seems incredible, many fortunes were thus made.

An eager petitioner presented his claim to the King, who consulted Trinity House on the necessity or advisability of establishing a seamark at the specified point. If the Corporation considered it advantageous a patent was issued. This was often to Trinity House itself, who then opened negotiations with the pet-titioner as lessee. The patentee or lessee then built the light tower and, paying an annual rent for the term of the lease (usually over a century) to Trinity House, surrendered the building and his own rights to the Corporation on its expiry.

This system persisted until 1836 when, under an important Act of Parliament, all remaining leases were bought out. By this time trade had increased to such an extent as to render it almost impossible to collect the dues, whilst the standard of service given by many of these lights was deplorable. Nevertheless enormous sums were made, as will be seen, and so eager were people to profit by this means that we find Lord Grenville writing in his diary, "to watch the king when he is in good temper to ask of him a lighthouse."

In Scotland the Isle of May light dates from a patent of 1636, though it was the only private light ever tolerated by Scots merchants, and in 1659 Trinity House recommended lights be established at Dublin, Wexford, Waterford and Youghal. Meanwhile the corporation built its own lighthouses under Crown patents at Winterton (Norfolk) in 1678, in the Scillies at St Agnes in 1680, and in 1694 on the Eddystone by sub-contracting Henry Winstanley to carry out the actual works.

The story of the infamous Eddystone is outlined in Chapter Four. It is one of triumph and tragedy, of endeavour and disappointment, for the Eddystone was to be the first true rock light tower, standing 13 miles south of Plymouth and exposed to the full fury of the Atlantic Ocean.

No fewer than five structures have been erected on this rock over a period of two centuries, four of them before steam power assisted either the transport of materials or their working. The fourth, Smeaton's tower, was only demolished because the rock was being undermined and the upper three-quarters stands today on Plymouth Hoe.

We are fortunate in having a vivid description of this lighthouse and its servicing from the pen of the only other man to have engineered the building of a rock tower in the age of sail. Before commencing work on the Bell Rock Robert Stevenson visited the Eddystone and saw how the station was tended. By this time Trinity House had acquired the lease and the details of the sailing tender are given in Chapter Four.

The interesting point about these early lighthouses is that whatever sea-going vessels the Corporation may have owned earlier, they possessed nothing suitable in which to visit the Scilly Isles during the building of St Agnes. In 1679 and 1680 we find "a royal ship being told off to convey the Trinity Brethren thither (to Scilly) and to await their pleasure".

At the same period Pepys admits the Corporation owned no river barges for ceremonial progresses, since he had to make "the usual" arrangements with the Admiralty for the loan of a naval barge. Since at about this time the Brethren ceased to exert any authority in the Royal Dockyard at Deptford, as well as losing their direction of ordnance and powder for the King's ships, it seems possible that they no longer owned a barge. This is a curiosity since one authority, Golding, claims they had one at an earlier period and Trinity House continued to license Thames Watermen until displaced by the Thames Conservancy Act of 1864.

Pepys's involvement with the navy and Trinity House demonstrates the close relationship of the two organisations. That it was sometimes strained will be seen, but it is one that persists. In her Silver Jubilee Review of the Royal Navy in 1977 Queen Elizabeth II, embarked in HMY *Britannia*, was preceeded by the Trinity House Vessel *Patricia*, in which the Deputy Master and Elder Brethren were embarked.

Pepys himself was elected Master of the Corporation in 1676 and therefore held its highest office. It is often asserted he was no seaman, let alone a captain. Curiously enough this is not so. That the diarist "commanded" the *Jerzy* is recorded in the Diary on 13th March, 1669:

"But that which put me in good humour, both at noon and night is the fancy that I am this day made a Captain in one of the King's ships, Mr Wren having this day sent me the Duke of York's commission to be captain of the *Jerzy* in order to my being of a court-martial for examining the loss of the *Defiance* and other things; which do give me occasion of much mirth, and may be of some use to me, at least I shall get a little money by it for the time I have it; it being designed that I must really be a captain to be able to sit in this court."

This sort of thing was by no means unusual at the time, although Acts of the sterner William III in 1696 stated that no person should be an Elder Brother that had not been a seaman, waterman, fisherman, lighterman, bargeman or keelman. The emphasis on what today would be a coasting qualification is interesting and demonstrates the royal insistence on the Brethren possessing a genuine knowledge of the waters around Britain.

During the 18th century Trinity House granted patents for a number of lights, of which three are particularly interesting. In 1723 the Caskets were lit by three towers and in 1751 the Lizard by two. The reason for this multiplicity of towers is simple. These were the days of coal fires, open grates or chauffers, which must have been dreadful things to look after. The only way to differentiate between one light and another was to burn a varying number of fires. When one considers the hit and miss navigation of the period, when the painstaking accuracy of a James Cook was the exception rather than the rule, it was not unusual for mariners entering the Soundings to wonder which flickering fire they were looking at as they ran into the Channel.

Thirdly a patent was issued in 1737 for the establishment of a lighthouse on Flatholm, an island in the Bristol Channel. Flatholm and Caskets were offshore stations and required the services of a tender. Whilst privately owned these were the responsibility of the lessee, and their tenders were probably local fishing boats, Caskets being serviced from Alderney, Flatholm from Cardiff.

Although leased lighthouses, they were built under some degree of supervision by Trinity House. At the Lizard there was a cunning feature in the design that can only have stemmed from a desire to increase efficiency. The senior keeper, or "overlooker", had his cottage between the two towers. At night he lay on a couch and by turning his head was able to view each fire through specially constructed windows! Should the bellows blowers faulter in their duties the overlooker prompted their activity by a blast on a cow horn!

The full story of these early lighthouses is given in D. Alan Stevenson's excellent book *The World's Lighthouses before 1820* (Oxford University Press

1959). It is a fascinating history and outside the scope of this work. However a brief resume of illuminants is given below.

The coal chauffer existed until 1822 when the last, at St Bee's, was replaced. The chauffer from the discontinued light at St Agnes is preserved at Tresco in the Scillies. Some idea of the problems of "keeping" these lights may be gathered from the fact that in 1801 the Skerries burned 150 tons per annum. Similarly in Scotland the single keeper at the Cumbrae light had to manhandle his coal from the tideline, where a tender dumped it, to the grate 400 feet above sea level.

Coal was not suitable for the first Eddystone. Winstanley used candles but Smeaton tried oil lamps (1756). These he found to be far too smoky and was forced to revert to a large candelabrum. However, a Swiss scientist named Ami Argand developed a smokeless oil lamp, the flame burning in a glass chimney that also increased its brilliance. Combined with the introduction of sperm oil in 1789, the Argand light gave markedly better performance than hitherto. Experiments in reflectors resulted in parabolic reflectors being contrived by embedding glass facets, or spangles, in a clay parabola. When towards the end of the century the Swede Norberg invented his revolving apparatus the combination gave lighthouses something of their modern appearance.

Further improvements in visibility were made by introducing vegetable oil in 1845 and mineral oil in 1873. Vapourised oil followed in 1901 and a year later this was burned in Matthew's incandescent burner. Finally Hood's paraffin vapour burner was brought into service in 1920 and the last went out of use in October, 1977, at St Mary's Tynemouth.

Incandescent oil and coal gases were used in minor lighthouses, as were "carbide to water acetylene", lythene and dissolved acetylene in the first twenty years of the present century. Dissolved acetylene remains in use for isolated unwatched lights such as the Monkstone in the Bristol Channel.

Electrification took place over a century before that last paraffin vapour lamp was extinguished at St Mary's. Both the South Foreland lighthouses (there were two which, in transit, cleared the south of the Goodwins) were electrified in 1872. Ten years earlier Dungeness had been electrified, but this had to be suspended for several months due to the "incompetence" of the keepers.

By the end of the 18th century, therefore, a considerable number of lighthouses existed around the English and Welsh coasts. They were all in private ownership except Caister, Lowestoft, Winterton, Scilly, Needles and Hurst. This private ownership varied from the speculative proprietorship of Mr Coke of Holkham who, in 1823, derived an income of £7,500 net from Dungeness, to the charitable profits of the North and South Foreland lighthouses owned by the Royal Naval Hospital at Greenwich and used by the Governor thereof as a source of income, some of which went towards the hospital.

That they were frequently poorly kept is attested to by no less a person than the Deputy Master of Trinity House. Writing a memoir to the new Master (a post which had by this time become honorary), the then Prime Minister, Lord Liverpool, Joseph Cotton informed his lordship of the doings of the Corporation. Writing in 1818, Cotton had this to say: "Long before the expiration of the lease of the Lizard lights, every reasonable inducement was held out to the lessee to adopt . . . these improvements; but the tenure of the lease, like Antonio's bond to Shylock, was coldly quoted . . . ''.

He says much the same of Spurn and Flatholm. Of the noble Eddystone he reports ''in a misty night, an East Indiaman passing the Eddystone was so close to it, that the light keeper hailed the ship, and enquired where she was going—a tolerably strong instance of the insufficiency of the light then exhibited.''

Much criticism has been levelled at Trinity House for the ambivalence of their intentions in respect of seamarks: ''It is difficult to assess the attitude of Trinity House towards the English coastal lighthouses at this time. Judging by its actions and not by its protestations, the determinination of the Corporation to erect lighthouses had never been strong; before 1806, whenever possible, it had passed on to lessees the duty of erecting them.'' Thus Stevenson in 1959.

It is true they had attracted bad publicity in the affair of the Nore lightvessel (see Chapter Three) but it is not entirely fair since, as we have seen, the English

The successive Eddystone lighthouses. *Trinity House*

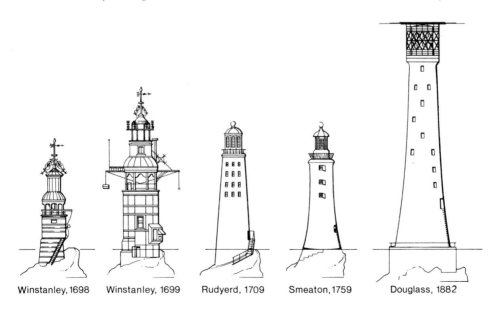

Winstanley, 1698   Winstanley, 1699   Rudyerd, 1709   Smeaton, 1759   Douglass, 1882

practice had the sanction of the Crown. Who were the Elder Brethren, deriving their powers from Royal Charters, to challenge the royal prerogative?

They were keenly interested in what was going on and carried out their duties as overseers with assiduity. We know they surveyed the site for the Lizard lights, that they visited the Spurn in 1777 and were ordering reflectors and copper lamps for Thomas Le Cocq, proprietor of Caskets. Presumably they accomplished much more of a similar nature.

The problem of proprietorship that so bedevilled England existed briefly in Ireland and scarcely at all in Scotland. Trinity House's six original Irish patents were granted by Charles II to Sir Robert Reading. He attempted unlawfully to collect light dues from fishing boats and in 1704 complaints forced Queen Anne to cancel the leases and form a commission to oversee the lights. In 1786 this board was reconstituted as the Commissioners for Irish Lights.

In Scotland, however, only one private light was built; that at the Isle of May as early as 1636. From then on the establishment of lighthouses was vested in various trustees which, in 1786, were formed into the Commissioners for Northern Lighthouses. After chartering supply vessels for several years, in 1799 they purchased their first ship, a sloop, and named her *Pharos*. It was in this vessel, the "Yacht of the Northern Lighthouse Board", that Robert Stevenson made his famous tours of English lighthouses, and a *Pharos* serves Scottish lights to this day.

Purchase of the Isle of May light from the Duke of Portland was accomplished in 1814 for the enormous sum of £60,000. It was hardly surprising, therefore, that the canny Scots merchants were opposed to private ownership! Taking a leaf out of their northern neighbours' book the Liverpool shipowners and traders, eager to have lights on the Isle of Man, were vociferously opposed to seamarks on the English pattern. It appears that northern dues were less than those of the south where the proprietors were motivated by greed and the neccesity of paying rent to Trinity House and gave a poorer service. The Liverpool men successfully petitioned that the new Manx lighthouses should be under the management of the Northern Lighthouse Board (1816) and so they remain to this day.

During the first decade of the 19th century Trinity House's pigeons were coming home to roost. The Eddystone light, built under a 99-year lease granted in 1708 at an annual rent of £100, passed to Trinity House in 1807. So in that year, with the prospect of an increasing number of leases reverting, the first true rock light tower became the direct responsibility of Trinity House.

CHAPTER TWO

The Sailing Yachts: Mutiny and War

" . . . express their Lordship's approbation of the zeal and activity
with which the gentlemen who directed these yachts co-operated
in this service."
April 1814   Mr Croker (Admiralty Secretary)
                                            to Mr Court (Trinity House Secretary)

IN AUGUST, 1745, the Board of Trinity House "ordered that Mr Widgeon
go down in the Trinity Sloop to clean the buoys in the South Channel."

At last! An authenticated mention of a Trinity House tender, and the only
one between the galley of Robert Salmon and the Trinity Yacht of 1777. Of the
latter we know a little more, but of this first buoy yacht we know almost nothing
beyond the bare bones of that single entry in a minute book.

It is necessary to flesh out these bare bones. Mr Widgeon was undoubtedly
the master of the vessel. There is mention in similar terms of a later and better
documented master of a later yacht, and the Elder Brethren, pedants on such
matters as social precedence, were careful not to elevate him to "captain". He
was undoubtedly the "Buoy Master", an official of the Corporation dealing
with the nuts and bolts of the buoyage service.

The name of his ship is more complex. It was common at the time to
append the vessel's type after her name: *Pallas*, frigate; *Argus*, cutter. The brief
entry may be separated into two parts, the latter describing her type.

Was *Trinity* the sloop's name? Personally I think not, but I believe the ship
was commonly called the *Trinity Sloop*, as succeeding vessels were known as the
Trinity Yacht, the *Trinity House Yacht* or the *Trinity Buoy Yacht*. That they
may have had more individual names is given credibility by a later Trinity Yacht
being called in one single discoverable instance *Zadora*. After the introduction
of steam destroyed traditional ideas each vessel bore her own name without
qualification.

As to the vessel's type, this is deserving of explanation. The contemporary
definition of sloop is given in Falconer's Marine Dictionary (1769) thus: "A
small vessel furnished with one mast, the mainsail of which is attached to a gaff
above, to the mast on its foremost edge, and to a long boom below; by which it
is occasionally shifted to either quarter".

The accompanying plate shows a vessel rigged as what we should call a
cutter, that is with more than one headsail. Referring to the article "Cutter" we
find that vessel "rigged as a sloop".

The difference, obscure to us but instantly recognisable to an 18th century seaman, was twofold. The sloop was a fuller version, built with a standing (fixed) bowsprit usually shorter than the huge running spar fitted on a finer cutter. The latter possessed the huge bowsprit to spread enormous areas of canvas and was usually found in official service (i.e. the Revenue, Admiralty despatch boats, etc). In private craft this bowsprit usually denoted a smuggler, or at least a potential one, and the large spar is sometimes referred to as "the illegal bowsprit". Perhaps it is this that encouraged the use of the term yacht, which is discussed below.

So much for Mr Widgeon and his sloop. He was not the first man to attend the buoys in the Thames Estuary, for there is a reference to them being removed in 1688 when Dutch William and his English queen were on passage to oust James II, Pepys's old patron. Buoy keepers existed at Harwich and Margate, but

An eighteenth-century sloop, from Falconer's Marine Dictionary.

the maintenance of these buoys was by an anonymous hand. Mr Widgeon is, therefore, the first named master of a Trinity House Tender.

His sloop glides down the Lower Hope, the hands preparing to clean the buoys in the South Channel. It is August, 1745. Johnny Cope is marching to quench the flames of rebellion lit by Charles Stuart, grandson of the deposed James. He was sent scuttling back to Berwick. England was in a ferment, with fighting in Flanders and revolt at home.

Notwithstanding all this, Mr Widgeon proceeds upon his business, in and out of the pages of history a single sentence in a dusty and almost forgotten minute book. Yet the service upon which he went was one of importance to men of all nations and one that transcended the pride of princes.

At about this time, therefore, appeared the regular beginnings of what was eventually to become known as the Steam Vessel Service of Trinity House. If this was to sound a little grandiloquent, then the original organisation was no less splendid. It was to the "Yacht Establishment" that officers of the Corporation were appointed, with its headquarters first at Deptford and later at Blackwall.

As far as the Thames was concerned the Yacht Establishment was distinct from the dredgers and lighters of the Trinity Ballast Office, but as far as the foundation of a regular service to mariners is concerned it marked a watershed in the history of navigation. A hundred years later it was strengthened by the 1836 Act of Parliament and the introduction of steam propulsion which so facilitated the performance of the yachts' duties. Today many of the tasks originally carried out by Trinity Yachts, particularly those in the Thames Estuary, are carried out by the Admiralty's hydrographers and the surveyors of the Port of London Authority, and the use of Trinity High Water has long been moribund.

Before considering the development of the Yacht Establishment it is as well to clarify the use of the word "yacht". It is still employed occasionally when describing the Trinity House flagship and conveys an entirely erroneous impression of the function of the vessel. The etymological error has been made by the most eminent of historians. In their excellent account of the naval mutinies of 1797, *The Floating Republic*, Messrs Dobrée and Manwaring mention an Elder Brother, Captain Calvert, as "returning from a little pleasure trip in his yacht". In fact Calvert was on official duty in the *Trinity Yacht*.

A yacht was not necessarily a vessel intended for pleasurable purposes, though the term "yachting" had early become associated with cruises and races since it had become fashionable at the court of Charles II who, with his brother James, Duke of York, diverted himself in this manner.

In a Dutch-Latin dictionary published in 1599 the noun "jaght" is shown derived from "jaghen", meaning to hunt or pursue, and a vessel so called was therefore a light, swift warship. The gift of a "yacht" by the States-General to Charles II ensured that court influence on the vernacular tongue made "yacht" a fashionable word. What is usually overlooked is that the term eclipsed an older English word, "pinnace".

In an English/Netherdutch dictionary by Henry Hexhams (1660) the word "pinnace" is translated as "een snet zeylande jacht". Another dictionary gives fifteen alternative spellings and defines "Jachtschip" as "a ship for chasing, a light sailing vessel, a fast piratical ship". In his autobiography of 1613 Phineas Pett uses the term "youathe".

Though much has been made of the Merry Monarch's more frivolous use of the craft, including his habit of naming them after his mistresses, there is ample evidence that there were other yachts in government employment. From 1674 onwards (until 1939) the Admiralty maintained a yacht at Portsmouth. There was another at Chatham in 1716 and in 1718 the Government Yacht *Queenborough* was stationed at Sheerness and spent her entire time surveying in the estuary. Other yachts were in general fleet service as tenders and despatch vessels. The Lord Lieutenant of Ireland had a yacht to convey him to and from

Dublin and the Lord Lieutenant of Hampshire maintained one for passage to the Isle of Wight.

The Revenue Service also employed these "fast piratical ships". Writing of the first decade of the 18th century Smollett, who saw service with the navy, mentions Roderick Random taking passage aboard a smuggler and being chased by "a Custom House Yacht".

To bring this digression full circle, it was not surprising that Trinity House, with its close naval and governmental ties, used the term for its own ships. Although the name "tender" was used for vessels operating under local agents, it was entirely in accord with the temper of the times that those craft under the direct orders of Trinity House should use the title "yacht".

The British lighthouse tender is descended from four separate and distinct roots. The aristocratic vessels of the Yacht Establishment based on London "cruised" on inspections and surveys and attended the ever-increasing number of buoys that appeared annually upon the coast. There were also vessels brought into service solely for the purpose of constructing lighthouses, many of which were sold soon afterwards and disappear from the records. Thirdly there were, and still are, those boats employed locally for a specific purpose, chartered by the various Agents at first, and later by the District Superintendents. Finally there were local permanent tenders of contemporary fishing boat size, acting under an Agent and attending one or two offshore stations. These vessels acted in a logistical role to the lightvessels or lighthouses. The modern District Tender is a direct descendant of these small ships.

The first depiction of a *Trinity Yacht* is in a painting of 1778 which shows "The Trinity House Yacht approaching the River Humber to inspect the new lighthouse on the Spurn Point on 17th April 1777".

In 1778 a party of the Elder Brethren embarked in this yacht to view the new spangle light in Lowestoft. The local Agent from Yarmouth saw the new light on two nights in October from distances between four and five leagues and a petition from mariners attested to its value. The Brethren increased the candle-power suggested by the Agent, so must have made their observations after his inspection, clearly demonstrating the yacht was employed throughout the year.

It was in this same yacht that the Brethren visited France about 1787, to view improvements in the French lighthouses. The full records of the visit were lost in 1940, but shortly after a small revolving light had been installed at Dieppe it was copied on a larger scale at St Agnes, Scilly.

These instances, bare of details though they are, do give us some idea of the use to which the vessels were put. It is important to emphasise they were regular seagoing craft, although based on the Thames.

At Deptford was the Ballast Office, until its removal to Ratcliffe in 1818, and here the junior or Nether Warden kept his boat and "two watermen" from which he measured all ships using the Thames.

Trinity Yachts off the Eddystone, a detail of a painting by Butterfield showing buoy yachts off Smeaton's tower, c. 1800.   *Trinity House*

Whilst the senior or Rental Warden assisted the Deputy Master in London, the second senior was a frequent visitor to Deptford. He was in fact known as the Buoy Warden and had under his supervision the Buoy Yachts as well as the principal yacht. It is not certain how many of these there were, but it is likely that there were at least two at London by the end of the 18th century.

The Buoy Warden's responsibilities were all the buoyage and beaconage in the Thames and its vast estuary and approaches. His precise duties are best described by Joseph Cotton.

"It consists in the examination of all the channels, placing and replacing the buoys and beacons, directing their construction, repairs & c; in the discharge of these peculiar duties, he must frequently be himself afloat, and exposed to the vicissitudes of the weather and other casualties. The charge of the yachts is solely with him, and they are under his direction and control, as well as the floating lightvessels, with all their establishments, equipment and stores, the number of them, and of the buoys, which of late years have been trebled, and which will constitute a part of the following detail, must verify the assertion as to the increased extent of this duty.''

The Deputy Master goes on to enumerate the nature of the buoys then in use, their function and the reason for their establishment.

''The utility of buoys and beacons, to mark the limits of particular sands, which are in the line of the navigation, to caution those who have the conduct of the ships or vessels using the channels, to mark out the several

NAMES, SIZES, COLOURS, AND NUMBERS, OF THE BUOYS IN THE DIFFERENT CHANNELS—MAY 1818.

Names.	Size.	Colour.	Number.
Wreck in Sea Reach...	6 fee	........Red.........	" Wreck" on it.
Nore	7 „	........White......	Name on it.
Shoeburyness.........	7 „	........Black.......	1
West Oaze...........	7 „	........Red........	27
East Oaze	7 „	........White.......	26
Mouse	7 „	........Black........	2
Maplin.............	7 „	Black & white chequered	Name on it.
Swin Middle........	7 „	........Black........	3
North Hook Middle ...	7 „	black & white chequered	Name on it.
Whitaker Beacon Buoy.	10 „	Red, with staff and vane	Do.
Ridge..............	6 „	........Red	4
West Buoy...........	6 „	........black.......	5
Knoll	6 „	........White.......	Name on it.
Eagle	6 „	........black.......	Do.
Wallet Spitway	3 „	........Red........	6
Swin Spitway	6 „	........Black.......	" Spitway " on it.
Heaps	3 „	White, with staff and vane	8
Wreck off Gunfleet ...	7 „	........Red	" Wreck" on it.
Gunfleet...........	7 „	........Black........	9
West Rocks..........	7 „	Black and white striped	Name on it.
Cork Ledge.........	7 „	........White......	Do.
Altar..............	6 „	........Red.......	Do.
S. W. Buoy Shipwash...	8 „	........White......	Do.
N. E. Shipwash......	7 „	........Red	Name on it.
Rough	7 „	........Red	10
Bawdsey Sand........	7 „	Black & white chequered	Name on it.
Cutler.............	7 „	........Black.......	
S. W. Whiting.......	7 „	........White......	
Hook Whiting.......	7 „	........Do........	
N. E. Whiting.......	7 „	........Do........	11
West Buoy of Middle Hosely Bay.......	7 „	........Black.......	
East Buoy of do.....	7 „	........Do........	
Aldbro' Knapes.......	8 „	Black & white chequered, with staff and vane	Name on it.
Wreck in the Downs (1st)	7 „	........Red........	" Wreck" on it.
South Brake	7 „	........Black......	12
Fork...............	8 „	Black & white chequered	Name on it.
North Brake........	7 „	........Red	14
Gull Buoy	7 „	........White......	
Elbow Buoy.........	7 „	........Do........	
Total..............59			Sota

Names.	Size.	Colour.	Number.
South Buoy, leading to Ramsgate	7 „	........Do........	
North do. do.........	7 „	........Red	
Old Cods Channel.....	4 „	........Black	Name on it.
E. Buoy Margate Sand...	7 „	........Do	15
East Tongue..........	7 „	White, half-white, half black bottom	16
North Spit	7 „	........Black.......	17
West Tongue........	7 „	........White.......	18
Wedge Buoy	7 „	........Red	19
Pan Patch	7 „	........White	20
Pansand Beacon Buoy ..	10 „	Red, with staff and vane	Name on it.
South Knoll..........	7 „	........Black	21
West Pansand Buoy	7 „	........White.......	22
North Kroll	7 „	Red and white striped	Name on it.
Girdler Buoy	7 „	........Black	23
Shivering Sand Buoy...	8 „	Black & white striped, with staff and vane.	24
Knob	7 „	........Red........	25
Spile..............	7 „	........Black	28
Middle Ground	7 „	Black & white chequered	Name on it.
West Spaniard	7 „	........White.......	29
Gillman	6 „	........Red	30
East Spaniard	6 „	........Black	31
Columbine	6 „	........Red	Name on it.
Spell Buoy	6 „	........White......	32
Woolpack	6 „	........Red	33
West Last	6 „	........Black	34
Hook Last	6 „	........Do........	35
East Last	6 „	........Do........	36
Scart..............	6 „	........Do........	37
Hook, Margate Sand ..	6 „	White, with black cross on large end......	38
Gore Patch	7 „	Black & white chequered, with staff and vane	Name on it.
Horse	6 „	........Red	Do.
Cant Knoll	7 „	........White......	" Cant" on it.
Sheerness Middle	6 „	........Black	" Middle Ground" on it.
Redsand............	7 „	........Red	Name on it.
Wreck in the Downs (2d)	7 „	........Red	" Wreck" on it.
Wreck off Dover.....	7 „	........Black	Do.
Total 36			
Brought forward 59			
Grand Total 75			

A list of buoys maintained by Trinity House in the outer Thames Estuary and the Downs, from Cotton's Memoir of 1818.

dangers on their right hand or their left, or to guide them in the fairway . . . The buoys are in general constructed of a size corresponding with their particular situations . . . they are painted red, white, black, chequered; some have vanes upon a staff six feet above the buoy . . . termed beacon buoys . . . The numbers have of late been very much increased rendering navigation more secure, although, it must be confessed, a multiplication of them, indiscriminately placed, leads to confusion, and often to the neglect of other precautions. The drifting from their stations also, which is unavoidable, from vessels getting foul of them, and in consequence sometimes of heavy weather, is productive of great inconvenience, and it is therefore with great consideration the Court (the full Board in formal session) concur in the increase, unless where new channels are to be buoyed out.

In the year 1684 there were sixteen buoys and beacons maintained by the Corporation of Trinity House at a cost of £144 annually. In 1776 there were only twenty one buoys . . . In the year 1816 there were sixty five buoys between the South Foreland, Orfordness and Gravesend . . .

The beacons referred to . . . are vessels which are sunk and whose masts bear a mark of discrimination to denote the sand upon which they are deposited.''

Some of these were particularly handsome, that at the Gunfleet bearing a wooden cage surmouted by a carved fish. Cotton goes on to describe other work done from the yacht.

"Surveys upon the coast, at particular periods, become essential: the lighthouses, floating lights, and every variation of the sands, are attentively inspected, and reported on by a committee, who proceed in the yacht. The examining and buoying out new channels, or improving the marks, buoyage and beaconage of the old, constitute also a duty of importance; and it is but an act of justice to remark that several of the Brethren volunteered, during the late very hazardous war, notwithstanding the risk and danger of a coasting voyage, from one extremity to the other of the coasts, from Scilly to Fern (Farne) Islands and persevered in this part of their duty, not deterred by any personal considerations.''

Writing in 1818, Cotton referred to the Napoleonic War during which British coastwise trade was harried by French corsairs. The Brethren, responsible for examining the masters and mates in H.M. ships, had to maintain a familiarity with all the navigational hazards of the coast. On 5th April, 1810, Cotton wrote to Lord Mulgrave, First Lord of the Admiralty, that the Brethren intended to proceed down Channel in their yacht to inspect the south coast and the King's Ports "so as more precisely [to] examine the Masters in His Majesty's Navy and to ascertain the navigation thereof''. This letter was minuted at the Admiralty "Vice Admiral Campbell to order a sloop of war or a gun brig to accompany the yacht for her protection when employed upon this service, and to give particular directions to the commander or lieutenant not to interfere with the course or management of the yacht, but solely to attend for the purpose above mentioned''.

The yacht was extensively employed on this surveying with or without the Brethren aboard. It is clear this work was carried out for others: "Other surveys also, on the requisition of proper authorities, they (the Brethren) have ever considered a matter of public duty''. Rudimentary though this surveying may have been, it was undoubtedly time consuming and demanding and it may be assumed that the yacht crews clearly knew their business and were trained to a high degree. Cotton's claims tend to overshadow the fact that the principal and buoy yachts were commanded by their own masters, officers subordinate to the Brethren but who were the working "skippers" of the vessels.

That Trinity House was "at all times disposed to render every service . . . gratuitously to government" was fulsomely, though not quite gratuitously, demonstrated on two major occasions during the long wars with France between 1793 and 1815. The first was during the naval mutiny at the Nore in 1797, the second was the defence of the Thames during the prolonged invasion scare of 1803 to 1805.

The causes of the great naval mutinies at Spithead and the Nore are well documented elsewhere. Suffice it to say that Richard Parker's economic blockade of London with the Nore fleet rapidly hardened opinion against his cause. For Parker decided to blockade the metropolis until his demands were met, a circumstance that reversed the traditionally liberal sentiments of the city's mercantile classes so that the justice in the seamens' claims was swiftly forgotten in the manner of their claiming them.

Although Sheerness rapidly filled with troops, the fairways of the Thames remained open for the mutineers to use as they pleased. For Parker had a contingency plan that, as time dragged on, seemed to be the only course the mutinous fleet could possibly take: defection to republican France or the new Dutch republic.

To facilitate navigating the fleet during such a desperate venture Parker had retained the Sailing Masters of the warships when the other officers had been bundled ashore. These warrant officers provided the fleet with its navigational expertise, and ironically it was the very organisation that gave these men their qualifications that now frustrated Parker, robbed the mutineers of their initiative and led to the eventual piecemeal capitulation of the ships.

As early as 1647 the Crown, bereft of a standing army, had considered Trinity House a suitable body to appoint for the manning of Tilbury and Gravesend forts, though the Dutch were virtually unmolested during their infamous descent on the Thames twenty years later.

During the invasion scare of 1779 when the combined fleets of France and Spain outwitted Admiral Sir Charles Hardy, the Admiralty requested Trinity House submit a plan for the defence of the Thames. It was recommended that warships "of some force be stationed to give the alarm" off the North Foreland, the Galloper and Orfordness. Each of these cruisers was to have a cutter as messenger, and revenue vessels with fishing smacks were to be requisitioned to destroy the buoys and beacons in the outer estuary. How far this plan was valid may be judged from the fact that Admiral Lord Keith followed these dispositions some quarter century later when fears of a Napoleonic invasion were at their height, leaving Trinity House to form a second line of defence in the lower reaches of the river itself.

But to return to 1797. By the beginning of June the situation of the Nore fleet had become critical and the Admiralty were apprehensive that the defection of the entire fleet was imminent. The Admiralty Secretary, Evan Nepean, contacted David Court, Secretary to Trinity House, with a view to the Brethren and their yacht masters rendering assistance.

Accordingly Captain Bromfield, an Elder Brother, posted to Harwich where he arrived on 6th June. With the assistance of Mr Bean, the Corporation's local Agent, he assembled a squadron of fishing smacks led by the buoy yacht *Argus*. Bean was despatched "with two vessels" to remove or sink the Whiting, Rough and Gunfleet buoys in the northern approaches to the Thames estuary.

Before leaving himself Bromfield reported that "John Poulter (Yacht master of the *Trinity Yacht*) is gone with two vessels to the East and West Ooze (Oaze), Shivering Sand, Girdler, West Pan Sand, Pan Sand Beacon, Tongue and c". These buoys and marks extended from the North Foreland almost to the anchorage of the Great Nore.

Bromfield himself undertook the destruction of the buoys from the Naze through the Swin channels to Foulness, thus erasing the seamarks from the principal route for vessels escaping into the North Sea.

It was five in the evening of 7th June before Bromfield returned to Harwich, having met with Poulter the previous evening near the Nobb (Knob) channel through which the *Trinity Yacht* was proceeding on her passage of destruction. Work was hampered by light winds "in the night and greater part of the day. The Gentry at the Nore keep a sharp lookout all the day, therefore we did not think it safe to attempt anything until 10 last night and we began above (i.e. upstream) so as to be out of their sight when daylight came this morning . . ." Thus Bromfield reported to Court, and he had some reason to be apprehensive, for the mutineers, having got wind of Trinity House attempting some such measure, had threatened to hang any of the Elder Brethren that fell into their clutches. To this end they had guard boats out down channel from the Nore.

In London on the morning of 8th June Court reported the substance of Bromfield's despatch to the Admiralty. A serious problem existed with the Nore lightvessel. "There may be some difficulty in getting that (the Nore's removal) effected as it lays near the mutinous ships . . ." Court and his Board were also anxious to communicate with the lightvessel.

The position of the Nore was distinctly invidious. Once the mutineers learned of Trinity House's action it was possible that they might revenge themselves on her crew as she lay under the guns of Parker's "flagship", H.M.S. *Sandwich*.

Poulter, in the *Trinity Yacht*, had already been the recipient of some abuse from the mutineers. Completing work in the Nobb and Queen's channels, he had "met with some alarm from a row-boat of the delegates who swore at him and the vessels, and said 'they would be with him presently' ". Poulter put into Margate, probably to discharge his hired fishing boats. Due to proceed to join Bromfield he found Anthony Calvert, another Elder Brother, waiting for him. It seems that Calvert had instructions to attempt some communication with the Nore. The *Trinity Yacht* proceeded westward, bound for the lightvessel.

The *Trinity Yacht* was "arrested" by boats from the fleet and Captain Calvert was dragged on board *Sandwich* for a drum-head court martial prior to being hanged. Fortunately the delegates were charmed by the "openness and manliness of his conversation and manner". He was asked about public opinion and, with considerable courage, told the mutineers their cause had lost all public sympathy. After being waylaid by the kidnapped sailing masters, who implored his help in obtaining their release, Calvert was hustled back to the yacht and suffered to proceed, though apparently without contacting the lightvessel.

Plans to move it were dropped and the Whiting buoy was replaced as it was vital to ships, barred the passage of the Thames, in seeking the shelter of Harwich harbour.

Whether Calvert's intelligence inclined the mutineers to attempt the defection of the fleet is not clear, but late on the evening of the 9th John Poulter sent off a letter to David Court informing him that he had learned from a fisherman that a frigate had been seen flying the red flag, proceeding down the Swin and anchoring as a seamark on the end of the Middle Sand. A second had been similarly anchored near the Maplin Bank.

Two days later Court informed the Admiralty that Poulter had been sent to destroy the buoys in the shallow channels over the Kentish Flats to prevent any of the smaller ships with the mutiny's leaders from escaping. A week later the mutiny collapsed when Parker hoisted the signal to weigh. One by one his ships slipped into the Medway to await their fate. Parker was hanged but one boat, with some eight men aboard, escaped to an unknown fate.

But from the romantic to the pragmatic. Trinity House presented the Admiralty with a bill for the replacement of their seamarks. With a nicety we are compelled to admire, it totalled £1,260 0s 3d.

Nevertheless, whether for defence of the Thames or possible repetitions of the Nore affair, a year later the Admiralty directed that in a future case the Revenue Cutters should assist the work and be placed under the orders of Trinity House, also that the use of fishing boats should be restricted. In 1798 a rehearsal was carried out. Five smacks based at Harwich were hired at £60 per month, a vessel called the *Pocock* was engaged as tender to the Buoy Yachts and Revenue Cutters on station, and five additional smacks, at £50 each, held at Ramsgate to operate in the south channels.

A few years later Trinity House were again called upon to take up arms.

The end of the Peace of Amiens, "the peace that passeth all understanding", found England facing the seven army corps that comprised the Army of England. Defence of the Narrow Seas was undertaken by Admiral Lord Keith commanding the North Sea station. A second line of defence was established in the river itself where the marshy banks drew together at the Lower Hope. It was composed of a line of ten elderly frigates that were laid up at Deptford and Woolwich through lack of men. Trinity House recommissioned them at its own expense, having no trouble recruiting since they offered press exemptions, and a force of 1,200 men was quickly raised to serve under the Trinity Ensign.

The force was constituted as a volunteer battalion with Prime Minister William Pitt, then Master of the Corporation, as Colonel. Joseph Cotton, Deputy Master, was restyled Lieutenant Colonel and on October 3rd, 1803, at a public dinner at the London Tavern the officers of the Royal Trinity House Volunteer Artillery were sworn in. Pitt was in attendance with a friend, the diarist George Rose.

> "The sight was really an extremely affecting one—a number of gallant and exceedingly good old men, who had, during the best part of their lives been beating the waves, now coming forward with the zeal and the spirit of lads, swearing allegiance to the King, with a determined purpose to act manfully in his defence, and for the protection of the Capital."

A view of the Lower Hope Reach, 1803-05, with the Trinity blockships and, on the extreme right, the Trinity Yacht. *Trinity House*

Joseph Cotton, to judge from his correspondence, eschewed his former title without regret and adopted that of Lieutenant Colonel with enthusiasm. Two crews were appointed to each vessel, every crew being commanded by an Elder Brother using the title Captain in its military sense, the senior Warden being Major. About 600 men were therefore afloat in the blockships at any one time, though the Elder Brethren were not continuously on board until an alarm was given. One was in constant attendance, however, quartered aboard the *Trinity Yacht*, still under the command of the yacht master Johnathan Poulter.

The permanent officers aboard the blockships were lieutenants who appear to have been Younger Brethren or pensioned naval officers. They commanded a motley force of "seamen, landsmen, volunteers, pilots, lascars, Harbour Volunteer Marines, River Fencibles, Greenwich Pensioners, Trinity Pensioners and East India Company Pensioners".

The *Trinity Yacht* lay under the Essex shore, and from time to time she weighed and proceeded up or down river as tender to the squadron. She was also administrative office to the blockships. The government attached so much importance to the ships that a Post Office conveyance left East Tilbury, where store houses had been erected, at noon daily with mail for London. An order was passed that all letters, returns, etc, for London should be delivered daily to the *Trinity Yacht* by "half past eleven o'clock".

The *Trinity Yacht* was not the only yacht in the squadron. Also included were the Royal Yachts *Royal Charlotte* and *Princess Augusta*, ship-sloops commanded by Captains Neale and Grey, R.N., both receiving pay and privileges of captains of first rates. Neither of these officers, nor their successors Towry and Foote, were of much assistance to Cotton, and both turned a blind eye to the actions of certain unscrupulous naval officers who attempted the impressment of some of the volunteers. Relations between Trinity House and the Admiralty wore somewhat thin at times.

From the Kent to the Essex shores the cordon comprised the frigates *Daedalus*, *Vestal*, *Retribution*, *Iris*, *Heroine*, *L'Unite*, *Modeste*, *Quebec*, the yacht *Royal Charlotte*, *Solebay*, the yacht *Princess Augusta*, *Resource* and the *Trinity Yacht*. Partially rigged and secured to heavy moorings, they constituted a formidable barrier. Most of the frigates had been built under the 1783 establishment. *L'Unite* had been the French *Imperieuse* taken in 1793, *Modeste* another Frenchman taken in the same year by the *Bedford*, 74. *Retribution* was the former British frigate *Hermione*, whose crew mutinied against the savage brutality of her captain and handed her over to the Spanish. She was retaken in a cutting out operation by the boats of H.M.S. *Surprise* and so renamed.

The full complement of officers to be on board in case of invasion was two captains (except *Solebay* who bore the one major), six lieutenants, one sailing master and his mate, a purser, two midshipmen and five extra warrant officers. *Solebay* had three additional middies. Each of the crews consisted of between 50 and 60 men so that, in time of invasion, with both crews embarked, each frigate had about 120 men to man her guns. *Solebay* bore 58 "gunners" and 30 lascars in each of her crews.

The barrage was not established without difficulty. In October of 1803 Second Lieutenant John Chessel wrote of the Woolwich yard which was preparing some of the ships,

"Why the same orders are not given at Woolwich (as at Deptford) I am at a loss to know—they will not give us even an old lead line to hoist our colours with. The fire screens and lanthorns have never been demanded, the former of which is quite indispensible—I am quite disheartened when I see our ships so far behind-hand, and at any time, attention and expenses thrown away."

It is a lament familiar to ship's officers of all times.

In May of the following year Pitt inspected the defences and Cotton gave instructions to Quartermaster Parsons, commanding a detachment of Trinity Volunteers attached to the East India Company hoys further up river, "fire a round as the Trinity Flag approaches them to Deptford and when abreast to give three cheers". The three hoys were to be anchored in line ahead from Durrand's Wharf to the Dog and Duck, which shows that Cotton possessed a proper appreciation of waterside landmarks!

While the men of the blockships waited for the invasion they were not suffered to remain idle. Lighters of hemp "junk" were brought alongside from the Royal Dockyards and the hands were employed picking it for oakum. This was then made into artillery wads at the Woolwich arsenal.

A glimpse exists into the internal life of the squadron. One Christopher Hindes, boat coxswain of the *Modeste*, was tried for disobedience and striking his superior officer, Lieutenant William Brabazon. The court of three lieutenants found him guilty and he was sentenced to 36 lashes, though his offence was mitigated by Brabazon having first laid a hand upon his shoulder. Reviewing the sentence, Cotton ordered the number reduced by 12 in view of Brabazon's conduct and a further 12 if Hindes apologised.

If the French attacked, the very comprehensive General Orders issued to the squadron were to be followed. The vessels hauled out of the cordon to allow the passage of traffic were to be hove into their correct stations and then, depending upon the wind and tide, a complex combination of cables and springs was to swing the ships with their broadsides downstream. The instructions also contained orders that boarding nettings be put up immediately the alarm was given, "particularly around the bows as they will take time to secure . . . more perhaps than will be allowed us". This fear of boarders is expressed elsewhere: "The gunports not in use should be barred in and not a rope suffered to hang over the side. Three persons in each top with hand grenadoes and blunderbusses would do great execution . . .".

Trafalgar and Austerlitz removed the threat of invasion and the RTHVA was disbanded. It had cost Trinity House some £10,000 in the two years of its existence, and the Corporation was thanked by Parliament in late 1805 when Viscount Castlereagh moved a vote of gratitude.

As a final flourish to its involvement in the great French war, the *Trinity Yacht* and one of the buoy yachts joined a squadron under the command of the Duke of Clarence (later Master of Trinity House and eventually William IV) in Dover after Napoleon's first abdication in 1814. They assisted naval ships in conveying the household of Louis XVIII back to French soil and earned from the Admiralty "their Lordship's approbation . . . ".

It was a fitting conclusion.

Thomas Whitcombe's painting of the Trinity Yacht off the Caskets, 1788. This shows Poulter's handsome yacht soon after its building.   *Trinity House*

During the two years that the *Trinity Yacht* had attended the blockships the other London Buoy Yachts had continued with their normal duties. Obviously it was necessary that the Nore lightvessel and the growing number of "floating lights" elsewhere were serviced regularly. The story of these is described in the following chapter.

Poulter's command, the *Trinity Yacht*, made a public appearance in 1806 at the opening of the East India Dock. A description of the event in *The Globe* for 4th August runs thus:

"Shortly before two, the signal of the Royal Salute was fired . . . for the . . . ships to enter at the time of flood; immediately upon which the elegant little yacht of the Trinity House, decked to her masthead in the naval finery of flags and streamers of all nations, led into the basin in very elegant style, followed by the *Admiral Gardner*, East Indiaman, with the British Anchor at her foretopmasthead, the Royal Standard at her main and the Union Flag at her mizen; and displaying from the lower rigging the colours of all nations, the French under all."

But what kind of vessels were these yachts owned by Trinity House? Several paintings exist showing the principal yachts of the period and a number of specifications for the building of two of these and two Buoy Yachts are also extant in copy form.

Between 1775 and 1835 there were three principal yachts. The first was replaced in 1788 and the second in 1828. This vessel was displaced by a steamer within a decade of commissioning, though sailing tenders were to exist until the end of the century.

There is no name for the first *Trinity Yacht* but two paintings of her show her to have been a handsome vessel. The first, by Francis Holman, is shown on page x. The second is a watercolour by John Holl of "the *Trinity House Yacht* off Margate as it appeared on board a yatcht (sic) in 1785 the Church Tower South West".

From these two pictures we learn the vessel was about 60-70 feet long, with a square stern and a tan hull. She probably bore the rampant lion figurehead of unrated warships, bearing the Trinity dagger. Her underbody was payed black with pitch and she had tiller steering. Her quarterdeck was raised, with a low gunwhale painted sky blue and set off with gilding. This was surmounted by a rufftree rail which also extended across the stern. The sky blue and gold decorated transom bore the Corporation's arms in its centre, flanked by sash windows shuttered off in heavy weather. The transom carving showed Neptune reclining at luxurious ease among his sirens. There is a lower waist where the boat, showing towing astern in the Holman painting, was stowed inboard.

Rigged as a sloop with a fixed bowsprit, two headsails and a large gaff mainsail, she crossed a square topsail and, if required in a following wind, a lower course. The lower yard could be dropped to the deck or cockbilled if required.

This early yacht was pole-masted as, although she carries what appears to be a doubled topmast, the topsail and peak halliard blocks secure to the lower mast. In fact the unstayed upper spar is merely a flagmast.

The arrangement of flags in the Holman picture is interesting. Although on a visit of inspection and, judging by the ten tricorne hats on her quarterdeck, with the Brethren almost certainly embarked, yet no flag flies at the masthead, beyond the standard pennant. The Elder Brothers' flag may not then have been flown as a "command flag" but it is clearly visible at the extremity of the bowsprit as a jack. This flag, a St George's cross quartering four Tudor ships, is properly flown at the mainmasthead when an Elder Brother is on board. However it is still called, in common usage, a jack, even when so flown. speculation leads one to wonder whether this is a relic from its original position.

Holman's painting is also the first known depiction of the Trinity Ensign. This colour is the oldest British ensign still being flown in its original form, the red, white and blue ensigns having undergone several reallocations but the Trinity Ensign with its distinctive fly motive of St George's cross and four ships remaining basically unchanged, given the addition of St Patrick's saltire in 1801. The flag has been occasionally misrepresented. On one print showing a buoy yacht and yacht either side of the Corporation's Arms the ensign is shown as a white ensign, the three unoccupied quadrants of which have a Tudor ship. More recently a book showed it as a blue ensign, which must have turned a whole purgatory of Brethren in their graves.

Nevertheless the position of the fly emblazon has undergone subtle shifts over the years, as can be seen from the plates. In early paintings the ships are shown as contemporary craft, while some which existed into the 1900's show Tudor galleons with guns blazing.

Holman's picture shows the ensign flying from a specially fitted staff at the extremity of the boom where it benefited from the air flow out of the bunt of the mainsail.

By contrast with this early yacht, several representations of her replacement, built in 1788, are in existence. It was this ship which acted so dramatically during June, 1797, and as tender to the Thames blockships. During this period she was commanded by Johnathan Poulter, whose family were yacht masters and superintendents of the Yacht Establishment for several generations.

She was launched "by or before the last spring tides in May (1788)". The extreme length of her hull was 61 feet, with a keel length of 46 feet. Her beam was 20 feet 3 inches and her burthen 100 tons. Built at a rate of £12 per ton by Messrs Randall and Brent, of Rotherhithe, she was specified simply as "one good, new strong and substantial yacht or vessel". Her hull was of oak and her decks of "good, sound $2\frac{1}{2}$ inch Dantzick Deal".

Poulter's yacht in later life seen off Ramsgate in another painting by Thomas Whitcombe, 1810.
The cutter on the right is a naval vessel. *National Maritime Museum*

It is certain that she was capable of buoywork, for she had "a good windlass, with good pawls, and a capstan with a drumhead and six bars, to have a proper davit, fixed in the room of a cathead, on the starboard side, with 2 large shevers (sheaves), and a proper cathead on the larboard side, with sufficient bowsprit partners". Obviously the sheaves on the starboard side were for buoy moorings, as was the capstan. The windlass and "proper cathead" on the port side were for the bower anchor. At this date a davit was a heavy spar used for stowing anchors, etc., and not for hoisting boats.

Whitcombe's two paintings of this vessel show a handsome little ship with a white payed bottom, black spirketting and yellow topsides. Her gunwhale and fore and after topgallant rails are sky blue, gilded and decorated with gilt stars. A rufftree rail is fitted, painted scarlet, and six guns are mounted on the quarter deck. The yacht has a stempost with a false beakhead, elaborately carved and terminating in a lion guardant with drawn dagger, a variation of the Corporation's rampant lion crest and known popularly as "the monkey and marlin spike".

The stern of Poulter's yacht is shown in a number of pictures. The date of J. T. Serre's "Firing a Salute, the Trinity House Yacht and a view of the Thames", is given variously as 1787 and 1789. Captain Chaplin, who researched the matter, is adamant that the latter date is correct and this seems certain to be the new 1788 yacht. The decoration lacks father Neptune and his harem but has

A Trinity House Yacht firing a salute and a view of the Thames, by J. T. Serres, c. 1788. Note the awning and the masthead pendant.

Trinity House

the heavily decorated oval quarter windows of Thomas Whitcombe's fine painting. The Corporation's arms are in the centre, flanked by carved pillars, and this is corroborated by a print by Gendell of 1801.

Serres shows the masthead pennant despite the ceremonial awning, presumably in honour of a Dutch dignitary in the adjacent yacht, whilst Whitcombe's paintings off the Caskets and Ramsgate and the Gendell print show the Elder Brother's flag at the masthead. The Ramsgate painting also shows the Trinity Ensign at the peak. No doubt the passage of twenty years between Whitcombe's two pictures had resulted in the abandonment of the boom staff that harked back to an earlier flag etiquette.

The provision of guns was for signalling as much as self-defence, and Trinity House were the last to operate muzzle loading cannon as signal and warning guns on lightvessels up to the middle of the twentieth century. They were used to salute George IV in 1822 when he visited Scotland.

No previous Hanoverian monarch had ever visited North Britain, as it was then called, the last Royal visitor having been Charles II. The proposed voyage initiated a vituperative correspondence between Trinity House and the

Admiralty on the subject of pilots. This matter was eventually solved and founded the privilege of Royal Escort in which the *Trinity Yacht*, and no other vessel including warships, precedes the sovereign.

When, on being asked for the names of two reliable pilots for the Royal Yacht, Trinity House recommended Thomas Duncan and Matthew Rutledge an unholy row exploded. Rutledge had formerly piloted a Royal Yacht from Dungeness to the Owers in 1817. His name was objected to because he had charged fees for a 2nd Rate, and both candidates were turned off the yacht *Royal George* by her Captain, William Mingaye, R.N. After a furious exchange in which the Navy Board claimed the yacht was listed as a 6th Rate a compromise was reached. The pilots' services were declined since the "misunderstanding" arose "as to the particular description of person required . . . " and two others were selected in Mingaye's presence. The objection to Rutledge on fiscal grounds was patently rubbish since Mingaye himself, as captain of a Royal Yacht, was paid the salary for that of a 1st Rate.

In addition to the approved pilots the Elder Brethren were to embark in the *Trinity Yacht* and her commander was ordered to contact the commodore, Sir Charles Paget, to receive his orders. Thus was started the tradition that has endured as a prescriptive right up to the present time.

In 1828 a contract was signed between Jacob Herbert, on behalf of Trinity House, and Thomas White, of Cowes, for the construction of a new yacht at £13 per ton. The quality of her build was high: "The keel to be of good, sound Beach of English growth, the garboard strake to be of elm, the entire frame to be of best quality African oak, the bottom planks, wales, topsides, planks, shears, waterways, shelf pieces, beams, keelson and ceiling planks all of the best African oak.

"To be completely copper fastened throughout—to have one hanging iron knee to each mast beam and to the two beams in wake of the runner and tackles . . . " Her beams "to be 3′ 6″ apart, her topsides 2″ thick", her decks were to be "of the best Dantzic Deal $2\frac{1}{2}$″". To give some idea of the size of her rigging, her four shrouds secured to channels eleven feet long, 11 inches wide and 4 inches thick. In all she was about 120 tons, being 63 feet overall in the hull with a beam of 21 feet 2 inches, and a hold depth of 9 feet 8 inches. Unlike Poulter's yacht, she was fitted with only a windlass and was not intended to service buoys. She was launched on the spring tides of September, 1828.

Her rig was taller than that of her predecessor and a gaff topsail had replaced the square topsail, although a yard for a running course was still carried

We know little of this yacht beyond Chaplin's observation that she was "a very handsome vessel with fine stern carving and figurehead as was indicated by a fine model of her unfortunately lost in 1940". Eight years after commissioning she had fallen from grace, replaced by the hideously efficient steam yacht *Vestal*, and two years after that was sold for £1,750. Presumably that failure to fit her for buoy work prevented her continuing a useful if relegated life as a buoy yacht, as happened to the first *Patricia*.

There is one other fact known about this yacht. As the final payment for her building, one of £500, was made in November, 1828, she had clearly been accepted into service by August, 1829, when we learn that the Trinity Yacht *Zadora* was at Cowes. Perhaps this was her name, for we know so little about these intriguing vessels or about the men who sailed them. A name here and there, the reference to a gratuity penned in the Warden's ledger by a disinterested clerk. Few reminiscences remain to convey an impression of life aboard them. Lieutenant John Boeteler, R.N., was an officer of the Royal Yacht *Royal George* who took command of her tender. She was smaller than *Zadora* or her sisters, with a crew of twenty men, but his description is brief and graphic. It is not out of place to include it here.

> "It being my turn with the other two lieutenants, I took command of our tender, the *Seagull*, a cutter of fifty tons only, a good sea boat, but very wet in the winter months. She was a sort of half tide rock, as much under as above water. I wore fisherman's boots above the knees, as the only way of keeping tolerably dry."

The *Zadora*, the last sailing yacht, off the Caskets, by an unknown artist. Her gaff topsail replaces the squaresail, though a yard is retained for running.
Trinity House.

CHAPTER THREE

The Sailing Yachts: Lightvessels and Buoys

" . . . the petitioner, having with great study, labour and
expense, found out and invented a new method for dis-
tinguishing of lights whereby one light (erected for the guidance
of shipping) may be perfectly known from another and consequently every ship's crew or single mariner be informed . . .
where they are . . . as well in the night as if it were day . . . ''
Robert Hamblin's petition to the King, 1731

THE introduction of lightvessels brought into being the local tenders of
Harwich, Wells, Great Yarmouth and Ramsgate. The establishment of that
at the Nore was not without problems. As early as 1679 Sir John Clayton
proposed a vessel with a cresset at the masthead, but Trinity House had opposed
it on the grounds that it would be ineffective. The difficulties of maintaining
such a fire are not hard to imagine. Nevertheless fifty years later the Nore *was*
established, although the manner of its doing was irregular.

Robert Hamblin, a barber of Kings Lynn, had interested himself in nautical
matters as a consequence of espousing a shipmaster's daughter. He had secured
for himself a share in a collier along with his new bride. Hamblin's career was as
unsuccessful as a shipowner as it had been as a barber and he was reduced to
penury and lawlessness. He became involved with an adventurer named David
Avery who saw possibilities in Hamblin's idea of mooring lightships round the
coast. For these two unlanded men the prospect of high light dues was too
attractive to be denied so Avery, knowing they had but a slender chance of
obtaining a patent, hit upon a brilliant subterfuge.

Given that the main problem in lighthouse design was the identification of
one light from another, Avery hit on the idea of Hamblin claiming to have
invented such a method as set out above. His petition was successful and he
received a 14-year patent dated July, 1730.

By some means he and Avery purchased a small collier, reduced the masts
to a single main and topmast, crossing a solitary spar, and suspended two
lanthorns, one from either yard arm. The vessel was moored insolently close to
the Nore buoy.

The Elder Brethren were furious. They objected vehemently once they
learned the pair intended fitting out more such craft and invited the Admiralty
to join them in taking proceedings against the two adventurers. However the

practicability of such "alarm vessels" was being seriously considered by their Lordships and they declined the Trinity House invitation.

Trinity House then approached the Attorney-General and after two years persuaded the King to revoke the partners' patent. The clerks then had the vexatious and unprecedented task of drawing up an instrument of revocation.

Opinion was now on Avery's side. The lightvessel had been on station long enough to prove valuable and mariners using the Thames raised an outcry at its proposed removal. In a sensibly conciliatory tone Avery now approached Trinity House and applied for a lease. He stated the outlay had been £2,000

Faced with such a *fait accompli*, the Brethren reconsidered their decision and with good sense granted Avery his lease at £100 per year for a period of 61 years from 1733. Three years later Trinity House had done an about face and were suing certain ship owners for evasion of light dues. The lightvessel had arrived as a feature of the coastal seascape, and although the Nore has long been discontinued the last vessel to occupy the station is now preserved at St Katherine's Dock, London, almost within sight of the Trinity House it once challenged.

So popular was the Nore with her flag by day and twin lights by night that mariners trading off the flat and lethal coast of eastern England were soon clamouring for more lightvessels.

A Captain Waggett of Yarmouth had advocated an alarm vessel on the Dudgeon Shoal as early as 1724, and with the success of the Nore Avery sought a second patent. Despite the exposure of the station Trinity House decided there was sufficient sea room for her safety if she broke adrift and in 1736 Avery got his patent. Trinity House nevertheless tried to discourage a proliferation of such vessels by charging Avery and his associates £200 a year, increasing to £300 after two years. In 1739 a patent was refused for a lightvessel at the Cockle Gat. The Gatway marked the northern entrance to an inshore passage fron Wintertonness to Lowestoft, and it was argued that the alarm vessel could break adrift with fatal consequences to her crew and to other mariners who might be misled by her movement.

Notwithstanding this, the success of the Dudgeon soon encouraged more lightvessels. In this the Navy Board were active, never having shared the Elder Brethren's misgivings. The feasibility of a floating light on an exposed station was further confirmed by Smeaton whilst building his tower on the Eddystone. To provide a temporary light and to enable a continuous levy of light dues to be made Trinity House obtained a Crown patent and on 13th August, 1756, moored the brigantine *Harlequin* as a temporary lightvessel two miles north west of the rock. A ship called the *Neptune Buss* was also used as an accommodation ship. *Harlequin* was insured with the London Assurance Co. for £850, and she remained on station until Smeaton lit his famous tower on 16th October, 1759.

It was the Admiralty that pressed Trinity House to establish floating lights in the approaches to Portsmouth. In 1788 a specially constructed lightvessel costing £4,500 was moored south of the Owers shoal. She demonstrated what has often subsequently been observed, that a ship moored in shallow water will frequently give more trouble than those in deeper water and on more exposed stations. The Owers broke adrift several times, once driving across to France and bringing up at St Valery-en-Caux. Getting her back on station must have been a daunting task, as the local Agent's cutter based at Littlehampton could do no more than "assist" her. Bearing in mind the cost of these custom-built alarm vessels compared with the yachts mentioned in the last chapter, it seems certain that they had a capability to sail themselves.

The establishment of the Newarp lightvessel was, as such things so often are, the consequence of disaster. In a heavy gale on the night of 30th October, 1789, two convoys of merchantmen ran foul of each other in the Cockle Gatway, one bound north, the other south. In the ensuing chaos 23 ships foundered, 20 ran ashore and some 600 seamen lost their lives. The Brethrens' decision not to lay a lightvessel in the Gatway was not considered to be the cause of this loss, the weather excepted. It was the Caister leading lights that were held to be misleading, a situation only worsened by the terrible weather that prevailed during the night. The Caister lights were forthwith discontinued. In their place two lighthouses were erected at Happisburgh, Norfolk, and at a cost of £4,500 a lightvessel was fitted out with two horizontal lanterns and laid on the Newarp station in December, 1790.

But of all the banks and shoals around the British coast none has taken such a toll as the Goodwin Sands, the "Great Ship Swallower". Proposals for beacons and floating lights had been dismissed for various reasons but the loss of life was continuous. In the great gale of November, 1703, in which Winstanley and his Eddystone perished, an entire fleet was lost on the sands, and on another occasion no fewer than 30 ships ran on to the banks. The local boatmen from Kent were not slow to take advantage of these wrecks and with typical English sententiousness it was asserted that "the bare interest of the *property* (author's italics) lost on the Goodwin Sands in one year would maintain a floating light as long as this world continues".

Eventually a patent was obtained and in August, 1795, a lightvessel showing three lanterns in a triangle was established off the North Sand Head and named "Goodwin". The discontinuance of the low South Foreland lighthouse and subsequent mooring of other lightvessels round the Goodwins altered her name to "North Goodwin". A lightship rides on that station today and remains the most liable to drag upon the coast.

The optimism that originally attended this light was not borne out. Vessels continued to be lost on the Goodwins and, worst of all, the lightvessels themselves have broken adrift, notably in December, 1929, and November,

1954. These incidents recall the Brethren's tragically prophetic caution two centuries earlier: "A lightship would not ride, would break adrift and drown all the people".

Quickly following the Goodwin, and at the same £5,000 cost, the Sunk was fitted out as a mark for vessels entering the Thames from the north. Although the patent was dated July, 1796, there was a delay of over three years before the Admiralty gave permission for its laying as there was fear of the French making use of it.

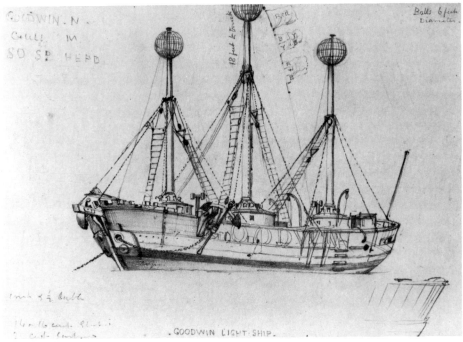

A lightship of about 1830, seen in a drawing by E. W. Cooke.   *National Maritime Museum*

The Admiralty were keener on a light near the Galloper shoal but Trinity House did not concur as to its usefulness to commercial shipping and their Lordships were compelled to fit out a vessel, which was laid in 1803. However, its supply was put in the hands of the Trinity Agent at Ramsgate, Mr George Strivens. The annual cost of its maintenance was £1,800, of which Strivens had £30.

The Gull Stream or Gull lightvessel was established by a similar process in 1809. Her two horizontal lanterns marked a passage inside the Goodwins, and this close proximity to the North and South Forelands induced the Admiralty to foist the maintenance on to Greenwich Hospital, which in turn could levy the dues. However, the Hospital took legal advice and in 1816 the Admiralty consented to pay.

In May, 1811, their Lordships asked for a light off Bembridge to mark the Ledge in the approaches to Portsmouth and Spithead. They requested the Elder Brethren appoint a master for the vessel then fitting out at the naval dockyard. The Littlehampton Agent recommended the mate of the Owers, William Loosemore, as a fit person and he asked that a single carronade be fitted as a warning gun. This was approved, as was the Admiralty request that the light-vessel be stored and supplied by the Trinity Agent and paid for in the same manner as the Galloper. Trinity House then recommended that two lanterns be exhibited to avoid confusion with the Owers and undertook to publish the necessary notices to mariners. On 10th September, 1812, the Commissioners informed the Brethren that the trow *Maria* was fitted and ready and that the Corporation's personnel should take charge of her and of the arrangements to lay her moorings, and that she should be "ignited" on 29th September.

The subsequent request for a "mooring lighter" and assistance indicates that the heavy chain moorings were laid out from a barge and then passed to the lightship. The *Maria* was laid on station and on 1st October the vessel (tug?) *Eliza* "who laid the (light) vessel on station returned and stated the reason for mooring the vessel off the Nab Rock instead of on . . . Bembridge Ledge . . . the tides on the edge of the Ledge are very strong and run in eddies, the ground there is rocky and foul and that the buoy of the Nab being no longer necessary may be taken away".

The three "Government lightvessels" continued to be paid for by the Admiralty and may be why ex-naval officers were again admitted to the Trinity Board about this time. In 1824 the charge for the Gull was £1,024 and that of the Bembridge £763. The latter seems to have been on a diminishing scale, for in 1813 it had cost £2,075, while by 1836 it was only £390. There exists a full description of the Galloper in 1826 when a Danish naval officer was permitted to inspect her, his government being desirous of establishing one off the Trindelen Rock.

Moored to a mushroom anchor and 200 fathoms of 1 1/8 inch patent chain, she carried two spare anchors, each with 100 fathoms of chain, and had sails to regain her station. It was agonising work weighing chain cable by hand, for this was shortly before chain cables came into use for even the largest battleships. We are compelled to admire those hard-bitten lightship sailors. When a naval fire-ship was detailed to act as a lightvessel off the Skaw during the Napoleonic Wars (the Skaw lighthouse having been extinguished) the duty was irksome and unpleasant. In the end the Royal Navy cut and ran: there is no record of a Trinity House lightvessel having been reduced to that!

The two lanterns were exhibited by night and a large scarlet flag by day.

Her crew were a master, mate, lamplighter, cook and nine seamen. Relieving was carried out so that the master or mate and eight others were always aboard.

Once the Napoleonic War was over lightvessels appeared in ever-increasing numbers. In 1815 the Stanford was laid off Lowestoft. In 1832 the South Sand Head (later the South Goodwin) followed, fitted with the new chinese gongs sounded in fog at intervals of ten minutes and replacing the confusing ship's bells used hitherto. In 1837 the scarlet flags were replaced by wooden balls at the mastheads, struck if the lightvessel dragged off station.

In 1849 the Leman and Ower lightvessel was laid on the extensive banks off Norfolk. She showed two lights, a fixed light aft 27 feet above the sea, and a revolving light forward, hoisted nightly to a height of 38 feet. So the floating light, or alarm vessel, had reached a state of development not far from its modern counterpart in terms of concept. True it used spermaceti oil rather than electricity, but the revolving light had arrived and the hoisting lantern continued in use until the Second World War.

By the time the Leman and Ower lightvessel was laid steam power had arrived to facilitate towing operations. How those ancient mariners managed their ungainly craft can now only be imagined.

The local Agents who tended their needs were often men of considerable resource who carried a great deal of responsibility, far more than that borne by individual Elder Brethren whose decisions were always made collectively. The Agents were in the front line when things went wrong and were the counterparts of today's District Superintendents.

Virtually nothing is known of the Littlehampton men who attended the Owers and Bembridge lightvessels beyond the fact that they supplied the ships with their stores and periodic reliefs. However, it is known that the Littlehampton Agent possessed two small cutters by 1820. The *Vigilant* had been built at North Yarmouth* in 1819, was cutter rigged and measured 30 52/94 tons, and the *Betsey* was of 38 54/94 tons. Built at Blackwall in 1818, she was for some time the Bembridge tender but is also listed as being stationed at Blackwall. Since the Blackwall Depot was opened some time later, she would appear to have started her service based at Littlehampton. She remained in use until sold for £228 in July, 1842. At this time Trinity House decided to abandon Littlehampton in favour of a wharf and store at East Cowes, which was purchased in 1842.

The tender to the Dudgeon lightvessel was based at Wells (a name by which the Dudgeon was formerly known). In June, 1786, one Allison Davie was appointed Buoy Keeper at Great Yarmouth and by 1809 was responsible for both the Dudgeon and the Haisbro lightvessel, known at this time as the Newarp.

Davie has left details of his charges. The Newarp was a vessel of 112 tons anchored in 11 fathoms to a 16 cwt mushroom anchor and 120 fathoms of chain.

*The old name for Great Yarmouth, Norfolk.

The chain was fabricated in the "King's Yard" of two-inch iron bar, the links being 11 inches overall. Her station was one mile from the north end of the Newarp bank and her crew were a master, mate and six men holding "protections" from the press. The crew served two months at sea and one ashore. During the latter period they worked in the buoy yard.

The Dudgeon was a little larger at 131 tons and had similar moorings except that these were supplied by the Limehouse company of Huddart & Co., owned by Captain Huddart who happened to be an Elder Brother! This lightvessel had leather chafing gear around her hawse and her lamps were in gimbals.

The Dudgeon had dragged twice in the period 1789 to 1809 through stress of weather, and the vessels were often run into. In this little has changed, the Dudgeon being holed last in 1977 by a German coaster. Her station was twenty miles from her base at Wells and Davie had a 60-ton tender there to carry out regular consignments of sperm oil and stores. In 1827 a new tender, the cutter *Dudgeon*, replaced Davie's original tender (probably of the same name). She was built at North Yarmouth and measured 62 20/94 tons.

Another 60-ton cutter was at Yarmouth and, under Davie's supervision, attended both the Newarp and the buoys around the Cockle, Scroby and Corton Sands. There were 22 of these moored to 13 cwt square stone sinkers, about 18 inches thick with a central hole. The chains, which varied from 7 to 15 fathoms "according to depth and dangerous situation", were considerably shorter and the weights lighter than those in use now. Spare buoys were kept in a buoy yard ashore and cleaned, overhauled and painted by "off-duty" lightsmen. Davie probably employed a full-time cooper and blacksmith. Spare sets of cables were also held for the two lightvessels and "at every good opportunity, now and then, to observe the effect the salts may have in corroding the iron" the chains were examined. Davie also had to make arrangements every three years to bring the lightvessels off station for cleaning and repairs.

The sandbanks off the coast, particularly those around the Cockle Gat, were continuously surveyed, and this work was carried out by a little 20-ton cutter. Davie altered the buoys to conform with the channels and exercised wide discretionary powers over his squadron. In 1820 two larger vessels were stationed at Yarmouth. The *Diligent* was built at Cowes by Thomas White and was a cutter of 59 68/94 tons. She lasted until 1839 when she was in service in the Bristol Channel and on 3rd November was wrecked on Flatholm.

Diligent was joined a year later by the prosaically named *Trinity Buoy Yacht*, a larger cutter of 95 tons. She was 58 feet 3 inches on the keel with a beam of 19 feet 8 inches, her hold depth being 10 feet 4 inches. Her hull was "of English growth, properly season'd, and free from sap, strake or Defect, the whole of the frame well grown and square . . . ' Her decks were of Dantzic deal 2½'' thick and she was "framed with proper carlings and partners—the main hatchway coaming to be 6'' thick and 10'' deep".

For buoy work she had a rufftree rail fore and aft and an ''Iron roller fix'd in a solid chock forward; a windlass with iron necks and iron Pawls; to have sufficient bitts for receiving the bowsprit and for Pawling the Windlass, together with proper Carrick Bitts, secured in the upper deck, by sufficient carlings and knees . . . '' and ''a good substantial winch to the mast or bitts''. The cost of this Buoy Yacht was 15 guineas the ton.

This vessel with her rather uninspiring name was still at Yarmouth in 1845. In 1833 she had been joined by the *Eliza*.

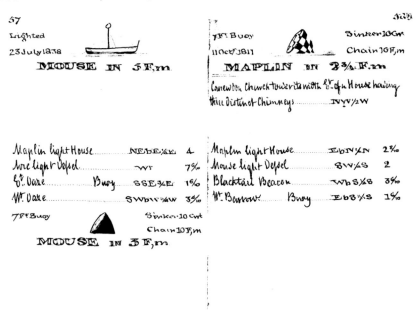

A page from a detailed record of all Trinity stations kept by Captain George Probyn, 1843. Probyn, an Elder Brother, recorded the marks and bearings for all seamarks from Northumbria to the Solway in this book.   *Cruising Association*

Eliza may have been intended for use in the Bristol Channel, since she was built at Milford Haven in that year, 1833. In 1820 Flatholm lighthouse was raised and improved with an oil reflector lantern. Although the proprietor's lease had a few years to run, a tender was built and stationed at Cardiff. Curiously this vessel was built at North Yarmouth and named *Yarmouth*, being a cutter of 59 13/94 tons. It seems that the introduction of buoys on the Wolves Rock and other dangers in the Bristol Channel demanded a Buoy Yacht and that *Yarmouth* and *Diligent* were sent on that service while *Eliza* came to Yarmouth. *Eliza* was of similar size, being a cutter of 51 21/94 tons. According to Chaplin she was still at Yarmouth in 1841. Indeed it is possible that she and the large *Trinity Buoy Yacht* remained on this important station until the commissioning of the second steam vessel named *Argus* in 1856.

Further south the Ramsgate agency looked after the Goodwin area. George Strivens had been appointed Collector of light dues at Ramsgate about 1790 and when the Goodwin lightvessel was established five years later he accepted the agency for an additional annual salary of £30. In due course the Gull and Galloper became his responsibility, as has been shown, bringing his income up to £90. In 1813 this was increased to £40 per lightvessel with an additional £10 for work "in the buoy department".

Clearly Strivens was attending both lightvessels and buoys, for it was at this time that buoys supplemented the alarm vessels round the Goodwins. In 1796 the Elbow and Gull buoys were laid, in 1819 the Broadstairs Knoll, and the Ramsgate Fairway as early as 1783. It also appears that Strivens was the first man to use that contentious seamark the green wreck buoy on some of the wrecks that still occurred. At Ramsgate Strivens rented a warehouse for stores and buoys at £80 per year from 1817, and founded the Depot which lasted until 1914.

To carry out his duties Strivens had the *Antelope*, a cutter that remained in service at Ramsgate until 1839 when she was replaced by *Lyra*. She is thought to have been sold off as a going concern and to have lasted even longer. Strivens manned *Antelope* with the "off duty" lightship men, and judging by his activity these unfortunate men can have had little time at home. *Antelope* was hard pressed to maintain the three lightvessels, particularly with the Goodwin so liable to drag. Strivens frequently had to hire assistance, for in November, 1825, the master of the smack *Ezra* was paid £70 for towing the temporary lightvessel at the Galloper into Dover.

Some idea of *Antelope's* movements and duties can be gauged from extracts of the log of the Goodwin lightvessel for 1804:

"tender off after placing the North Brake buoy.
"16 June. Tender took the moorings and the Goodwin Light went to Ramsgate (to be cleaned), fix'd the lamps to the tender."

The Goodwin was back on station on 30th June and a few days later leaked 13 inches in six hours. It was a question of pumping until 17th June, 1805, before the Goodwin again left her moorings to *Antelope*, proceeded to Ramsgate for cleaning and paying, and returned the next day.

On another occasion: "Saw *Antilope* (sic) going to the Galloper" and again "sent a letter home by a mackerel boat". The standard of contemporary navigation is vividly illustrated in the entry "Brig hove to and inquired if we were Galloper". On the other hand it had its compensations, for on 1st March, 1806, "Picked up five casks Brandy and one of Rum".

In 1839 the *Lyra* (O.N. 19958) took over from the *Antelope*. She was a cutter of 67 21/94 tons burthen built at Limehouse and may be the cutter shown with the steamer on page 60. She is mentioned in a journal dated June, 1840, and is known to have had a long life, "first at Ramsgate and later at other stations".

In 1832 the South Sand Head lightvessel had come under Ramsgate's jurisdiction, but by this time Strivens had retired after 46 years' service, 32 of which had been as Agent for lights. His pension was £40 annually and he enjoyed nine years of retirement before his death in 1836.

His successor, Stephen Holmes, retired through ill health and was replaced by Richard Davies, who was granted two shillings per day when afloat on duty. In 1839 the store was enlarged and after 1844, the Harbour Trustees having purchased a steam tug, this was frequently chartered at £1 the hour for buoy laying and attending the lightvessels. The number of the latter had been increased by the laying of the Varne and East Goodwin ships, although the Galloper had passed to the Harwich Agent about 1828. By 1847 Davies was referred to as the "Superintendent" and he died in 1854.

The Harwich Agent was Mr Harcourt Runnacles, who in 1826 was apparently unfit. Mr Mayor, master of the Sunk lightvessel, was

> "called in and questioned on the mode in which the buoy service is at present conducted and it appearing that the execution thereof afloat has rested principally with himself, and that he has been in the service of the Corporation as master of the Sunk lightvessel for 24 years and . . . on board the Owers lightvessel for 8 years, resolved to . . . appoint him . . . as agent to the Sunk lightvessel and Buoy Keeper at Harwich. And having regard to Mr Mayor's great length of service and practical knowledge recommend that he be allowed a salary of £100 p.a."

His appointment coincided with the arrival of a new tender. The unimaginatively and dolorously named *Sunk* was a cutter of 60 62/94 tons built at Limehouse. It is possible she may have replaced the *Argus* mentioned in Bromfield's correspondence.

In the previous chapter allusion is made to the apparent upkeep of buoys after the Restoration. In his apologia on Trinity House John Whormby gives fuller details. In 1669 the Court of Trinity House appointed two Buoy Keepers for the Thames Estuary. One, based at Margate, was to attend the buoys in the south channels for a salary of £18 yearly, which rose to £25 by 1742. The north channels were attended to from Harwich, where the buoy keeper had £16, increased to £18 in 1687 when the Ooze Edge buoy was added. From this it is fair to deduce they had about nine or ten buoys to look after. However these gentlemen apparently took advantage of the perquisites that accrued to their appointments and a contract had to be drawn up wherein Trinity House supplied all buoys, chains and stores from London, bore the cost of all smith's and cooper's work, allowing the Buoy Keepers £70 a year for everything else.

Out of this amount the Buoy Keeper had to man and operate his tender.

The situation remained thus until 1742 when the Brethren decided to have their own Buoy Yacht, and the result of this resolution was, as we saw in Chapter Two, Mr Widgeon's *Trinity Sloop*. The unsatisfactory Buoy Keepers were discharged on midsummer's day, 1742, which indicates that the *Trinity Sloop* was in commission by that time and the Yacht Establishment, under the Buoy Warden, may be dated from this period.

Eighteenth-century buoys were coopered from ash or oak staves, bound with iron work, some bearing topmarks as outlined in Cotton's Memoir to Lord Liverpool, all brightly painted and named or numbered. By 1820 some buoys bore warning bells actuated by waves, but by and large those tended by the sailing yachts and tenders before the steam age were of this simple type.

How then did the masters and crews of the Buoy Yachts manage?

"A proper davit," as portrayed in Falconer's Marine Dictionary.

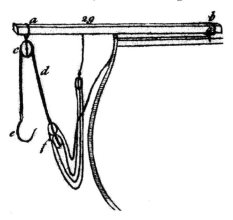

In 1791 a contract was signed with Messrs Randall and Brent for a new Buoy Yacht of about 100 tons. It is possible that this vessel was the cutter *Argus* which was commanded by a "Captain Saunders" and assisted Bromfield in the destruction of the buoyage in 1797. Be that as it may, the Buoy Yacht had a keel of 50 feet, a beam of 18 feet and a hold depth of 10 feet 6 inches. She was built in oak with the deck of the customary Baltic pine. Clearly on the London Yacht Establishment, she was grander than her contemporary sisters at the outports, for she had "a light handsome carved stern, and quarter pieces and the Trinity Arms on the Center (sic) and Two Quarter Badges". She had sliding sash windows glazed with crown glass giving light on to a cabin "fitted up in a plain neat Manner with four bedplaces with sliding doors two on each side, and . . . a Water Closet and Store Closet." She mounted six guns on her quarterdeck and a galley was fitted up against her forward bulkhead. A platform for the buoys was made " . . . as directed" and this probably constituted a light, sacrificial spar deck which could easily be replaced.

As usual she had her "Capstand (sic) with Drumhead and six bars" and "a proper David (davit) with a large sheave fix'd forward". It is clear from the specification that there was no special lifting gear above the level of the rail although the davit head could, and probably was, adjusted by a masthead topping lift as was just being introduced in the navy for the hoisting of quarter boats. There was rarely any special lifting gear on a sailing vessel, the derrick being an invention necessary to steam, for whilst yards, masts and stays existed these were employed to lift weights inboard and outboard. The "yard and stay" technique, however, was scarcely suitable to a cutter since the yard in question was a light, sliding spar.

It is therefore probable that tackles were led from the lower mast hounds to transfer buoys from the davit head to the deck. To direct the buoys horizontally, or keep them clear of obstructions, handy billies (small, portable tackles) were rigged where required. The bowsprit housing had "sufficient bowsprit partners to fit all Kevel Ranges, Blocks . . . & Co.". The Kevel, or Cavil, was a thick, horizontal timber bolted to partners to form a very heavy cleat.

It is quite likely that in changing buoys the yachts used to carry out one at a time, especially those of the largest class, eight and ten feet in diameter. Loading the clean buoy from the sheerlegs and lighter at Deptford, the sinker alongside it and the chain fleeted in the waist, the Buoy Yacht would have dropped downstream as wind and tide served. It is most unlikely that the buoys were towed, as their drag would have seriously hampered a sailing vessel in the then crowded waters of the Thames, although a boat was undoubtedly streamed astern. The carriage of buoys on the foredeck would have rendered the staysail virtually useless, hence the advantage of a big jib out on its long bowsprit, counteracting the mainsail and making the cutter handy in stays.

Given fair weather the Buoy Yacht would approach the buoy to be serviced and moor to it, heaving it alongside her gangway, just forward of her mast. A short chain snotter or weighted rope dropped over the buoy would capsize it and when hove upon at the capstan, bring the mooring chain up in the "large sheave fix'd forward".

The buoy could now be disconnected and passed astern out of the way. If new moorings were to be laid the old chain and sinker were hove up and the Buoy Yacht's own anchor let got. If not, the mooring was examined through "the thrash", that part of it that rises and falls on the sea bed due to the action of the wind and tide and consequently suffers the greatest wear.

With the old sinker hove up to the davit head, the masthead tackles lifted it inboard and the operation reversed would have the new one over the side. With stone or iron sinkers, renewal would be infrequent and short lengths of heavy ganger chain would remove the need to bring the weight inboard, allowing it to be stopped off prior to the fitting of a new chain.

Wrought iron forelock shackles and chain were used, usually with long links

Trinity House, as seen in a nineteenth-century print.

to reduce cost. The new buoy was got over by the masthead and davit tackles, lowered and slipped to its relaid mooring. Lying back on a rope, the dirty buoy could then be hauled back alongside and hoisted aboard.

By comparison with the above, buoy painting and cleaning was probably fairly easy. The davit would lift the head of the buoy, the capstan the "arse", so that the whole thing lay overside but horizontal. Men could then scrape off marine growth while the buoy was slowly parbuckled, completing the job with a coat of paint and tar.

Whilst the mate carried out these operations forward, the yacht master would check the position of the buoy by its various marks and/or angles. If adjustment was necessary he would manoeuvre the Buoy Yacht accordingly. A second mate might also be sent off in the boat to sound for the bank or shoal.

A painting by Butterfield shows two Buoy Yachts off the Eddystone. Although dated 1815, the ensign is the pre-1801 type without St Patrick's saltire. Flying Elder Brothers' flags at the masthead, they are on an unspecified visit, perhaps the principal yacht was elsewhere at the time but they are certainly vessels of the London Yacht Establishment.

The Buoy Yachts carried crews of about 40 men. Poulter's *Trinity Yacht* had a mate and two second mates.

It is clear that such work was only carried out in the summer months, and this was the general practice until within living memory. Today the vast number of buoys, the reduction of the tender fleet and the distances involved has meant the work goes on continuously.

The mysterious "schooner" *Charon* seen in a painting by an unknown artist, 1841. Note the seaboats hoisted on her quarters and the Elder Brethren's flag at her foremasthead.

National Maritime Museum

We do not know how long the Buoy Yacht of 1791 lasted. She was probably replaced about the same time as Poulter's yacht, some time around the middle 1820's. At all events, in 1827 a new vessel was registered. She was named *Charon*. The ferryman across the Styx, whom one paid when passing to Hades, provided perhaps not such an inappropriate name for a vessel looking after seamarks intended to guide the mariner through the shades of night. One wonders whether any of her crew were classical scholars enough to appreciate the allusion.

She was built at Harwich, probably at the Navy Yard since her construction was certified by the surveyor of the Navy. Registered as a schooner, her rig in

1842 was something of a curiosity, more like the then accepted form of a brig with a fore spencer (see opposite). Ninety-seven feet between perpendiculars with a beam of nearly 15 feet and hold depth of 10 feet made her narrow gutted. She was carvel built with a square stern and what is described as a "sham gallery" with the Corporation's Arms. She hoisted boats in davits and bore an immensely long jib-boom.

Charon was stationed at London but was not registered until 1849 when a 33 foot long engine room is given. As there is no mention of engine details a possible proposed conversion to steam auxiliary power may have been suspended, for on 12th December, 1853, *Charon* was sold to William Philip Beach, of Globe Dock, Rotherhithe.

One Jonathan Poulter was her master in 1848, and as he appears to have successively commanded the Corporation's new ships as they commissioned he seems to have been the principal officer, or Superintendent, of the London Yacht Establishment. The Warden's minutes refer to his promotion in late 1824, so he may well have been the son of the master and commander of the *Trinity Yacht* of 1788. As late as 1858 a Mr Poulter is referred to in connection with finding a replacement on the sudden death of one of the tender masters.

Before concluding, some mention must further be made of lightvessel cable-work. Before the steam age any work with chains was hard and exhausting. Even the largest ships used rope cables with their anchors, for it was the handling of such brute things that took time and energy. Anchor handling was facilitated by cat-heads and davits, cables were a more difficult and dangerous task. When *Antelope* laid out the Goodwin's moorings, how was it done? We can only conjecture. From the evidence available concerning the Bembridge lightvessel her moorings were laid out by a "mooring lighter" and transferred to the lightvessel when she arrived on station. There is no such lighter mentioned in connection with the later custom built vessels which, unlike the converted trow *Maria*, had their own windlasses. Probably they had their own cable lockers and the low geared, hand operated barrel windlasses that seem to have been available at the time enabled the chains to be laboriously veered or weighed. Whatever the method it must have been slow and arduous. In these operations the tender's crew would assist, since one of the functions of these vessels was, and still is, to provide a mobile labour force. Hence the Buoy Yachts and tenders carried large crews and the work on which they were engaged was sufficiently dangerous to warrant a large insurance premium in 1824 when the Warden's minutes record a sum of £3,500 being paid.

The decade that followed this payment was to see the last of the sailing yachts, but before leaving them we must turn our attention to the lighthouses that were appearing on the rocky promontories and reefs of Wales and Cornwall that jutted out into the wild fury of the Atlantic Ocean.

CHAPTER FOUR

The Eddystone and other rocks

"His only man . . . upon whom was all his dependance in landing at the (light) house where nobody els could or wou'd venture."

The Plymouth Agent, 1st May 1702

THE tower on the Eddystone has a special place in the iconology of lighthouses. It represents the unremitting determination of certain men to overcome natural barriers, and remains so to this day when these limits, forced further outwards by science, are largely beyond the comprehension of the common man. Today the Eddystone light is an immensely impressive monument to human achievement.

No fewer than five towers have been erected on the reef, four of them during the age of sail and oar. By any standards it posed problems, and the only thing in the builder's favour is that the Eddystone, unlike the Wolf Rock, does not cover at high tide.

Before the building of the first tower the Eddystone had been a fearful danger to mariners, lying in wait for ships approaching Plymouth:

"... a wicked reef of twenty three rust red granite rocks lying nine and a half miles south of the Rame Head on the Devon mainland, great ragged stones around which the sea constantly eddies, a great danger . . . for if any vessel makes too far to the south . . . she will be caught in the prevailing strong current and swept to her doom on these evil rocks."

Thus wrote Christopher Jones, Master of the famous *Mayflower*, in the first half of the 17th century, and he aptly encapsulates the fears and protests of mariners and merchants.

So vociferous did these protests become that the Crown was petitioned for something to be done and in 1694 William and Mary issued a decree that

"... having regard for the many gallant seamen who have perished round these dangerous rocks, these said captains, shipowners and merchants are agreed and willing to pay to the Corporation of Trinity House one penny a ton outward and . . . inward for the benefit of a warning light."

The Elder Brethren protested the impossibility of such a scheme, saying they had no experience or expertise in the matter of such an undertaking. Although the light at Scilly had just been completed, it was a very different locality from the wave-swept Eddystone.

Eventually a wealthy Plymouth merchant undertook financial responsibility and a gentleman adventurer named Henry Winstanley was chosen to design and build the proposed tower. Winstanley describes the site thus:

> "Although the weather seemed most calm in other places, yet here (the sea) would mount and fly more than two hundred feet . . . and therefore all our works are constantly buried at these times, and exposed to the mercies of the seas; and no power on earth able to come near to make good or help anything."

Winstanley thus describes the effect of the Atlantic ground swell which, even on calm days, makes the ocean heave like some vast sub-aqueous respiratory system. His persistent endeavours were crowned with success and a light was exhibited from his bizarre, pagoda-like structure on 14th November, 1698. He had triumphed in an incredibly short time over the forces of nature and the malice of man, for the War of Spanish Succession was in progress and French privateers abducted his workmen. By special order of Louis XIV, who may have nurtured ulterior motives, Winstanley and his men were repatriated in a cartel.

Smeaton was to have similar problems with the press gangs of his own nation, and this is perhaps the place to mention the importance of these early lighthouses in the tangled diplomacy of the times. It is remarkable that as early as the eighteenth century a special treaty was drawn up between those ancient enemies France and England to guarantee the maintenance and safety from raid of Vauban's lighthouse at Pointe Le Stiff, Ushant, lit for eight months of the year "in peace as in war".

Returning to Winstanley's tower, it was found to be too ornate and was simplified and strengthened into his "second tower". But alas, man proposes and God disposes. Visiting the tower with workmen in the fall of 1703, Henry Winstanley, his workmen, keepers and the entire structure were utterly destroyed in the greatest gale ever recorded in Britain, which swept the south of the country on the night of 26/27th November.

Little time elapsed before a stone and wooden tower followed. Inspired by boatbuilding techniques, it was designed and built under the direction of John Rudyerd and completed in July, 1708. It stood successfully until 1755, when it was destroyed from within by fire. The keepers escaped, huddled on the rocks below, for it was a calm night. One died later, and a nugget of lead that he had swallowed when molten was discovered in his stomach.

It was now the turn of Smeaton, and he describes conditions at the lighthouse in his account of the building.

"I was astonished to find that the account given by Mr Winstanley did not appear to be exaggerated. At intervals of a minute and sometimes two and three, I suppose when a certain combination happens to produce one overgrown wave, it would strike the rock and building conjointly and fly up in a white column enwrapping it like a sheet . . . I particularly noticed the manner in which the waves began to gather as soon as they came so near . . . as to be sensible of the sloping rocks under them. Those waves, by degrees towering higher . . . formed a deep hollow sea at the foot of the building; then falling into it, struck it with all imaginable force . . . Even when the sea was smooth and unruffled by the slightest breeze, where the groundswell meets the slopes of these the sea breaks upon them in a frightful manner."

When Trinity House took over the light in 1807 the candles were replaced by Argand lights and reflectors. The local Agent in 1813 was the collector of customs at Plymouth, Mr Tolcher, and under his direction was the *Eddystone Tender*. In 1811 this cutter replaced a smaller vessel, which was withdrawn as soon as Trinity House had acquired its own replacement.

The *Eddystone Tender* was 48 feet "upon the deck", of 14 foot beam, with a hold depth of 6 feet. Her burthen was about 36 tons and her crew comprised a captain aged "about 70", a mate "of about 65" and "Pollard aged about 50". Visiting the lighthouse in 1813, the famous Scots engineer Stevenson, contemplating a passage in the vessel, considered that "the crew being so very far advanced in life I thought it advisable to procure another man or two to enable me to make a push at landing when I should go off". He obtained the services of the son of Mr Churchill, the mate. Early in the morning of 13th September they left Plymouth "with the wind at the south west blowing fresh". It was to be the beginning of a memorable day.

"A great number of coasters for company, but the *Eddystone Tender* beat the whole fleet for sailing. At two p.m. the tender hove to on the south west side of the lighthouse at the distance of about half a mile from the tower, and the boat being manned, she stood till within a cable's length, when I got into the boat with my frail crew consisting of young Churchill and the captain, who pulled the after oar while I steered. As it blew fresh and threatened to be heavy weather it was judged advisable to leave two men in the tender . . . In rowing towards the rock the old captain was thrown off his seat and fell back by his oar unshipping . . . and as I was approaching a strange place and one of which I heard much of the dangers, I felt no small uneasiness at being so ill-provided with a crew. The seat of precedence in a boat is . . . at the stern oar and the captain took it,

The Eddystone Tender delivers stores to Smeaton's tower at the time of Stevenson's visit, seen in a sketch by the author after a print by an unknown artist.

but as the most commanding oar is the bow, it was with difficulty that she could be kept in her course as the young man's exertions had the effect of turning the boat . . . However we approached . . . with safety though not with ease, as there was a cross head sea running. On making the entry into the gut, or landing place, a heavy sea fell into it over the south west ledge and this sea, coming round the north west into the gut, obliged us to set the boat stern off, to prevent her from being filled, but before this could be done, and from the weakness of her crew, there came on board a considerable quantity of water and wetted the bowman.

"Watching for a smooth, the boat was rowed speedily up to the rock. The lightkeepers threw a rope into the boat, and I veered out rope astern from the grappling (grapnel, a four-fluked stockless anchor, very light and efficient on a rocky bottom, the method is used to this day at the Eddystone and other rock lighthouses) which we had previously let go. In this manner the boat got close to the rock, though not . . . without shipping more sea, as the lightkeeper threw the northmost rope into the boat, which did not haul her enough ahead of the roll of the sea which came round the rock in that direction. But when this was rectified and the rope shifted I got close to the rock, when I speedily ascended a ladder . . . ''

Poor Stevenson's relief can only have been tempered by apprehension for the return trip. He regained the deck of the tender without incident, only to have the mate, Churchill, at the helm, pass perilously close to the rocks while ''the captain and crew cried out in despair''.

On his return to Plymouth Stevenson mentions the floating light moored in the fairway to guide shipping clear of the breakwater then under construction. He concludes '' . . . we made the floating light about 6 p.m., got safely into Sutton Pool, when I landed with a thankful heart that I had got so safely over this trip''.

I make no apology for quoting extensively from Stevenson because he gives an authentic picture of a boat landing at a rock lighthouse and the only one extant for the period. Leaving aside the aged and comic crew, the performance of the *Eddystone Tender* herself was clearly impressive. Plymouth built, she remained in service until 1846 when she was lost on the Isles of Scilly.

The age problem seems to have been peculiar to Plymouth. Doubtless the activities of the naval press had much to do with a lack of suitable manpower. Even six years after Stevenson's visit Tolcher's successor, John Arthur, was writing to Trinity House on the same point but with a different crew. The men given as manning the *Eddystone Tender* are ''John Burgoin aged 73, Daniel Pallot aged 72 and Allen Churchward aged 68''. Arthur goes on to say

''the youngest in point of years are the most incapable, but all from age and Infirmities are wholly incompetent to the management of the vessel intrusted to their charge, unless it is very moderate weather, and even then require assistance, consequently the lighthouse is not visited as often as directed . . . some accidents have occurred and my fears are excited whenever the vessel goes out''.

Neither Tolcher nor Arthur seems to have possessed the energies of a George Strivens. Neither appears to have ventured to sea, presumably detained by their duties at the Custom House. The problem of manning the tender to the Eddystone was not new to the incumbent of the post of Plymouth Agent. As early as May, 1702, the then Agent protested that his boatman, James Bound, had been impressed aboard the *Rochester*, man o' war. He expressed the distress in which Mr Winstanley then found himself as a consequence of having "his only man taken from him upon whom was all his dependance in landing at the house where nobody els could or wou'd venture". Stores and materials were urgently required and Bound's return was imperative "so as that wee may proceed with savety to carry ye candles and things to the house which lye now reddy by ye water side to goe off".

It seems likely that the crew of the *Eddystone Tender* were amongst the first to have an exemption from the Impress Service, so it is difficult to understand fully why successive Plymouth Agents had so much difficulty recruiting. Pay was quite good, 2s 6d per day for the mate and third hand, and by the end of the Napoleonic Wars, the disbanding of the armed forces and a recession and unemployment throughout the land should have cured at least Arthur's problem.

Arthur was anxious about accidents and in particular the handling of the small boat. How small it was is revealed by some correspondence of 1815 between Arthur and James Court in London. Tolcher enclosed a quotation from Messrs Moore and Son for "A Compleat copper fastened well finished boat with skeg and stem band also three coats of paint. Length 14' 6" Breadth 5' 8" Depth 2' 3". Compleat at £13 1s."

The subject of Agents is one upon which Stevenson waxes scathing. On his last English lighthouse tour in 1818 aboard *Pharos* he visited Caskets in the Channel Islands. "The Governor of Alderney is said to be the agent for the lights—and contractor indeed! Be that as it may this important lighthouse establishment is very unlike a public one and seems to be little attended to either in keeping or putting up".

The supply of necessities for the lighthouse was undertaken by a boatman from Braye, on neighbouring Alderney. He was summoned "when they want beer and other stores, they make signals by a telegraph to the island of Alderney for the attendant boat or vessel, according to the state of the weather".

Caskets is barely an island, more a cluster of rocks, but it supported "one man and his family with a girl who acts as a servant, but is rather in the character of a nun. She has been here five years and said she had been a very bad girl and had come here to reclaim herself". Stevenson's solicitude for the girl did not extend to the keepers. "The keepers are said not to remain here more than seven years when they expect a pension". His sense of outrage continues, especially as the salary was "£25 per annum and his victuals".

But complaints of the Caskets pre-dated Stevenson's visit. The standard of light keeping was frequently poor but as there were originally three fires to attend to, each in its separate tower (named St Peter, St Thomas and Dungeon) that is, perhaps, understandable. Although the first fires had been lit on 30th December, 1724, twenty years later Admiral Balchen's flagship, HMS *Victory*, was lost on the reef at a cost of 1,100 lives.

The facility with which keepers are now flown by helicopter to these isolated stations is in great contrast to lighthouse work before the 1840's. The combination of the 1836 Act and steam power which made possible the great building programme of the second half of the nineteenth century obscures many of the difficulties overcome by the early tender crews. In addition to the Eddystone and Caskets lights, both the Longships and the Smalls were offshore rock stations whilst St Agnes, on the Scilly island of the same name, required a tender by virtue of its isolation.

The Corporation had had an agent at Penzance for Longships and the Scilly light, whilst servicing of the the Smalls, off Pembrokeshire, was undertaken privately.

The Longships had been lit on 29th December, 1795, and had keepers of ''a very ragged and wild like appearance'' in 1818. Stevenson contradicts Cotton's assertion that the Brethren frequently inspected all the lights: ''No person to inspect has been here for four years''. Although the Longships was privately built, Trinity House almost immediately assumed responsibility since the builder, Lieutenant Henry Smith, was declared ''incapable of managing the concern''.

At the turn of the century a man named John Millet was agent for the Longships, which had four keepers who did a month on and a month off in pairs. Reliefs were rowed out from Sennen Cove, where a store was built, and no sailing tender was allocated to the station.

The main tender was the cutter stationed at Scilly used for supplying St Agnes lighthouse. Running between the island and the mainland, she may have doubled as a packet as well as for more obscure Kurnowic purposes. The building of the Wolf Rock lighthouse (1861-1869) made Penzance the pre-eminent station and eclipsed Scilly. By that time St Agnes had been discontinued and James Walker's first Bishop Rock tower had been built (1858). The keepers of the Bishop lived on St Mary's and until the introduction of helicopters, like the men of Longships, were conveyed thither by local boat. In 1910, the steam boat having broken down, the relief was undertaken by the St Agnes gig, entailing a round trip of twenty-five miles under oars.

After 1841 the Scilly tender *Billow* also had the Sevenstones lightvessel to look after. Although no details survive of the first tenders on this station, the locally built *Scilly* was commissioned in 1827. At 46 60/94 tons burthen she probably replaced an older vessel of the same name.

Scilly was succeeded by *Billow* (O.N. 20327) variously described as a sloop or cutter of 34 tons and built at Charlestown, Cornwall, in 1834. There is no apparent reason for *Scilly's* short life except perhaps an unrecorded wrecking. Nevertheless, when Walker began the Bishop Rock tower *Billow* was joined by *Diligent.* The open iron lattice structure was designed as an improvement on the rickety but successful Smalls, allowing the sea to pass through its web of girders. It was completed at the end of 1849 and was ready to receive the lighting apparatus when on 5th February, 1850, it was destroyed in a gale at a loss of

£12,000. The granite tower built in its place was strengthened several times, finally by Sir James Douglass, who virtually encapsulated Walker's tower, adding to its height until it weighed 5,720 tons.

There is a record that both *Diligent* (the second of that name) and *Billow* were at Scilly in May, 1849, in connection with the building work. *Diligent* was a cutter of 50 registered tons built at Falmouth in 1845 (O.N. 5810). This is the only record of her, and she may well have been a chartered vessel or loaned pilot cutter. The record may be an error, and it is possible that the tender with *Billow* was the even more mysterious *Tortoise*, for reasons discussed in Chapter Six. *Billow* lasted forty years, for with the *Wolf* she attended the building of the Wolf Rock light and went on to serve at London, but *Diligent* fades into oblivion.

The Smalls lighthouse is situated on a cluster of rocks 15 miles west of the red coast of Pembrokeshire. The reef was as dangerous to shipping making for Liverpool as the Eddystone to Channel traffic. On 1st September, 1776, a light was first shown from the grotesque pile lighthouse then newly completed. Although doused for some months for strengthening, it was relit in September, 1778. The undertaking was supervised by Henry Whiteside, whose apprenticeship for lighthouse construction had been served as a musical instrument maker! Built on long oak piles, the dwelling and lightroom were said to move in a gale to such an extent that on one occasion the terrified keepers sent off a distress message in a bottle. It reached St Bride's Bay and was found. The would-be rescuers eventually found the keepers well, if a little shaken by the experience. Stevenson was not impressed. The tower struck him as a "raft of timber rudely put together . . . " and he intimated Whiteside should have stuck to violin manufacture. Scarcely fair from a man whose only qualification was as a metal "Hammerman". Whiteside's tower stood 77 years before Douglass built his stone tower, confounding its critics and puzzling James Walker, whose enthusiastic copy on the Bishop met with the fate described above. The stumps of Whiteside's tower may still be seen.

As early as 1759 a bell buoy had been suggested for the Wolf Rock. Its isolated needle point is perhaps the most lethal danger on the Cornish coast and several efforts were made to erect beacons upon it. All ended in failure until Walker's granite tower was lit on 1st January, 1870. It remained the most difficult station to relieve until the introduction of the helicopter, and its keepers were frequently days, occasionally weeks, overdue in their reliefs.

The apparent inability of Trinity House, or anyone else for that matter, to establish a seamark on the Wolf worried the Admiralty a great deal. When their lordships heard Stevenson intended a tour of English lighthouses they saw the possibility of this brilliant engineer being encouraged to consider such an undertaking. With this in mind they went to the unusual end of placing a vessel at his disposal. Stevenson concludes this chapter in his own words, words that graphically describe the difficulties inherent in wind-driven ships. It sums up the personal risk that was the daily lot of seamen at this time where hazard was commonplace.

Taking ship in HMS *Orestes*, a 25 (sic) gun ship-sloop, Captain Smith commanding, Stevenson had to traverse a distance of 68 miles from Plymouth to the Wolf Rock. Boarding in the afternoon, they were still "plying to windward" that evening. All the next day they "kept working along the shore", beating west and at 7 p.m. anchored in Mounts Bay, where the services of a pilot from Mousehole were secured.

All the next day they were becalmed, weighing at 6 a.m. the following morning and "the wind shifting from south west to east with a fine breeze, and at 11 a.m. got up with the Wolf Rock. At 12 noon two boats were manned—one commanded by a midshipman and the other by Lieutenant Fallick, into which I went, and after pulling round and round the rock with both boats, sounding all the while, he made preparations for landing. Mr Fallick arranged his boat's crew and let go a grappling over the stern, then veered away upon this stern rope watching for a smooth, and when the boat was near enough, the young man . . . appointed to land with a bow rope to make fast leaped upon the rock and upon these two ropes the boat was hauled off and on with great ease and facility".

The keepers at the Wolf Rock being relieved by a method which only fell into disuse when the helicopter arrived. The boat could never lie alongside the rock.   *F. W. Taylor*

CHAPTER FIVE

The Act of 1836 and the Age of Steam

" . . . Whether it is expedient with a view to the utmost
efficient and prompt execution of the Public Service, that a
Steam Vessel should be employed by the Corporation . . . "
Captain Woolmore, Deputy Master, 3 October 1833

THE very exclusivity of the Brotherhood of St Clement and the Glorious and Undivided Trinity has, from time to time, excited the jealousy of others. This is nothing new. Secretary John Whormby produced an "Apologia" as early as 1746, and Joseph Cotton was at pains to refute allegations of culpability. In an age of great corruption in public offices the Trinity House seems to have been morally exemplary. But the Elder Brethren were easy targets, possible kettles for black pots to point at. Indeed, during Cotton's tenure of office they were often known as "The Merchant Brethren", with all the disparaging connotations that contemporary society associated with "trade"!

The activities of Trinity House were the subject of a number of Parliamentary Enquiries. The first two were concerned with pilotage matters but those of 1822, 1834 and 1845 were directly to do with lighthouses, buoys and beacons. The 1834 enquiry led to the Act of 1836 and is significant in our story.

In 1822 the Select Committee on Foreign Trade recommended that all lighthouses came under Trinity House control, with a consequent reduction in dues and encouragement of trade. The result of this was that in the next decade Trinity House acquired a number of lighthouses for which the private owners demanded substantial compensation. In 1823 Flatholm lighthouse was bought for £15,829, in 1825 Farne Island cost £36,000 and Burnham leading lights in Somerset £13,500. The North and South Forelands purchased from Greenwich Hospital came at the bargain price of £8,400 the pair in 1832.

Several government lights were transferred gratis in the period 1827-37. They included the Gull and Galloper lightvessels, Gibraltar and Heligoland lighthouses. The island of Heligoland in the German Bight had been captured from the French in 1807, principally as an entrepôt for the trade with Europe that Napoleon strove to prevent.

The Parliamentary Act of 1836 (6, 7, William IV, Cap 79, 13 August 1836) which followed the 1834 Royal Commission was of profound importance to the history of lighthouses. It was in effect an act of nationalisation, bringing the seamarks of England and Wales into line with those of Scotland and Ireland.

Section 3 empowered Trinity House to buy the Crown leases of the two lights of Harwich and Orford; to purchase Dungeness, Winterton and Hunstanton; to buy out the Trinity leases of Smalls and Longships (this cost £37,000 alone); and made provision for special Acts to take over the perpetual leases of Spurn and Skerries. All succeeding construction was, of course, undertaken by Trinity House.

It proved an immensely expensive business. Even by today's standards huge profits could be made by lighthouse owners. I have already alluded to Mr Coke's £7,000 from Dungeness. As a further example Mr Morgan Jones made a gross profit of £14,479 from the Skerries between 1827 and 1833. Even deducting costs, he had £12,525. Purchase of his perpetual lease cost Trinity House £444,984! The owner of the Smalls complained the Trinity House offer was not large enough and took the Corporation to court. Oddly enough the court agreed and the final settlement was £170,000.

Funds were raised by various expedients. Trinity House and Pilotage funds were dipped into, a Treasury loan was negotiated and Corporation Bonds issued. The effect of the Act was to establish Trinity House as the pre-eminent lighthouse authority in the world, a curious about-face after the ambiguous attitude of the previous century. The coincidence of other factors consolidated this position. The expansion of the Empire and following of the flag by trade saw to it that British ports, especially London, became immensely wealthy. The expansion of the Mercantile Marine increased the income from both light dues and the ballastage. Trinity House thus participated in this new prosperity.

Eager to give the Corporation some ballast of its own and perhaps provide for pensioned officers, the Royal Commission of 1834 recommended naval officers be again eligible for election to the Board. It may also have been to prevent the sort of acrimonious row that had blown up over the case of Captain Foulerton, an Elder Brother. The Admiralty had arrogantly ordered him to undertake survey work which had entailed his absence from other duties. The Master and Wardens were understandably furious and Foulerton, having fallen between two stools, was fined on his return. In addition there was a trend towards greater official control of bodies like Trinity House. The Honourable East India Company was under considerable scrutiny at this time and the beginnings of an imperial bureaucracy are evident.

Finally the Brethren were accorded their due status by Queen Victoria, being given their precedence in the realm immediately after Captains of the Royal Navy. This was obviously more than just a social matter, since it gave them a certain amount of ''muscle'' in an age when to have been a ''gentleman'' was of far greater importance than to have been a ''mariner''. However, they were soon in frequent conflict with officials of the Board of Trade, whose officers in the Customs Service acted as collectors of light dues, and whose officials effectively controlled the Corporation's finances.

The acquisition of additional lighthouses, the increase in shipping and demand for more seamarks meant that the practical side of the service was stretching beyond the resources of sailing tenders. The records show a vast increase in lightvessels and buoys in the 1830's and 40's. The local Agents were having to give more and more time to the Corporation's affairs and it was manifest that they would have to become full-time employees of Trinity House. As already noted, about 1847 the title Superintendent had come into use and it was apparent that a major reorganisation of the sea areas and their management was increasingly necessary and that the Brethren, through the London Yacht Establishment, would have to delegate some of their powers. They were, in any case, becoming more involved with the business of Empire, involving themselves in lighthouse establishment in the Bahamas, the Falklands, on Minicoy and what was then Ceylon. They were also involved in the internationally managed light at Cape Spartel, near Tangier in Morocco.

So from this time British lighthouse administration began to take on a semblance of its present form. Agencies existed at Great Yarmouth, Harwich, Ramsgate, Littlehampton, Scilly, Cardiff (after the acquisition of Flatholm) and Holyhead (for Skerries). Each had a cutter or cutters, but the whole was still rather amateur, after the manner of most public services in the preceeding century.

The appearance of steam was to change it all, and even as the politicians were sharpening their knives for the 1834 enquiry the matter of steam propulsion was being debated at Trinity House.

This is not the place to digress upon the development of marine steam engines, even supposing that I felt competent to do so, except to say that by 1830 double acting engines, condensers and side lever engines were all available. By 1840 the design of valves and improvements in boiler design had made possible use of the expansive working of steam in the cylinder that James Watt had earlier abandoned as impractical. In 1812 Henry Bell had run a service on the Clyde with his *Comet* and in 1833 the Canadian built *Royal William* arrived in London after a 19-day voyage across the Atlantic almost entirely under power.

There is a reference in Chaplin's notes to "a steam vessel of 279 tons . . . launched for the Honourable Corporation of Trinity House . . ." in April, 1826, but judging from the subsequent debates it was not a yacht or tender and remains something of a mystery. Word of the House's interest in steam must have been current among London shipping circles, for in March, 1833, a Mr Harby offered his steam vessel *King of the Netherlands* for sale. It was declined on the grounds that no such purchase was contemplated. However on 3rd October the Deputy Master, John Woolmore, stated to the full Board (or Court) that he thought the matter of the introduction of a steam vessel should be considered "instead of the present Buoy Yacht". This statement suggests that the London Yacht Establishment had two vessels, the principal yacht *Zadora*

Vestal, the first steam yacht, smoky and inelegant, in a painting by an unknown artist. Note the cutter on her quarter flying the Trinity cornet, probably *Lyra*. *Trinity House*

and the schooner *Charon*, then based at the new wharf at Blackwall.

Captain Woolmore went on to state the advantages of a steamer.

"The prompt and efficient execution of the . . . Buoy Service within the Department of the Buoy Warden, not only under favourable circumstances, but also under such as would render their immediate execution impracticable by a sailing vessel. The great facility which a Steam Vessel affords for the examination of Sand Banks and . . . channels. The ready means which it would provide for conveying Oil, Stores, Chain Cables, Buoys and Buoy Chains, Mushrooms, Sinkers . . . to many of the Light Establishments upon the coast . . . The Towing of Lightvessels and Temporary Lightvessels to and from their stations (and) Generally the certainty and promptitude with which any required service might under emergencies be . . . carried out".

Woolmore was not entirely committed to the project on grounds of capital outlay and a committee was formed to debate "whether it is expedient with a view to the utmost efficient and prompt execution of the public service, that a Steam Vessel should be employed by the Corporation". On 7th November, 1833, the Court concurred with the committee's recommendation to build a steam ship.

Accordingly a request was sent to Captain Symonds, Surveyor of the Navy, to supply drafts of naval steamers, and those of H.M. Ships *Lightning*, *Comet* and the survey tender *Gulnare* were produced. Several builders offered to construct the new ship and Curling Young of Limehouse received the contract. She was carvel planked in wood, 130 feet 6 inches between perpendiculars and of 173 37/94 tons. Completed in 1835, she was stationed at the new Buoy Depot at Blackwall.

Named after the maidens who tended the perpetual flame of the Roman hearth-goddess, she was called *Vestal*. No details exist of her engines, but they probably rated about 35 h.p. A painting by an unknown artist shows the enormous grey paddle boxes and stovepipe funnel awkward between her well-spaced masts. She was steered from aft, and one wonders whether Jonathan Poulter, who commanded her at her commissioning, enjoyed his new vessel. The plate shows her off the North Foreland with the Brethren's flag at the mainmasthead. A small black cutter is shown off her quarter. This is clearly a tender, for at her masthead is the Trinity cornet, a red pennant with the four ships in the upper hoist canton, traditionally the command pennant of an Agent or Superintendent. She may be the *Lyra* and provides a contrast with the much larger *Vestal* clanking her smoky way north.

Her mechanical gear gave trouble almost immediately, for on 5th November, 1839, it was decided to defer the refitting of the working parts and bearings of her paddles, which had been recommended. Again in June, 1841, the famous London engineers Maudeslay Son and Field, who built the engines for Brunel's *Great Western*, reported adversely on the state of her boilers. She was sold about 1853 and in 1854 appears registered in Liverpool under the ownership of James Bain.

Vestal was soon joined by another "Steam Schooner" built at the same yard, the *Beacon* of 112 21/94 tons, 73 registered, which was 97 feet between perpendiculars, 19.6 feet in the beam and 11.7 feet deep in the hold. Her engine room was 39.4 feet long and she was described as being carvel built with sham quarter knees and a figurehead. Again Poulter commissioned her. He seems to have been the senior officer of the Yacht Establishment, a sort of forerunner of the present Chief Superintendent. *Beacon* was stationed at Blackwall and appears to have spent her working life as a buoy tender on the London District until sold to Thomas Beglue of London in November, 1862.

Despite teething troubles, the steamers immediately bore out Woolmore's expectations. On their cruises of inspection the Brethren took with them cargoes of buoys to the buoy yards now being established, and details of one such voyage on the east coast of England in 1841 are interesting. Leaving Blackwall, *Vestal* visited the Maplin pile lighthouse and the Swin Middle lightvessel "of 150 tons burthen: revolving light". Next the Sunk and the Kentish Knock, which had a "revolving light, the vessel a splendid one". *Vestal* proceeded on to the Galloper, Pakefield lighthouse "kept by old Captain Goodwin formerly in the Jamaica trade", and the Stanford lightvessel, "two lights horizontally; six reflectors; formerly the old Owers L.V. fifty years old and now doubled all over". Lowestoft and Winterton lighthouses were next on the itinerary, then the Newarp with its triangle of three lights and the single light of the St Nicholas off Yarmouth. They appear to have omitted the newly established Haisbro lightvessel which had caused the name of the Haisbro Gatt lightvessel to be altered to Newarp (although long known by either name, the stations now had their names painted on the sides). The Elder Brethren went on to see the Happisburgh, Cromer, Spurn and Dudgeon lights. This sort of voyage, or cruise, became a regular occurrence during the summer months. The object was to observe that the lights were being properly exhibited for the benefit of navigation, interview the various keepers and persons involved with their upkeep, and resolve difficulties and disputes. In this they were fair and strict. Old order books record their comments. There is one particularly vitriolic entry in that of Orfordness resulting from the station being found in a dirty and disordered state.

In August, 1842, *Vestal* accompanied Queen Victoria and the Prince Consort on a voyage to Scotland. The Royal Yacht was the now elderly ship-sloop *Royal George* that appeared earlier in our narrative. From Woolwich she was towed downstream by the tug *Monkey* to where H.M. Steam Vessels *Shearwater*, *Black Eagle*, *Salamander*, *Lightning*, *Fearless* and *Rhadamanthus* joined as escort. The first two took the Royal Yacht in tow.

A vast number of steamers and spectators accompanied the squadron out of the Thames "displaying every manifestation of loyalty and affection". The voyage took 66 hours at a speed of about six knots, and so impressed was the Queen with her progress that she chartered the General Steam Navigation Company's 1,000 ton steamer *Trident* for the return voyage.

The following year *Vestal* was on the west coast carrying out inspections. On 14th July she closed with the cliffs of Trevose Head to land a party by boat. The boat was lowered and an Elder Brother, Richard Drew, together with a Captain Jenkin Jones (a guest?), were pulled towards the rocks. The weather was fresh, no landing could be effected and the boat headed back to *Vestal*. Seeing the boat returning *Vestal's* master turned to give her a lee but due to some circumstance of the sea or miscalculation the steamer ran the boat down. Rather typically the available records make no mention of the boat's crew. By inference they appear to have suffered the same fate as Drew and Jones; that of drowning.

Other duties that occupied *Vestal* included the towing of a sailing tender, either *Billow* or more probably *Tortoise*, back to London from the building of the Wolf Rock beacon, completed in 1839.

As part of a long continuing effort to mark the Goodwin Sands a beacon had been established on the eastern edge of the Swatchway, a passage through the sands now much enlarged and called Kellet Gut. It was washed away and on 24th May, 1841, *Vestal* towed into position a hulk which was fitted out with a beacon mast and sunk her in position on the south side of the Channel with sixty four tons of ballast. Two years later it had gone.

More successfully established was the long-demanded lightvessel at the Cockle Gat. Trinity House having decided to comply with the pleas of east coast seamen, HMS *Blazer* was despatched by a co-operative Admiralty to survey the Gatway and Yarmouth Roads. A contemporary account of 20th December, 1834, spins the yarn.

> "*Vestal*, Trinity Steamer, having the lightvessel in tow, was seen entering St Nicholas Gat (the then southern entrance to Yarmouth Roads) on Tuesday Morning when the vessels lying in Yarmouth Roads immediately hoisted their colours and as she passed alongside Her Majesty's Ship *Blazer* the crew manned the rigging and gave three hearty cheers by way of welcome. At noon the lightvessel was in her position . . ."

During this period *Beacon* had been working out of London on the increasing number of buoys in the Thames Estuary. Like *Vestal*, *Beacon* had been involved in work on the Goodwins. In September, 1844, she towed a Mr Steward's beacon to station, but it lasted only three weeks. In June of the following year Trinity House themselves had James Walker build a replacement for the Swatchway beacon lost earlier. It was towed out of Dover by the "Trinity Steam Buoy Yacht" *Beacon* but bad weather forced them into Ramsgate. Eventually on 6th July the beacon, a ball surmounting a staff, was established. It was removed in 1850 when the Swatchway shifted. *Beacon* also laid a mark displaying an inverted cone designed by Walker in 1849 but it was lost in a severe gale 30 years later and no further beacons were attempted by Trinity House.

The workload was increasing elsewhere, particularly in the Bristol Channel. In April, 1839, the Board had decided that due to:

> "The great extension of the light and buoyage service in the Bristol and St George's Channels . . . it is desirable that a steam vessel of sufficient size and power should be provided to be stationed at Milford, and that an efficient Sailing Tender should also be stationed at . . . Cardiff, and that . . . the several Agencies . . . from the River Usk to the South Stack inclusive be . . . placed in the charge of a Superintendent at Milford."

Orders were put in hand immediately, and in the following year the steam schooner *Argus* (O.N. 18971) was completed by Henry Fletcher Son and Fearnall at their Union Dock, Limehouse. She was 158 registered tons, 128 feet between perpendiculars and 19.4 feet in the beam. Her hold depth was 13.7 feet and her loaded draft 9 feet 4 inches. *Argus's* twin paddles were driven by two marine steam engines of 50 horse power built by Boulton and Watt. She had a round stern and lion figurehead.

On 7th April, 1840, she underwent engine trials "in a short run down the river" and Mr Brown, London manager of Boulton and Watt, reported very

The second *Vestal* in a photograph taken about 1860, with her gangway doors open and a derrick topped up on the foremast.   *Trinity House*

favourably on the result. A later record complains that her vibration was "so great that writing is extremely unpleasant and difficult".

Argus completed the initial building programme of steamers and remained at the new depot at Neyland, in Milford Haven. She was replaced by the third *Argus* in 1856, though not sold to the Patent Derrick Co. of Cornhill, London, until 23rd January, 1858. Like *Vestal* and *Beacon*, the Admiralty registered this second *Argus* (the first being the cutter of 1797 fame) to carry armament in time of war. The likelihood of this becoming necessary was due to the Russian crisis that culminated in the Crimean War. *Argus* and *Beacon* were capable of mounting one 9-pounder and two 18-pounders, while the larger *Vestal* was rated at one 12 and two 18's.

The depot at Neyland was acquired about 1840 and became important, supplying the "Neyland Rocks", as the Smalls, Skokholm and South Bishop lighthouses were called. Also on *Argus's* district, the floating lights at Helwick and the island light of Lundy required her services. The depot is now derelict and its unglazed windows stare across the Cleddau at the remains of Britain's first ironclad, HMS *Warrior*; two relics of a bygone age.

The efficient Sailing Tender despatched to Cardiff was *Diligent*, whose loss on Flatholm in November, 1839, has already been noted. The cause of her wrecking is not known but the prevailing strong tides may have contributed to it. No replacement was available until 1841 when the cutter *Satellite* took up her duties, so the *Argus* probably covered from Milford.

Satellite (O.N. 50031) was a cutter of 67 16/94 tons built at Limehouse in 1840. She was originally stationed at Yarmouth attending the southerly light-vessels on the Stanford and St Nicholas stations. However, in 1842 Trinity House received a letter dated 13th March from Mr Joseph Mayor, Master of the Bristol Channel (later the English and Welsh Grounds) lightvessel, in which he complains of the sailing qualities of *Satellite*, thus indicating her employment in the area. It was decided that arrangements were to be made to bring her to Blackwall "with a view to such slight alterations as may render her more handy in stays".

She did not return to Cardiff, for shortly after the Littlehampton base was closed and that at Cowes opened *Satellite* was allocated to the Solent station where the tides were less fierce. Here, in May of 1843, dry rot was discovered in her and Mr White, the famous boatbuilder, was called in to inspect her. He advised the repairs would not exceed £100. Incidentally, the officer in charge of the new Cowes depot was referred to as Superintendent contemporaneously with the Milford officer and Mr Davies at Ramsgate.

Satellite's replacement at Cardiff may have been *Yarmouth*, built in 1826 at North Yarmouth and sent originally to the west coast for reasons given in a former chapter, as her whereabouts at this time are not clear. There was certainly a degree of interchangeability with the sailing tenders.

By the time of the Great Exhibition of 1851 Trinity House and her sister Commissions of Irish and Northern Lights led the world in the provision of seamarks.

At London and Milford the steamships *Vestal*, *Beacon* and *Argus* demonstrated the triumph of the new technology. At the outports *Satellite* was at Cowes, the *Sunk* at Harwich. *Eliza* and the *Trinity Buoy Yacht* looked after the floating lights off East Anglia, supported by the *Dudgeon* at Wells attending the lightvessels off Norfolk and in the Wash. *Billow* and *Eddystone* were based at St Mary's and Plymouth respectively, whilst *Yarmouth*, *Charon*, and *Tortoise* completed the fleet.

The service offered to the mariner was indeed modern, and he could traverse the waters of the Narrow Seas with more confidence than was hitherto the case.

CHAPTER SIX

Imperial Splendour

"She combines High Speed and comfortable accommodation with great strength and carrying capacity. The former qualities are required to enable the Elder Brethren to perform their special duty of attendance of Her Majesty when afloat."
Illustrated London News, 11th July, 1868

A SUCCESSION of Parliamentary Acts in the second half of the 19th century extended the powers of Trinity House. That of 1854 made the Corporation the general lighthouse authority for England, Wales, the Channel Islands, Gibraltar and Heligoland. Power was also given to oversee local authorities and approve alterations in the Northern and Irish services. The 1894 Act gave to all vessels belonging to the three lighthouse authorities the entitlement "to enter, resort to, and use any harbours, ports . . . in the United Kingdom without payment of any . . . rates of any kind".

The financing of the lighthouse authorities underwent changes and by an Act of 1898 the General Lighthouse Fund was set up into which light dues were paid and which included in its outgoings disbursements for colonial lighthouses and Britain's contribution for Cape Spartel.

There was a strong connection between Trinity House and many colonial lights. In 1867 Mr William Douglass, brother of Sir James, the Engineer in Chief, was sent out to Sri Lanka to erect lights on the Basses and another member of the Trinity House staff, Mr T. Matthews, surveyed Minicoy, the cast-off member of the Maldive Islands in the Indian Ocean.

On the home coast the number of lighthouses increased. Douglass rebuilt the Scilly Bishop and the Eddystone, and Walker, his predecessor, rebuilt the Smalls and finally succeeded in constructing the Wolf Rock. The number of lightvessels also grew until in 1929 there were 46 stations with eight spares held in reserve. Like the Eddystone lightvessel used whilst Smeaton built his tower, they were often laid to mark the extremities of works. In 1901 No.24 (built 1847) was sunk by a careless ferry when marking the Dover Pier Works. Another was stationed off the great stone breakwater at Holyhead until the terminal lighthouse was lit. No. 51 lightvessel was built in 1879 for a very unusual purpose. Of composite construction, she was twenty feet longer than usual with a tonnage of 259.5 tons burthen. Rigged as a three-masted schooner, she sailed out to the Great Basses Reef where she lay until the lighthouses were completed.

As we shall see she was not the only Trinity House ship in those beautiful waters. No. 51 came home to be sunk by enemy action in August, 1943, while on the Helwick station.

Another interesting lightship was No. 58. Built at Fowey in 1862, the schooner *Wolf* was of 92 registered tons. She was intended to assist with the building of Walker's tower of the same name along with *Billow* and the steam tug *Solva*. *Billow* had replaced *Scilly* on the western station and *Solva* had been commissioned to assist in the replacement of Whiteside's pile light at the Smalls. *Solva* therefore came under the direction of the Engineer in Chief. The work at the Wolf went on from 1861 until December, 1869, *Solva* having five small 40-ton lighters to convey prepared stones from the mason's site at Penzance to the rock. On completion of the tower the mason's site became the new Depot and the *Solva* returned to London.

Wolf and *Billow* continued as District Tenders. A contemporary ''impression'', of the first relief of the Wolf Rock lighthouse shows the keepers landing from a small paddle tug named *Wolf*. This is an error, probably due to the fact that while *Wolf* was the official tender all work that could be done by *Solva* was done by her, and she almost certainly accomplished this first relief.

The new Superintendency at Penzance was under the direction of Hugh Tregarthen, formerly the Scilly Agent, who had moved to Penzance from Tresco. Not so keen to become mainlanders, the Scillonian crews of *Billow* and the Sevenstones lightvessel were rancorous. The resulting lack of co-operation resulted in a poor service to the new Wolf Rock and during the winter of 1872/73 *Solva* had to be brought back from London. The same practice was followed the following winter, but she was not afterwards returned to Blackwall for Tregarthen asked for a permament steam tender. £6,500 was set aside for this and in the meantime *Solva* remained at Penzance with *Wolf* while *Billow* was returned to lay up in London. These Penzance tenders used to act as committee ships for the Penzance regatta, and after attending that of 1875 *Solva*, relieved by the new woodent steamer *Triton*, was sold out of service and the *Wolf* was laid up. In 1883 the latter was converted into No. 58 lightvessel and was sold in 1898.

Tregarthen had assumed office in October, 1841, and by 1876 the Plymouth Buoy Store had been abandoned in favour of Penzance, though a small lighthouse store was left for the Eddystone. The Scilly store and boat house were given up when Tregarthen moved to Penzance. Tregarthen also absorbed the St Ives Agency, which had first looked after the Godrevy lightship and afterwards the almost inaccessible lighthouse there. Mr Tremorne, the Agent, was paid off for £150.

In 1858 there were 35 lightvessel stations and spare ships were held in readiness at Milford, Yarmouth and London. Trinity House were also responsible for 77 lighthouses and 420 buoys and beacons. Blackwall was the principal Depot and the Superintendent's duties extended far beyond the Thames estuary. While his primary role was "to send a lightvessel, steam vessel or buoy away at the shortest notice", he had also to keep buoys for the Bristol Channel. His pre-occupations with the nuts and bolts of the job were varied. Nominally commanding one of the ships on the station, the Superintendent delegated this duty to a First Officer while he himself managed the disposition of navigating and engineer officers. The manning arrangements were undertaken by his clerk, and his staff had to "test and prove all cables, moorings etc . . . to certify all bills as to Sundry Goods being received . . . to weigh all Oil, Tallow and Soap". As already mentioned the post was, for many years, held by a member of the Poulter family.

Special buoys were kept for various stations: "Convex bottom wood buoys as per West Barrows" and "Mast thro' iron wreck buoy for the Stein Rock Heligoland". This last is interesting since it is evidence that the Trinity Steamers looked after at least one buoy in the German Bight. The Superintendent was also responsible for the uniform clothing of "the crews of all the yachts and lights . . . to be measured and supplied between Christmas and Lady Day".

By 1858 the Blackwall Depot had attached to it two new steamers. *Vestal's* paddle gear had for long given trouble, and as early as 1849 purchase of an Admiralty Mail Packet had been considered. Also mooted at this time was the conversion of the schooner *Charon* to steam power, and this may have already

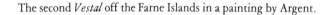

The second *Vestal* off the Farne Islands in a painting by Argent.   *Trinity House*

been put in hand, but in July, 1853, it was decided to sell her and build another new steam vessel to support *Vestal's* replacement.

Vestal had fallen from grace as the principal yacht on the commissioning of the first *Irene*. Deliberations as to her building had commenced in January, 1851, when Trinity House debated "Whether if a new steam vessel be purchased or constructed for the Yacht Service of the Corporation, it will be preferable that such a vessel should be of wood or iron, it was . . . decided in favour of wood".

Irene was built under the supervision of a Mr Lang, of Chatham Dockyard, and he made certain recommendations to the builders, Messrs G. F. Young, of Limehouse. Young's applied for an extension of building time and this was probably just as well since a month later the Elder Brethren had still not chosen a name for her. Eventually they succeeded, but no reason can be discovered for their choice.

Trials were carried out under Poulter and in attendance were the Elder Brethren, the engine builder Mr Penn, Mr Lang and Mr Young. Poulter took the sparkling vessel down the Thames. In Long Reach the engine telegraphs rang up "Full Ahead" and with the huge connecting rods throwing their massive weight behind the paddles which thrashed the yellow Thames to a yeasty froth, *Irene* ran over the measured distance. Three times she tore up and down the reach and with a curious reluctance to leave the shore that bore her, it is recorded that "her mean speed per Hour was 16.62 Statute Miles".

Irene was 157 feet between perpendiculars, with long overhangs, a depth of hold of 11.5 feet and a hull beam of 20.8 feet, her paddle sponsons increasing this to an extreme of 39.6 feet. Her schooner rig had a standing bowsprit with a figurehead of a "demi-female" beneath it, the accompanying scrollwork merging into a ribband which ran out round her sponsons and terminated in quarter badges. Registered at 149 tons net she had two 13-ton boilers and twin engines which combined gave a nominal 160 h.p. Her furnaces were fed with coal, later anthracite, 50 tons in bunkers, 15 in her hold and 20 "on deck".

With eight fires burning she consumed 28 cwts coal an hour at 13 knots. A more economical 10 or 11 was achieved with four fires and a consumption of 18 cwts. *Irene* (O.N. 8214) was said to have been a sister ship to H.M.S. *Vivid*, but faster. To run her Poulter had two mates, a carpenter, cook and steward, two engineers, six firemen, two coal trimmers and thirteen seamen. Last but not least, she carried three indentured apprentices.

Irene's first public appearance was as escort to Queen Victoria in her own new (and first named of three) yacht *Victoria & Albert*. The occasion, a review of the Channel Fleet, was held on 11th August, 1853, at Spithead. The Prince Consort described it as "the finest fleet . . . which England ever fitted out; forty ships of war . . . all moved by steam power but three . . . propelled only by the screw, 11 miles an hour against wind and tide!" The newly established Channel

The second *Vestal* alongside the coal hulk *Africa* off Blackwall about 1885. *Galatea* can be seen in the background.   *Trinity House*

Fleet consisted of wooden broadside ships of the line fitted with steam engines and screws. The media of the day were pleased to call *Irene* "The pretty little Trinity Yacht".

Irene escorted the Queen on a number of occasions and during her service probably had her boilers renewed, for in April, 1868, she again went over the measured distance in Long Reach, achieving a mean speed of 14.659 knots.

The committee that, in July, 1853, debated the addition of another steamer must have had in mind not only the deterioration of *Vestal* but also that of *Beacon* and *Argus* at Neyland. *Irene* initiated a new building programme, from which it is clear that Trinity House considered an establishment of three steam vessels, two at Blackwall and one at Neyland, to be essential and sufficient to the needs of the service. This number was augmented in succeeding years (as, for instance, at Penzance) and was supported by sailing tenders, several of which were still to be built. The next two ships were the second *Vestal* and the third *Argus*.

The year 1855 saw the commissioning of the beautiful paddle schooner *Vestal* (O.N. 26651) a ship markedly larger than the *Irene* and indisputably better looking than her forbear of the same name. She was 170 feet overall at building with a net tonnage of 199 tons. Her hull beam was 23.5 feet and her hold depth 13.3 feet. Materially altered in later life, her length was increased to 182 feet with an increase in tonnage to 207.47. New engines may have been fitted, as her horse power is re-rated from 160 to 180, the latter being generated by oscillating engines with cylinders of 48 inch bore and 48 inch stroke powered from tubular boilers. Buoy work was carried out with derricks from the foremast and she was well equipped with boats.

Soon after building she relieved *Argus* on the west coast, and by 1856 the latter was sold. Fitted out with accomodation for the Brethren, *Vestal* carried out inspection cruises, though in 1877 she was on the east coast laying one of "Courtney's Automotive buoys" close to the Galloper lightvessel for evaluation. In 1880 she was in London when her presence was urgently required off Land's End. On 26th April, hastily loading a mushroom anchor and 315 fathoms of chain, she left to attend the Sevenstones lightvessel that had broken adrift. Leaving Trinity House, Captains Nisbet and Burne hurried down to Cowes to intercept her. Having embarked the two Elder Brethren, the steamer continued her passage and on 28th took the off-station lightvessel in tow. Proceeding into the shelter of the Scillies, *Vestal's* crew toiled to stow the new cable in the lightship and at 20.00 on the 29th re-established her on station 1.5 cables ENE of her former position, the two Elder Brethren having concluded her original station had had a foul bottom.

Vestal remained a paddle steamer all her life and seems to have returned to Blackwall about 1872. She was probably relieved by the second *Beacon* (see below). Her last master was Captain "Johnny" Reading. Initially, however, the London District was served by *Irene* and the ageing *Beacon*. Little is known of the latter ship beyond the fact that she was the principal buoy tender and spent her working life on this important but obscure service.

Billow was, as noted, returned to London with the closure of the Scilly store in 1869. *Tortoise* is a mystery. The available evidence leads one to conclude that she was a small vessel with a crew of a master and a few seamen. The former was no more than a petty officer, his pay of £4 10s per month nine shillings less than that of *Irene's* carpenter and only 35s. more than his own seamen. She had a high allowance of coal and seems to have been exclusively used in lighthouse construction. She may well have had a steam winch for handling masonry and been built for this purpose. The mention of *Vestal* towing an unnamed sailing vessel from Penzance to London after the completion of the Wolf Rock beacon (remains of which form the present landing refuge) suggest that the vessel was a poor sailer, built for a purpose commensurate with a plodding image and name. As if to corroborate this theory, she was present at the building of the Needles in the summer of 1858 when James Ormiston, Clerk to the Works, wrote to Mr Poulter requesting a replacement for her master, James Stretton, who had died suddenly and now lies buried in Freshwater churchyard. Nothing further is heard of *Tortoise* after 1858.

By this time the old *Beacon* had already reached the end of her days. She was replaced in 1856 by the third *Argus*, which was to have a long life. Initially a paddle steamer, her original appearance is uncertain, for at some time she was lengthened and converted to a screw steamer. Her "clipper" bow with its shield and scroll figurehead disappeared in favour of a raked stem. Built by Wigram's of Blackwall, *Argus* (O.N. 12589) was commissioned in December, 1856. Of composite construction, she finished life 164.5 feet overall, 23.5 feet in the beam and 14.5 feet deep in the hold. Her final registered tonnage was 331 and her twin 80 h.p. paddle engines were substituted by equally powerful steam reciprocating engines driving twin screws.

Her complement was a master, two mates, carpenter, cook, steward and two engineers, six firemen and two coal trimmers, nine seamen (she carried only three boats) and three brassbound apprentices. One of the boats was a steam launch. Coal was stowed in bunkers (60 tons) and in the hold (40 tons).

The latter was taken aboard by the London ships from the coal hulk *Africa*, an old wooden warship, moored off the Blackwall wharf and convenient for a dusty berth.

A further steamer joined *Irene* and *Argus* on the London District in 1862, bringing the number of steamers to three working ships plus a "principal yacht". This new vessel was the second *Beacon*, a paddle steamer of 262 g.r.t. (181 nett) built at London. Her two cylinder engines developed 120 h.p. in a hull 146.9 feet overall, 22 feet beam and 12.5 feet deep. Few details are known of *Beacon* beyond the fact that she had accommodation for a Committee of Elder Brethren and later relieved *Vestal* on the Neyland station about 1870. *Beacon* (O.N. 45014) was in use until 1889 when a certain Sidney Castle Nash bought her, removed her engines and sold her to foreign buyers.

These paddle Buoy Yachts were elegant vessels. By the end of the 1860's they had a considerable number of buoys to attend to, particularly on the east coast and in the Thames estuary. Buoys were of wood or iron, the largest some 20 feet in diameter weighing 3¼ tons. The cost of one of these was the sum of £254. A 10 foot diameter wood buoy worked out at around £57. Although the buoys were made by contracted manufacturers such as Bwiney and Bellamy, Lennox and Co, Shuters or the un-nautical Ditchburn and Mare, the Depot at Blackwall employed smiths and coopers to carry out the work of repair and in 1869 expansion took place to include mechanical workshops.

Moorings consisted of cast iron sinkers, even then costing between £60 and £80 each, with a 1 1/8 inch buoy chain at 13s. the fathom. There is a record of the East Tongue buoy made of iron in 1846 at a cost of £239 16s. 8d. being, in November, 1858, brought ashore and galvanised.

The high manoeuvrability conferred by paddles must have been a boon to men trained in sail. Nevertheless these vessels, with their huge sponsons and vulnerable paddle wheels, can have made recovering and laying buoys no easy task. Letting go an anchor, the ship would settle back in the tide until sheered across the stream, when the buoy would be brought into the gangway. With the iron bulwark doors open and the big wooden derrick plumbing overside, the master would undergo a few anxious moments while the hands, under the vociferous direction of the mate, would clamber aboard the buoy and hook in the gear. With the buoy bobbing alongside close to the paddles the master must often have had his worries; it is not surprising that *Argus* at least was converted to a screw steamer.

Despite the advantages of steam power Trinity House were still building sailing tenders. In February, 1864, Messrs Hoad Brothers of Rye submitted estimates for the building of two vessels. These were to replace the old *Lyra* at Ramsgate and the unsatisfactory *Satellite* at Cowes. The ships were to be about 80 feet long and of some 65 tons net. Hoad's quoted £1,955 for an oak and £1,995 for a teak hull. The reputation for durability and non-reaction with iron fastenings had been established by a number of teak frigates built at Bombay, and it was the latter offer that was accepted.

Hoad's commenced the construction of the *Triton* and *Mermaid* in late 1864. *Mermaid* was a handsome two-masted schooner with a lofty sail plan on a

The second *Argus* as she appeared at the end of her long life in 1909. She had started life as a paddle steamer. *Trinity House*

The last sailing tender in service, the *Mermaid*, shown off the Needles in a painting by Argent. Note the derrick topped up to the foremast and the large boats in davits. *Trinity House*

flush decked hull 76.4 feet between perpendiculars, 18.4 feet beam and 9.6 feet deep. Her registered tonnage was 76.32. She had a midships hold, two davit-stowed boats and a small derrick forward of her foremast. Her trail boards, stern badge and name are preserved in the National Maritime Museum.

Mermaid was sent to Cowes on completion and the *Satellite* was paid off. For the next 32 years *Mermaid* attended the various lighthouses and lightvessels on the District, the Needles, Hurst, Warner, Shambles, Owers and Bembridge. The practice of changing the buoys in the area by a steam yacht from London was by now well established and *Mermaid's* duties were predominantly supplying and relieving the lighthouse and lightvessel stations, with emergency buoy work as circumstances demanded.

At the time of her commissioning all the buoys in the Solent and Spithead were under the Admiralty, but in 1867 their lordships claimed the area was a highway for merchantmen and this was properly the duty of Trinity House. The Admiralty offered a site for a Depot at East Cowes. The landing stage had been built in 1845 for Queen Victoria to land at when visiting Osborne and was contiguous with Mr Auldjo's store, purchased by Trinity House a little earlier as an oil store. Trinity House were to have free use of the wharf when it was not required by royalty. The directive for its construction in a local paper reads "Sir

The *Mermaid* moored at Cowes depot about 1895, some five years after the painting of the previous picture. The site for this depot was provided by the Admiralty.   *Trinity House*

John Pelley . . . of the Trinity Board for the immediate erection of a wharf at East Cowes opposite the old Custom House, for Her Majesty to land and embark without intrusion''. The Admiralty footed the bill, as they did for its renovation in 1896. In 1922 it passed gratis to Trinity House. The old Depot was damaged by an Isle of Wight ferry in August, 1962, and rebuilt 1965. Regular calls were paid by the Royal Yachts, particularly *Elfin*, conveying papers and the despatch boxes to Her Majesty when at Osborne.

Mermaid was stationed at Cowes under a Captain West until 1897, when she was transferred to Cardiff and probably either laid up or used as a fender vessel or coal hulk. In 1902 she was sold for further trading but disappeared in the First World War.

Her sister ship, *Triton*, had a life of similar length but dissimilar nature. *Triton* had no figurehead but was a flush-decked, carvel-built, two-masted schooner completed a little earlier than *Mermaid* and replacing *Lyra* at Ramsgate. The Ramsgate District had undergone few changes in *Lyra's* time. Superintendent Davies's use of a chartered steam tug from 1844 has been noted and his successor can scarcely have been pleased to receive another sailing vessel. Davies died in April, 1854, and in September, 1855, Mr Charles Taylor, ''a chief mate of the Yacht Establishment'', was appointed to his place. The delay in his appointment had been due to the Board's change of policy when they decided to abolish the Agencies and fill the vacancies with officers of their marine staff, a new policy which was not always adhered to. Hugh Tregarthen was succeeded by his son James in 1875 and Penzance did not receive a uniformed officer until 1888, while as late as 1907 the North East District of the Northumbrian coast was administered by a solicitor at Sunderland.

Taylor at Ramsgate, though mate in the London Yachts, had command of the local ship as well as the store, and this practice was common in the small outports. Taylor was succeeded by Mr White, late first mate of *Irene*, who retired in May, 1864, and White by a Mr Tucker, who was followed by the mate of *Galatea*.

Almost as soon as taking office Taylor petitioned for a steamer, with the result that he received *Triton*, but in March, 1868, £3,500 was set aside from the light dues for the provision of a Ramsgate steamer, the *Alert*. However, although later the Ramsgate tender, she spent no more than a few months there on completion. She was a small ship of 144 g.r.t. (98 net), with an overall length of 104 feet, 20 feet beam and 11 feet depth in the hold. She was built in Glasgow with twin screws and 35 n.h.p. horizontal engines. Her derricks were more for ornament than use, and her sea-keeping qualities were picturesquely described thus: "When she's in anything rougher than a mill pond she stamps twice between each wave and then turns round to have a look".

The pressing requirement for an additional steam vessel on the west coast meant that *Alert* was soon despatched thither and sanction was obtained from the Board of Trade on 8th June, 1869, to spend £2,000 on *Triton's* conversion to a screw steamer. In September Messrs J. Stewart were contracted to supply and fit a double cylinder marine engine for £1,325, inclusive of spares. *Triton* was now lengthened to 97 feet overall, her beam of 18.6 feet and depth of 9.5 feet remaining the same. Her net tonnage was reduced to 57 tons whilst her gross rose to 105. Steam steering gear, a winch and windlass were also fitted, and having completed her trials in March, 1870, she steamed to Holyhead to take up her station on the newly formed District. Her conversion had cost £3,618.

Triton's new base was the result of the expansion of the Bristol Channel District. Trinity House work on the west coast was divided into areas separated by large distances and the Neyland ship found it more and more difficult to maintain the required standard of seamarks. Approval was obtained from the increasingly important Board of Trade to create the St George's Channel District based on Holyhead, and later named after that port. A Depot was acquired without a wharf, the tender taking up moorings in the New Harbour and lightering everything off from a boat jetty. As soon as she arrived at Holyhead *Alert* was relieved and returned to Ramsgate, the port for which she had been built, but a few months later in September, 1870, she and *Triton* were ordered to exchange stations. Reasons for this are not clear, but it would seem *Triton*

The first *Alert* seen off Cowes in a photograph taken about 1900. Note the anchor and preparations to cat it. *Beken of Cowes*

suffered some deficiencies, and on arrival at Ramsgate a new propeller had to be fitted. However, apart from a short break of service at Penzance (see below), she remained the Ramsgate tender until 1902 when she was sold to a Whitstable coal factor. In this strike-bound age it is almost encouraging to note that in 1871 Messrs Cory's were unable to supply Nixon's Navigation Coal due to a dispute. A cheaper substitute was available, however, at 24s 6d per ton. Upon *Triton's* sale *Alert* returned, finally, to Ramsgate after service elsewhere.

Trinity House built their last and most opulent paddle yacht at this time. The Trinity Steam Yacht *Galatea* (O.N. 60819) was larger than *Vestal*.

"A handsome vessel . . . built by Messrs Caird and Co, of Greenock . . . She combines High Speed and comfortable accommodation with great strength and carrying capacity. The former qualities are required to enable the Elder Brethren to perform their special duty of attendance of Her

Majesty when afloat, and the latter for the conveyance of stores and supplies to the different lighthouses and stations on the coast, for the arduous duty of towing and shifting lightvessels and their moorings, and for handling and carrying heavy buoys; this last being a most difficult task in a seaway, and requiring solid construction to enable a vessel to perform the work without damage to herself. Sufficient accommodation is provided for a committee of the Elder Brethren when out on their duties at sea and a suite of cabins has been specially arranged for the use of the Duke of Edinburgh, * Master of Trinity House, when he is pleased to accompany the Elder

Galatea, the last and most opulent paddle yacht, which was built in 1868 and served until 1895.
Illustrated London News

Brethren. The decks are roomy and able to carry a large number of buoys, and on the quarterdeck is a large deck house, where charts and surveying instruments are kept, and where, in all weathers, the Elder Brethren can go on with their work. The vessel is steered either from the bridge or abaft (sic). She carries six boats . . . one of them a steam lifeboat cutter, which is found of great use in surveying . . . towing boats with stores when conveying oil and supplies to stations round the coast. The vessel has been named *Galatea*, in compliment to his Royal Highness's first command of the frigate so named.

At the trial trip . . . accompanied by a large party . . . including those officials of the Board of Trade closely connected with the Lighthouse Department, a mean speed of nearly 14½ knots was obtained. The dimensions of the vessel are length (b.p.) 220 feet; length overall 231 feet;

*Second son of Queen Victoria, he rose to be a Captain in the Royal Navy. He succeeded Palmerston as Master of Trinity House and the tradition of a Royal Master has endured from this time. Today the office is held by H.R.H. Prince Philip, Duke of Edinburgh.

Breadth 26 feet; Depth of Hold 13 feet 8 inches; gross tonnage 507 tons, and registered tonnage 319 tons; her draught . . . 9 feet 6 inches. She has a pair of oscillating marine engines of the collective power of 200 horses nominal or 1516 effective. The coal bunkers will carry 120 tons''.

This rather fulsome account adequately describes the function of the Steam Yachts and the difficulties of their duties. The assumption by association that the Elder Brethren ran the ship is a pardonable error on the part of the *Illustrated London News* but a pity for posterity. The Brethren boarded their vessels in the character of flag officers on their cruises of inspection. Their function was that of managers of the Lighthouse Service as a whole, answerable to Parliament and the purseholders at the Board of Trade. But the *Galatea* and her sisters were run by the officers of the Yacht Establishment, commanded by men whose schooling had been in the Corporation's ships and manned by prime seamen who undertook those ''difficult tasks''.

Galatea spent more time than previous London ships cruising on the west coast. She is recorded making annual visits between 1869 and 1889. She was at the grand ceremony of the opening of Douglass's Eddystone lighthouse in company with a flotilla of craft, both official and pleasure bound. For some inexplicable reason her registry was shifted to Swansea on 3rd May, 1892.

On 1st January, 1894, with Sir Sydney Webb, Deputy Master, and Captain Vyvyan, Elder Brother, on board, she arrived off the island of Heligoland. The occasion of her visit was the handing over of the island and its lighthouse to the newly unified German government, who promptly turned it into a naval base in time for the First World War. The lighthouse had been relieved from Ramsgate, the last visit being made by *Warden* (see below).

Galatea was sold in 1895 to the Mersey Docks and Harbour Board for about £3,000 and in 1896 received two new cylindrical multi-tubular boilers by Messrs T. Sumner and Sons to power her two original engines of two 52 inch diameter cylinders of 66 inch stroke. By November, 1904, repairs were required that were considered uneconomical, and while awaiting a buyer she was visited by Elder Brethren. ''Though the boilers and engines are said to be in capital order, the *Galatea* is to be sold for what she can fetch . . . '' That turned out to be a mere £1,500.

The first year *Galatea* cruised on the west coast, that of 1869, was that in which *Alert* was built, the *Cutty Sark* was completed and the Suez Canal opened. It was also the year in which two extraordinary ships were laid down for Trinity House. Both were identical, both were built by Seath's of Rutherglen, Lanarkshire. The first, *Arrow* (O.N. 63528), named after the then Deputy Master, Sir Frederick Arrow, was of 192 g.r.t. (130 net), 120 feet overall, 20 feet beam and 10.6 feet depth of hold. *Hercules* (O.N. 65375), completed in 1870, had identical machinery: a two-cylinder direct acting engine of 18 inch bore and

24 inch stroke built by David Rowan of Glasgow. The nominal horse power was about 36.

Their function was the construction, under the aegis of the Imperial Lighthouse Service, of the lighthouses on the Basses Reef off the south-east coast of Sri Lanka. Mention has already been made of No. 51 lightvessel in connection with these works.

Arrow arrived in Ceylon, as it was then known, on 27th February, 1870. under the command of Captain James Laing, seconded from the P & O Company. Her cargo of equipment and stores was discharged and part of her holds fitted for accommodation of native workmen. On 5th March she left Colombo for the Great Basses. Laing returned home to bring out *Hercules* and arrived back at Colombo on 19th October.

Both vessels were able to carry 120 tons of cargo, mostly stone blocks, at a speed of ten knots. Once on site *Arrow* had a complement of master, mate, two engineers, one stoker and two seamen of European nationality, a serang, six lascars, one bandaddy, three firemen, cook and steward of Asian origin. *Hercules* was similarly manned. It is not clear whether any of her officers were from the Yacht Establishment, but it seems likely since they possessed the required expertise for inshore work. Certainly during the early years of the First World War a Trinity House officer, Mr Kendall-Carpenter, served on secondment aboard two steam yachts of the Imperial Lighthouse Service based in Sri Lankan waters.

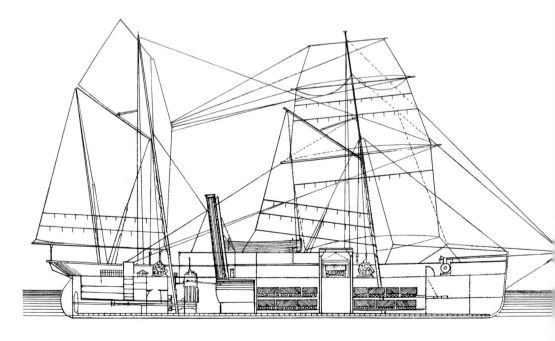

Sir James Douglass commenced his rebuilding of the Eddystone, occasioned by the undermining of Smeaton's Tower, in July, 1878. The lighthouse was built faster than any other tower and Douglass attributed this to *Hercules*. She carried 2,171 blocks weighing 4,668 tons in three years. This is an extraordinary achievement given the difficulties. Daily when the weather permitted *Hercules* would arrive with a fresh cargo of ready shaped blocks. Taking up a mooring buoy, she would be veered down close to the rocks where the wires for the hoist were picked up. Until the work was above sea level she pumped out the caisson and supplied compressed air for pneumatic drills. Blocks taken from her hold were rolled aft on a railway along her deck, picked up on travellers running on the wires connected to a stern gantry and hove ashore with her winches. In this manner ten two or three-ton blocks an hour could be landed. In September, 1888, she transferred to Liverpool registry and was sold. Not strictly a lighthouse tender and financed from the Engineer in Chief's budget, she was still part of the story. *Arrow* remained in the Indian Ocean for the completion of the second light on the Little Basses, after which she was sold at Bombay in 1879.

By 1873 Tregarthen at Penzance was pleading for a steamer to replace *Solva* and *Wolf*. Accordingly Seath's of Rutherglen were contracted to build an iron steam ship 126 feet overall, with a beam of 20 feet and depth of 10.6 feet. She was to be single screw, with a compound vertical direct-acting engine of 50 H.P. Commissioned in April, 1875, as *Stella* (O.N. 70710) at a cost of £6,500,

Opposite: A cutaway drawing of the *Hercules* and *Arrow*, built for service in the Far East.
Institute of Civil Engineers

Right: The *Hercules* helping to build Douglass's Eddystone lighthouse in record time.
Mansell Collection

she was placed under the command of Captain William Stephen Pascoe. However, her station was not to be Penzance, as the Board considered her too large, and the temporary stationing of *Triton* there in 1874 was not suitable, leaving as it did a gap at Ramsgate which *Stella* could not fill. *Stella* therefore steamed to Holyhead where, better able to deal with the buoyage in the Irish Sea, she relieved the *Alert* which went to Penzance. *Stella* remained at Holyhead until 1901 and served Trinity House for 52 years. She ended her career at Blackwall in circumstances closely resembling farce, as will be duly related. However in 1875 she represented a new breed of "working ship" and from now

The first *Siren* about to lift a buoy. Note the sails on booms.   *E. C. Scott*

on the term "yacht" is less frequently heard, the idle rich having commandeered for their pleasure the term that other men used with pride for their place of work.

The kudos of the Lighthouse Service remained with the lonely light keeper whose legend had been so remarkably enhanced by that high-Victorian heroine Grace Darling; or with the Elder Brethren, whose unique guild reached the apogee of its brilliance in an age of glittering pageantry. With a puissant navy and massive merchant marine, the Trinity Steamers became a rather insignificant part of the marine seascape. Their task was so taken for granted that its very unquestioned reliablity was perhaps the greatest compliment the little ships could receive.

Stella was flush-decked with a working foredeck. Forward a wooden-barrelled windlass was worked by chain and sprockets from the steam winch abaft the foremast. The main derrick plumbed the hatch and buoy deck, abaft which came the superstructure. Beneath the bridge was the galley, and in the main body of the hull, stokehold and engine room. The officers' accommodation was below decks aft. Cabins for the master, two mates and two engineers and an additional cabin for the superintendent were situated here, and the firemens' and seamens' "fo'c's'les" were amidships. Grossing only 176 tons, she was a small ship usually commanded by a First Officer. After 1901, when she was sent to Blackwall, a master was officially appointed to her but as he was usually the Blackwall Superintendent *Stella* was effectively commanded by her chief mate.

Stella was followed by *Siren*, and details of her building are available. The prompt despatch of British yards was impressive, though the wrangles between builders and owners have a timeless quality about them.

On 23rd March, 1877, the Board ordered plans to be prepared for a replacement of *Irene* with accommodation for themselves. The Board of Trade sanctioned the expenditure of £14,000, having failed to obtain a redundant naval vessel for the job. Tenders were invited and by 1st June that of Palmers, on the Tyne, had been accepted at £15,000. This was the cheapest, and statutory sanction was given to proceed. A month later Mr Millet, chief engineer at Souter lighthouse, was relieved so that he could oversee the building. On 20th June Palmers demanded an additional £800 for a second boiler and a row blew up over the wording of the contract, but by the end of the year *Siren* was framed up.

Launched in January, 1878, she was 175 feet overall, 25.2 feet in the beam and 14 feet deep. The following month Palmers insisted on appointing a chief engineer as they had built the engines, but were overridden by the arrival of Mr R. Jones from *Argus*. On 13th April the completed *Siren* left Jarrow for Blackwall propelled by her inverted direct-acting compound engine and single screw. On arrival in London she continued to be a bone of contention. The subject of payment for extras was only resolved after long and bitter correspondence and a resort to arbitration. A couple of months later Palmers sent a model of *Siren* to Trinity House yet, in March, 1881, were complaining they had lost £2,000 on the contract. No more money was paid.

Siren (O.N. 81579) was measured for tonnage at 421 gross, 219 net, allocated the signal letters KBJM and sent off to Neyland, releasing *Beacon* for service at Great Yarmouth. *Siren* was used extensively on the west coast and operated from Penzance for a short time during 1912. She carried out west coast cruises when *Galatea* was not available and spent most of the First World War maintaining stations in the Bristol Channel. Usually commanded by a master, she was involved in collision with a battleship when under the temporary charge of the chief mate (See Chapter Ten). After the war her age and the loss of the second *Irene* prompted the Board to acquire a new yacht and *Siren* was sold to Spanish buyers in June, 1920.

Irene was sold in September, 1880, having been downgraded in 1876 when she was principally carrying out lightvessel reliefs on the east coast, never having been equipped for buoy work.

The *Warden*, a new breed of tender with increased lifting capacity which later proved inadequate. Note the anchor stowage. *Beken of Cowes*

The Corporation continued the practice of building up the small steam tenders at the outports and Cardiff was the next to receive attention. At 119 g.r.t. (61 net) *Ready* was only 100 feet in length, 18 feet beam and 10 feet depth. Built by Seath's she had two compound direct-acting vertically inverted engines driving twin screws. Her engine builders were A. Campell's Ltd. *Ready* (O.N. 89501) was commissioned in 1883 and served exclusively at Cardiff until 1926, when the district disappeared, at which time she was sold to a Mr H. Pollard. She was broken up in 1930. It may have been to serve as a coal hulk to her that *Mermaid* arrived at Cardiff in 1897. About 1903 she underwent modifications to improve her stability but in January following the mate in charge, Mr Roskruge, who was also the local Superintendent, complained she still performed badly in a head sea. The worst hazard she encountered appeared to be the mud of Cardiff. On one occasion, grounding at low water, she refused to rise on the flood. As a result of the tenacious hold the mud had on her bottom the sea rose over her decks and poured into the engine room. It thereafter became the practice when the vessel was compelled to lie in the outer harbour for the ship's crew to muster on deck as the tide made. On the mate's whistle the stalwarts jumped up and down upon the deck in unison to break the vacuum beneath her!

It may have been the mud that prompted a detached remark by the inspecting Brethren in 1913. *Ready* was "in good order throughout, there was, however, a most unhealthy bilge stench in the cabin and this should be dealt with at once".

Ready relieved *Alert* at Penzance between October, 1888, and September, 1889, when the latter went for a refit. By this time a Service officer, Mr H. T. Reading, had been appointed Superintendent of the Penzance District. His previous post had been that of First, or Chief, Officer of the *Galatea*. He was not rated master of the tender, the local Chief Officer taking command of her when the Superintendent's duties prevented his going to sea.

Until now the ships built for the outports without accommodation for the Elder Brethren were comparatively small vessels with a poor buoy-working capacity. In 1884, however, the first of a more powerful and new breed of tender was brought into service. The distinction between the London Yacht and Buoy Yachts and the Steam Tenders at the outports was to blur so that what emerged was the District Tender, a workhorse of a ship, capable of many tasks. *Warden* (O.N. 91833) had her disadvantages, but she marks this transition. Built by Seath's with two compound direct-acting vertically inverted steam engines of 77 n.h.p. each by King's of Glasgow, she had a length of 134.2 feet overall, with a beam of 22.3 feet and depth of 11.1 feet. Her tonnage was 246 gross, 140 net.

She had a low hull with a low freeboard designed to facilitate buoy work but making her a very wet ship. The lack of fo'c's'le made it necessary to stow her anchors on a billboard, thus robbing the stockless anchor of its great advantage, the ability to stow in a pipe and avoid the tedious process of catting. Her early history is not clear. She may have started life at Neyland with *Siren*, for *Mermaid* remained at Cowes until 1897 when *Warden* became the Cowes District Tender. She remained on this station throughout the First World War and for the next decade. While lying at the Cowes wharf she was run into by a Cowes ferry. Trinity House sued for damages but lost their case as it was proved that no-one was on the upper deck of *Warden* at the time keeping a "proper lookout". As already related, the Corporation had the last laugh since on the next occasion there was no tender as a scapegoat and it was brick and timber the ferry hit.

In 1886 the second *Satellite* (O.N. 91933) was completed. Seven feet longer than *Warden* with a gross tonnage of 246, her longer engine room, housing a compound steam engine of 70 n.h.p., reduced her net tonnage to 96. Built by Dunlop's of Port Glasgow, she lasted until May, 1926, when bought by Dutch interests. A Dutchman, Walter Emerson, also bought *Warden* in October, 1929, and both these ships appear to have ended their lives as diving tenders.

Satellite was based principally at Harwich. This port was increasing in importance, having originally been no more than a "Store". Trinity House had a lease on Landguard Fort, where lightvessel supplies, mostly gunpowder for signal guns, were kept. As early as 1858 a "tender keeper", wharf engineer, coal hulk keeper, watchmen and labourers were being paid at Harwich from Blackwall. *Satellite* was permanently commanded by a master, an unusual circumstance at an outport or for any but the Blackwall Yachts, presumably to have a senior officer in the locality. It was 1932 before Harwich was granted Depot status and 1940 before it received the facilities that were to make it into the premier Depot of the Trinity House Service.

The second *Irene* off Blackwall, with a number of buoys on her deck.   *Trinity House*

On 21st May, 1894, there occurred one of those incidents for which the 19th century has acquired a certain notoriety. The Trinity Steamer *Satellite*, proceeding upon her lawful occasions, was ordered to stop by the officer commanding H.M.S. *Mersey*. *Satellite* was "dressed" for some ceremonial reason and at her masthead flew the white ensign. No protestation on the part of *Satellite's* master that the Corporation's vessels had long flown the ensign as a masthead flag would satisfy the zealous naval officer. At the time Admiralty contempt for all merchant marine officers had reached an apogee of senselessness. Upon the introduction of the Royal Naval Reserve their Lordships had generously allowed the rank of sub-lieutenant to the captains of merchant ships intimate with the oceans of the globe! Whatever the strictures placed upon *Satellite* on this occasion, Trinity House Tenders fly the white ensign at their foremasthead when dressed to this day, their commanders holding authority to do so as a consequence of this rather petty incident.

The Trinity Yacht *Irene* leads the Royal Squadron through Tower Bridge at its opening on 30th June, 1894.   *C. K. Kendall-Carpenter*

Two further vessels on the lines of *Warden* were constructed; *Mermaid* in 1897 and *Triton* in 1901. However, in the interim the Brethren had sold *Galatea* (1890) and finally disposed of the "pretty little" *Irene*, replaced by *Siren* (1890). Replacement of the *Galatea* as the principal yacht was achieved by the building of the second *Irene* (O.N. 98150), which arrived in time to participate in some of the most splendid celebrations of the Empire.

Her original gross tonnage was 442.5 with a net value of 159.58, but in 1914 she was remeasured and the deductions reduced, giving her a registered gross tonnage of 543 and net of 242 tons. Her displacement was about 1,010 tons at a draught of 9 feet 6 inches. Clearly the bitterness between Palmers and Trinity House had evaporated, for they built her and her engines. She is reputed to have done 18 knots with twin triple-expansion engines and forced draught boilers which developed 245 h.p.

A twin-screw iron steamer with a hull "like a razor blade", she epitomised the "steam yacht". Her masts carried hoisting gaffs with dummy sails which were removable when a derrick was fitted for buoy work.

Irene was perhaps best known for her many Royal Escort duties.

> On these occasions the *Victoria & Albert* (second of the name) with the Queen and Royal Family, the Lords of the Admiralty in attendance on board, is preceeded by the Trinity Yacht *Irene*, the *Alberta* (a 179 foot Royal paddle steam yacht of 390 tons built 1863) being on the starboard, and the *Elfin* (112 foot Royal paddle steam yacht, 96 tons built 1849) on the port quarter. Next came the Admiralty yacht *Enchantress*, and the Lords and Commons, generally in troopships such as the *Himalaya*."

Thus was the Royal Squadron composed at a full naval review.

The best known of these occasions were Queen Victoria's Golden Jubilee Review in which *Galatea* led the Royal Yachts, and her Diamond Jubilee Review in 1897 when the fleet of Admiral Salmon V.C. was inspected at Spithead.

Then on 22nd January, 1901, Victoria died at Osborne. In the gloom of a winter's afternoon a few days later her coffin was borne on a gun carriage from Osborne to the Trinity Depot at East Cowes where, followed by King Edward VII and Queen Alexandra, the Kaiser and Prince Arthur (Duke of Connaught and Strathearn, Elder Brother and later Master of Trinity House), the body was embarked on the *Alberta* lying alongside. The Royal party embarked on *Victoria & Albert* (herself on her last passage). The two Royal Yachts made their way through the grey lines of the Channel and Reserve Fleets. Eight Destroyers led the procession, followed by *Alberta*, the *Victoria & Albert*, the *Osborne*, the Kaiser's *Hohenzollern*, the Admiralty Yacht *Enchantress* and the Trinity Yacht *Irene*. The moored lines of warships, their crews manning the rails in silence and their ensigns drooping at half mast, fired minute guns as the squadron passed to entrain the coffin for London.

The new king pursued the *Entente Cordiale* as a cornerstone of British foreign policy, and in August, 1905, *Irene* participated in a review of the British and French fleets at Spithead. It was during this that, horror of horrors, her illuminations were considered inadequate! Accordingly a proposal was made that she should be "illuminated with a rainbow from bowsprit end to taffrail . . down the . . . rigging on both sides of the masts . . . a line of lamps along the gunwhale . . . covered with red paper outlining bridge . . . Funnels . . . to have four rows of lamps covered in red paper and . . . a small ring of lamps round each masthead", an organisational nightmare that necessitated buckets of bulbs being concealed about *Irene's* upper deck to replace the frequent failures that occurred. On one occasion lit thus *Irene* was anchored in Cowes Roads close to the *Standart*, yacht of Tsar Nicholas II. Threats of assassination were in the air and her crew mounted an armed guard over the last of the Romanovs. They were not impressed by the practice of *Irene's* irreverent apprentices who were wont to fling bulbs over the side to shatter them on *Irene's* plating. The practice, which resulted in loud popping explosions, was abruptly terminated on receipt of a complaint from a furious Russian officer.

Irene frequently escorted King Edward on his visits to France when the Royal Yacht, the brand new *Victoria & Albert*, invariably left Port Victoria, Sheerness, preceded by *Irene*. In March, 1904, one such escort took place with *Irene* doing 16 knots. The flag officer, Commodore Sir Alexander Milne, asked for an increase in speed and, although *Irene's* stokers fired their boilers until the paint actually began to blister off the funnels, she would go no faster and was ordered astern. This was recorded as "escort dispensed with" in *Irene's* log. The matter of her speed was a problem over a long period. On one occasion she escorted her sovereign from Liverpool to the Mersey Bar, where the cruisers *Dido*, *Leda* and *Juno* took over, *Irene* following to Swansea "at her best speed". She also burned a lot of fuel and experiments were conducted steaming on one boiler. Draught was to be supplied by the fan at the Chief Engineer's discretion to maintain a steam pressure of 150 p.s.i. At 86 to 90 r.p.m. she cruised on inspections at nine to ten knots.

In March, 1904, Swan Hunter's at Newcastle installed new boilers and strengthened her engines.

"At 9.30 on 9th March *Irene* left Neptune Works and proceeded north of Tynemouth where she was put over the measured mile. Maximum speed of 17.168 knots, a mean speed at 168 r.p.m. Between 11.10 and 17.10 . . . 16.573 knots at 2361 I.H.P., forced draught in use, a speed of 14 knots without forced draught."

Her last major occasion was the Coronation Review of King George V in 1912. Apart from her ceremonial duties she shared the cruises of inspection with *Siren* and in 1896, in company with the Northern Lighthouse Board in *Hesperus*, carried out a tour of Scottish lights. The *Irene* had on board, in addition to Elder Brethren, the President of the Board of Trade and the Chancellor of the Exechequer. She also carried out survey work. The periphery of the banks were continuously sounded to see if they were "well guarded" by the buoys. A record of June, 1905, is fairly typical:

"Throughout the inspection the greater portion of the buoys and Lightships were found in their assigned positions and as far as could be ascertained by the various lines of soundings taken the several shoals appeared to be adequately guarded in all the channels which were examined."

Bearing in mind that these were still the days of the hand lead, this was arduous work. There was also the occasional approbatory remark: "The committee would like to place on record their appreciation of the willing assistance they received from Mr Russell the 2nd Officer and Apprentice Lee who were more nearly associated with them in the examining work".

In a long life *Irene* had a succession of masters. In 1894 Captain J. G. Browne commanded her. He was relieved by Captain Mayor who was followed briefly by Captain Eastham. Mayor returned about 1904 but within two years "Johnny" Reading had her, only to hand over to R. V. Williams about 1907. Her final commander was Hugh Leopold Philips, who died when his ship was mined in 1915. Browne succeeded a Captain Hattersley as Superintendent at Blackwall and was in turn followed by Eastham. Reading became Superintendent at Ramsgate, later Cowes. Captain Mayor was Superintendent at Neyland when *Siren* was on the District (1909). *Irene's* masters were all senior men whose experience of the Narrow Seas exceeded that of the majority of the Elder Brethren, for the latter, in command of foreign going merchantmen or warships, could not possibly accumulate the expertise and knowledge that Reading, Browne and their colleagues had spent a lifetime absorbing. These men, therefore, provided Trinity House with a fund of intimate knowledge of the waters over which it held jurisdiction, and ensured that the marine affairs of Trinity House were carried out to a high standard of professional skill.

In the final years of the 19th century the service had grown to provide the pelagic sailor with an unrivalled system of seamarks on the British coast. The old Yacht Establishment had been displaced by the "Steam Vessel Service" and the

last vestiges of 18th century amateurism had vanished. The age of technology had dawned, and nowhere was that more obvious than in the marine world.

Lighted buoys had been in use for some time. In August, 1875, new experimental gas buoys were laid near the Mouse lightvessel and off Sheerness. In 1880 the East Oaze was lit. Various types of illuminant were tried but by 1909 the incandescent oil gas buoy had become standard. Although remaining in use for many years, it was gradually superseded by the dissolved acetylene buoy introduced about 1920. Combining longevity with simplicity and reliability, it remains in service today.

Communications had also improved. The elaborate system of lightvessel signal guns and rockets had been phased out. In 1887 a submarine cable was led to the Sunk for telephonic communication, but it was constantly fouling the cable. Telephone cables were fitted elsewhere but did not last. They were replaced by the wireless transmitter, introduced about 1905 to all tenders and lighthouses. Lightvessels received them to an extent, but they were all removed for security reasons in 1914. A lightvessel seaman was trained as an ''operator instructor'' and borne on *Irene's* books. His trainees were paid 2d per day for their new skill.

In 1908 there were 54 lightvessels, and between 1877 and 1929 no fewer

Opposite: No. 15 lightvessel under tow in the English Channel in December, 1978, seen from the T.H.V. *Winston Churchill.*
  Ambrose Greenway

Right: A tender's seaboat and crew relighting an extinguished gas buoy about 1880.
Illustrated London News

Men of the second *Mermaid* signalling by semaphore to keepers on the Wolf Rock lighthouse.

than eleven were sunk by collision. All were lost except No. 38, which was raised from the Gull station. In 1894 No. 22 was under tow by one of the tenders when she broke adrift and was wrecked at Seaford, while No. 27 parted her moorings at the Selker Station and drove ashore in heavy weather at Drigg.

Handling lightvessels was, and continues to be, a hazardous operation. The wooden *Triton* and *Galatea* were in collison in January, 1874, when changing over the South Goodwin lightvessels and the *Argus* lacked towing bitts aft at all. Two wires were led forward to her windlass. The consequent chafing of the wires laid out along her deck on the corners of her deckhouses was a cause for concern and when towing at 100 r.p.m. her cylinder tops vibrated "perceptibly". By this time *Argus* had been displaced from the London District by the second *Irene* and had gone to Yarmouth where she relieved *Beacon*, sold off after 28 years' service. Also at Yarmouth was the steam launch *Ariel*. Built about 1900, she was a sea-going craft whose duty was the relief of the local lightvessels close to Yarmouth: the St Nicholas, Cockle, Corton and, in fine weather, the Cross Sand. She was also used for survey work, carrying out a survey of Lowestoft Roads in July, 1905, with Superintendent Thorpe and several Elder Brethren on board. She was usually commanded by an "off duty" lightvessel skipper.

By the turn of the century *Argus* had been lengthened and converted to a screw steamer, as already mentioned. Her district rapidly extended northwards. At this time the lighthouses north of the Tyne were part of the North East District, still administered by an Agent. Later, by some bureaucratic quirk due to geographical distance, they became part of the Holyhead area! At all events in 1904 the Filey Brigg buoy was taken over from the Tees Commissioners as they "hesitate to send their small vessels so far from their base".

In December, 1903, it was recommended *Argus* be extensively strengthened, but it was clear from the work then put in hand that her days were numbered. In 1909 a replacement was well under way and it is sad to record that a vessel 53 years old should end her life with a tragedy. On the night of 30th January, 1909, a collision occured between the S.S. *Dundee* and a sailing barge. The latter immediately sank close west of the Cockle lightvessel. Her crew were all drowned. The following day *Argus*, Captain Emerson, arrived to remove the barge's mast and clear the wreck to a safe depth. The weather was fresh and unsuitable for divers so Emerson decided to sweep in explosives from a boat. He despatched Mr Bound, Chief Officer, with five seamen and a seaman diver. Bound swept in two small charges with no effect but at the third a terrific explosion flung the boat upwards as high as the Cockle's lantern, shaking the lightvessel and *Argus*. As the water subsided Emerson and Moss, his 2nd Officer, anxiously searched the area. The boat capsized and only Bound survived. When the wreckage surfaced it was discovered that the barge was the ketch *Good Hope*, which at Faversham had loaded a cargo of 40 tons of gelignite.

The Mayor of Yarmouth launched an appeal for the bereaved relatives to which, in addition to the pensions, Trinity House paid £500. Bound was never a fit man again. He was almost continuously sick until his death, and although promoted master he left the Yarmouth District in 1914. This was the second such incident, the victims of an earlier wreck dispersal lying buried in East Cowes Churchyard.

The completion of the four ships of the *Warden* "class" was undertaken between 1897 and 1901 with the building of *Mermaid* and *Triton*. The second *Mermaid* was intended to replace *Alert* at Penzance. Building commenced in August, 1896, at Cragg's Middlesbrough yard. Her cost was a little under £10,000 and work proceeded slowly. In December, 1897, she ran over the measured distance off the Maplin Sands, attaining 10 knots but her stability was unsatisfactory and in July, 1898, £1,100 was spent on permanent ballast. It seems the problem was never overcome and in some respects she remained a failure. *Mermaid* (O.N. 108254) was 135 feet overall, 22.1 feet broad and 12.2

feet deep. Her propulsion was by twin triple-expansion engines of 10 inch, 15 inch and 25 inch diameter bore with a stroke of 18-21 inch giving an i.h.p. of 55. The engines were built by Sir Christopher Furness, Westgarth and Company.

Wrangling over *Mermaid's* stability and the financial liability for the extra work involved in compensating for it went on for some time. The final payment was not made until 1902, and then only under protest. *Mermaid* was sent to Ramsgate until the matter was resolved, and it was only after that final sum had passed to the builders that she exchanged with *Alert* and the latter finally arrived at the station for which she had been built. *Mermaid's* arrival at Ramsgate displaced *Triton*, whose eventual sale to a Whitstable coal factor has already been related. *Alert's* spell on the Penzance District had been interrupted only by her annual dockings in August when a tug from Falmouth carried out local reliefs.

A log book for *Mermaid* survives from which it may be learned that the Superintendent, "Johnny" Reading, technically master of the vessel, usually left the sea duty to the Chief Mate, Mr G. T. Thompson, who, with 2nd Officer H. J. Hudson, took her to sea. In July of 1907 *Mermaid* underwent a boiler clean for five days and a 16-day drydock in August. By December she needed another boiler clean. In July both *Irene* and (the new) *Vestal* were in the area, the former bringing *Mermaid* and the Penzance Depot their annual supply of stores. During early August *Mermaid* persevered in dispersing the wreck of the ketch *Bona* off Prawle point. The sunken vessel refused to settle and work was hampered by fog, rain and south-westerly gales.

It is an intriguing record of everyday activity. Seaman Ellis injured his foot and was "sent home in a trap", while a day or two later special leave was granted to men for R.N.R. training; they were probably glad of a relief from the apparently constant servicing of the steam steering gear. When the Elder Brethren inspected her they found her "scrupulously clean and in excellent order, with the exception of the steam steering gear . . . which jams when the helm is put a-starboard . . . the Superintendent thought it so unreliable that he . . . proposed to use . . . hand gear on his . . . visit to the Channel Islands''.

The Penzance District had been extended in 1904 to include Hanois lighthouse off Guernsey, Caskets, and Braye Harbour lights. After 1912 Alderney and in 1913 Sark were also added. This reorganisation had the effect of down-grading Ramsgate to a sub-district under Cowes. The *Alert* was proving a poor sea ship in the short seas of the Dover Straits and had once made five attempts to relieve the crew of the Varne lightvessel, all of which ended in failure. She was also quite inadequate to service the North Goodwin four-arm mooring or lift the larger Goodwin buoys. To circumvent the problem she exchanged stations with *Warden* every summer for a week or two, and it is Cowes where she appears in the illustration on page 77. Whilst here the visiting

Brethren animadverted on her weedy topsides, as a consequence of which the white ribband between boot topping and topsides was discontinued on all except *Irene* and *Vestal*.

In 1913 the Ramsgate sub-district was abolished and incorporated in the new London and South East District, upon which *Alert* was sold to Russian buyers. Also at this time *Mermaid* at Penzance was laid up with stability problems and *Siren* moved down from Neyland. The war was to bring *Mermaid* back into service.

The last of the *Warden* "class" was *Triton* (O.N. 112847), completed in 1901 by Ramage and Ferguson of Leith. 126 feet overall with 22.6 feet beam and 11.9 feet depth, her triple expansion engines of 10 inches, 16 inches and 20 inches bore generated 79 h.p. Her tonnage was 234 gross and 53 net and she steamed at 10.5 knots. Her station was Holyhead, from where the *Stella* was sent to London to assist *Irene* and the new *Vestal*. Under the command of Chief Officer W. A. C. Akaster, *Stella* had once rolled her cook, a Mr Rees, over the

The unsuccessful tender *Mermaid* in Penzance with the Runnelstone Buoy alongside. This class of buoy was formerly towed on station. *Trinity House*

side and back on board again. History does not relate which part of this story was most appreciated by his shipmates!

The new *Vestal* (O.N. 11018) was built in 1898 to a design by Mr Goodall, Surveyor of Shipping to Trinity House. She grossed 576 tons (133 net), having an overall length of 183.5 feet, 28.3 feet beam and depth of 15.2 feet. Her twin triple-expansion engines of 14 inches, 23 inches and 37 inches bore had a 24 inch stroke and were of 169 h.p. Built by Stevenson of Hebburn, she was an extremely handsome ship. Although straight stemmed, she had scrollwork on the bows and quarters and elegant yacht-like lines. But all that glisters is not gold, and she was curiously constructed with a very shallow draught forward and deep draught aft, so that in drydock one walked perceptibly downhill! Her lines forward were very hollow, giving her so fine an entry that she proved dangerous working out of Neyland in the 1920's (of which more later). For the time being she was employed as a London District Tender and a committee yacht for inspections. During one of these voyages a guarded reference is made by the Brethren to her stability and movement in heavy weather. In 1913, under the command of Captain H. J. Lile, she was "found in good order and the discipline on board was of a high order and the duties on board all well and quietly performed". She graced several festive occasions. In 1904 she conveyed the then Master of Trinity House, the Prince of Wales, and his Princess (later King

George V and Queen Mary) down the Thames to the training ship *Worcester*, and her last such appearance was in the lines of George VI's Coronation Review in 1937. Although a "yacht", she had to content herself with *Irene's* cast-off garland flags!

The *Warden* class of ships were not coming up to expectations. The growth of the outport districts and the increase in buoyage plus the increased incidence in buoy work occasioned by the frequent necessity of recharging oil gas buoys had long since rendered the London ships' buoy shifting visits a thing of the past. Now each tender had to look after its own parish, with the consequent necessary annual exchange of *Warden* and *Alert* already mentioned. But in 1913 *Warden* herself failed to lift the Blanchard buoy and moorings. This buoy, marking a fang of rock in surrounding deep water, lies in an area off Sark that is subject to fierce tides. Superintendent Reading, asked to despatch *Siren*, commented that he did not think even *Siren*, which had had a new mast and heavier derricks in 1911, could cope. *Warden's* masts were both in bad shape and she was obliged to leave the Blanchard. The complaint was soon dealt with and the new *Alert* was sent down to lift the buoy. *Alert* and *Argus* were bigger ships intended for the heavier buoys then coming into service.

In 1909 the fourth *Argus* replaced the third at Great Yarmouth. She, too, was destined for tragedy. The new ship (O.N. 129055) grossed 653 tons and was

Opposite: The second *Triton* recharging an oil-gas buoy in the 1920s.   *Trinity House*

Right: The *Triton* aground on the Shingles Bank building the N.W. Shingles beacon.   *S. T. Cope*

The fourth *Argus* alongside Yarmouth depot. Note her low bridge. Alongside the Swarte Bank lightvessel is the steam launch *Ariel*. Note also the semaphore tower on the depot roof in this photograph of about 1911.   *R. N. Thompson*

a powerful twin-screw steam ship with triple expansion engines and Scotch boilers. She had excellent lifting gear, though a low bridge made it almost impossible to take bearings on large arcs of the horizon obscured by the chart-room. Difficulties were also being experienced in finding the correct positions for lightvessels and buoys in the grey wastes of the North Sea as the general standard of navigation improved. The usual method was to sound for the bank and lay the seamark accordingly.

Following *Argus*, the second *Alert* (O.N. 132704) of 700 tons was also a twin-screw steamer with equally powerful lifting gear. She was stationed at Blackwall with *Irene* and *Stella*, making a useful addition to the district and more than adequate to the task of lifting the 11-ton Blanchard. In 1915 Captain Marshall, an Elder Brother, took passage in her to observe the operation and was duly impressed. But *Alert's* life was short. War clouds were gathering over Europe and in the fateful month of August, 1914, we feel a little of the quickening of the nation's heart.

Siren was on the Penzance District inspection on 2nd August, lying anchored in St Mary's Road, Scillies.

"Being Sunday mustered crew and inspected quarters. The Master was served with a notice that Naval Reserves were called out and Mr Dorien

The third *Vestal*, built in 1898, in service as a yacht on the East Coast in the 1900s. Note the low bridge, which gave insufficient visibility under certain conditions and was later raised. *Trinity House*

Smith of Tresco sent on board requesting a passage . . . for his son who is Brigade Major of the 4th Reserve Rifle Battalion . . . The *Siren* . . . left for St Ives, the Superintendent being instructed to meet her there and the eight Reserve men were landed . . .''

Just prior to the outbreak of war the disposition of the ships had undergone certain alterations connected with the abolition of the Ramsgate District. The responsibility for the Channel Islands was transferred to Cowes which met the London District at Dungeness. The three Goodwin lightvessels, the Gull and Varne were manned and relieved from Harwich, which relinquished some of its hold over the southern Yarmouth lightships for which it seems to have shared responsibility with Yarmouth.

Mermaid's stability had given cause for concern so that in 1913, as we have seen, *Siren* took her place. *Siren's* place at Neyland was taken by *Vestal*. *Triton* was still at Holyhead, and *Ready* at Cardiff. East Cowes boasted the ageing *Warden* with *Satellite* at Harwich. *Mermaid* was laid up until 1914, when the demands of war solved her stability problem automatically. At London *Irene*, *Alert* and *Stella* could be found, with *Argus* and the launch *Ariel* at Yarmouth completing the Corporation's tender dispositions on the eve of hostilities.

CHAPTER SEVEN

War and Peace

"Commenting upon the expeditious manner in which the Corporation's vessels performed the work of laying buoys during operations recently carried (out) on the Belgian coast, the vessels shared with H.M. Ships the risk of destruction by the enemy batteries and aircraft."

Vice Admiral Bacon, Dover, 1918

THE slow descent of Europe into the First World War had as its symptoms two Balkan Wars, international tension, incidents and assassination. In July, 1914, a "mobilisation" Review of the Home Fleet had taken place at Spithead before the capital ships of Jellicoe and the battlecruisers that Beatty was to take coursing in the North Sea dispersed to their stations. But all wars depend upon supplies, and the rising power of the submarine was first felt in its blockade and destruction of British merchant shipping. To this menace was added the mine-field, littering the continental shelf with devices that demonstrate man's almost divine ingenuity when it comes to murdering his own race. The combination of mine and submarine reduced Britain's corn supply to six weeks in April, 1917, and resulted in one in four ships being lost.

Lloyd-George overruled his naval advisers and imposed the convoy system on all merchant shipping, which at least made the problem manageable. In March, 1916, the Ministry of Blockade had been formed and the network of boom defences extended. That across the Dover Straits was designed to force U-boats wishing to plunder the Channel Approaches to travel round the north of Scotland. Also based in Dover was the Dover Patrol, a mixed force of warships under Admiral Roger Keyes used for harrying the right flank of the German line and maintaining communications with the Allied armies in France and Belgium.

The Corporation's ships became associated with the work of the Dover Patrol and of the minesweeping flotillas keeping the channels clear. The booms, channels and "gates" were buoyed, and it became the duty of a Trinity House tender to operate with the patrols. In addition to these duties the day-to-day running of the Service had to go on. In this the Trinity steamers had as much to contend with from "friendly" mines as from the worst endeavours of the enemy. In early 1916 *Vestal*, which had been returned to the London District, was despatched to attend the East Goodwin lightvessel which had broken adrift in heavy weather. Before her spare anchor could be let go the lightvessel had drifted into an advertised British minefield to the north-east.

Vestal's master took the ship in at full speed, hoping the bow wave would help keep any mines clear, all boats were turned out and the hands kept at the falls wearing lifejackets. They were fortunate, and towed the lightvessel into Margate Roads, fitted a new anchor and cable and relaid her on station, but the four hours they had spent in the minefield had been "long ones, very long".

The effects of bad weather were one thing but the threat of bombardment or invasion led to the removal of many channel buoys. At the outbreak of war the Cowes tender, *Warden*, Captain P. J. Yeates, was sent to assist on the east coast. Lifting buoys in the northern Thames estuary while the *Koningin Emma* was sunk away to the north, they were then sent to Plymouth to collect a lightvessel and tow it to Dover for use as a gate mark in the Dover boom. Here *Warden* avoided attack by a U-boat which sank the Downs examination vessel, H.M.S. *Niger*. *Warden's* next task was to steam into Belgian waters and withdraw to Harwich one of the Hinder lightvessels.

In April, 1915, *Irene* towed No. 51 lightvessel, that which had seen service on the Basses, out of the Thames and into the Dover Strait. She met *Satellite* off Folkestone with No. 21 lightvessel and the two tenders laid their respective marks on the Folkestone gate.

> "The wind and sea increased during the afternoon and evening and No. 51 did not pick up her moorings till 6-15 p.m. and the men sent on board to moor her till 9-45 p.m. when there was a strong wind and high sea."

Some idea of the laborious process of handling moorings may be gathered from this brief excerpt. This work, which once embarked upon cannot be stopped until its completion, indicates something of the labours of the Trinity seamen.

The first loss sustained was that of *Irene*, mined near the Tongue lightvessel on 9th November, 1915, when on "special service". Her master, Captain Hugh Leopold Philips, and twenty-eight men lost their lives, among them 2nd Officer Thomas and Chief Engineer Dewar. Apprentice John Reading, being a strong swimmer, rescued several men and pulled them on to the chart house top "which was floating like a raft". First Officer Plimsaul and 2nd Engineer Agar were among the survivors.

The sinking of *Irene* resulted in the immediate transfer of *Vestal* from Neyland to Blackwall. Her place at Neyland was taken up by *Siren*, and *Mermaid* was hurriedly recommissioned at Penzance. A consequence of *Irene's* loss was the provision of an armed escort to attend the Trinity Steamers, now being regarded as useful vessels; rather too useful to be wantonly risked.

Upon her arrival on the east coast *Vestal*, Captain McCarthy, joined *Triton*, Captain Bound (late victim of the Cockle explosion), which ship had exchanged stations with *Stella*, *Satellite*, Captain Reynolds, and Yeates's *Warden* on the north east coast. The task of the four ships was to lay a line of buoys marking the swept channels from the Humber to Berwick. These were marked by unlighted, conical buoys at intervals of five miles. Shortly after this the tenders again dispersed, but were kept constantly coasting, maintaining, repairing and laying seamarks as occasion demanded.

Servicing the Bridge buoy off the Needles, *Warden's* hands were witnesses to the mining close by of the steam ship *Rumanian*, 5,000 tons. Captain Yeates ordered the buoy over the side and, getting a towing hawser on deck, manoeuvred alongside the mined vessel. *Rumanian* had had her bows blown off and was listing badly. Getting his hawser across, Yates began to tow her into the Solent where a naval officer ordered him to anchor. Yeates protested that if he turned her head to tide her bulkhead would burst, a view shared by *Rumanian's* master. What he intended was to beach her in shallow water, but to do this he had to pass the gate of the Spithead boom. This the naval officer could not allow. Upon anchoring, the bulkhead burst, "She turned on her port side and went down flat . . . The old captain of *Rumanian* was very much annoyed and told the lieutenant-commander he had lost the ship". *Warden* then had to lay a wreck buoy on her.

Warden herself had several narrow escapes. Off Anvil Point the port propellor struck an obstruction,. Both the 2nd Engineer and Yeates's steward, who had been in the captain's after harbour cabin, came up to the bridge. Reporting the matter to the naval authorities at Portland sweepers subsequently

Officers and seamen from the yacht *Irene*, the steamer *Stella*, and lightvessels with the Blackwall wharf staff. This photograph was taken on *Irene's* foredeck about 1915, but a few months before many of those in the picture lost their lives.   *Trinity House*

discovered a line of mines in the area. Later, in the same position with Captain Lee, the District Superintendent, on board, Yeates shaped his course from the Point to the Shambles. Going into the chart room to write up the log some premonition warned him to keep to the north and he amended the course accordingly. Nervously walking to the port bridge wing, Yeates looked down to see "a large mine, just awash, about three feet clear of the vessel's side". Turning about, Yeates tried to sink the mine by rifle fire without success, but two small minesweepers arrived and did the job. Shortly afterwards one of the sweepers struck a second mine and exploded, killing ten of her crew instantly, another dying later and leaving only two survivors.

On another occasion *Warden* had a narrow escape from a submarine. Crossing the Channel bound for Hanois lighthouse with the armed yacht *Vanessa*, Lt-Cdr. Cockerell R.N.R., as escort, she rescued three Dutchmen whose ketch had just been sunk by a U-boat. Returning from the Channel Islands a few days later they ran into thick fog. *Vanessa* closed up on *Warden* and Cockerell asked Yeates what he proposed. The two ships proceeded at full speed in silence, and at one point the lookout reported an object to port. Nothing more could be seen and, having run her distance, *Warden* altered course for Sandown when, a few moments later, the fog horn at St Catherine's Point was heard. When the two vessels anchored in the examination anchorage Yeates was asked aboard *Vanessa* and Cockerell showed him several signals, one of which told of mines laid in the Needles passage, their alternative return route, and another gave the positions of several submarines. It was clear from one of the positions that the object seen by the lookout had indeed been a U-boat.

Warden survived the war and with her these reminiscences. Less lucky was the second *Alert*. This ship and *Argus* were the best buoy working ships Trinity House owned and as a consequence of this it was *Alert* that was sent from Blackwall to join the Dover Patrol in 1916. Under the newly formed Ministry of Blockade the war effort began to assume different characteristics, but *Alert's* employment under naval control was not without its problems. For a start the tender's master had to tolerate the presence of a naval liaison officer, and this clearly rankled. These officers were invariably reserve commanders or lieutenant-commanders, and like all men in advisory capacities tended to overbearance towards those on whom the real responsibility lay.

Secondly the work on which *Alert* was engaged was exceedingly dangerous. Along with the drifters and trawlers under Admiralty requisition, the Trinity House ships were undertaking nerve-wracking tasks. It was not surprising that the seamen, who regarded themselves as noncombatants, requested at least a cash allowance when under naval direction. This discontent eventually prompted the Deputy Master to visit the Admiral of Patrols, Sir Reginald Bacon, and discuss the matter with him.

"The Admiral was very appreciative of the services rendered but . . . stated that there was no special grant made to any men in the Naval Service for such work . . . He said . . . that if the Elder Brethren consider a case in which they in their service would make an exceptional grant he would be prepared to support it although he could give no promise that such a recommendation would be approved by the Admiralty."

It was not approved, and with the introduction of wholesale conscription the plight or plea of the Trinity Seamen was insignificant. Besides, nasty noises were coming from the wastes of Russia and attitudes of dissent were firmly discouraged.

Then on 15th April, 1917, while buoy working for their Lordships off Dover, *Alert's* anchor fouled a mine and the resulting explosion destroyed the ship and deprived eleven men of their lives. Captain Wynne, 2nd Officer Davies and Apprentice Raven were among the survivors.

Remorse is an emotion the Admiralty are not known for, but the loss of a ship was another matter. Both the Admiralty and Trinity House were seriously concerned about *Alert's* loss, from the operational point of view. The Admiralty had no ship to undertake the essential work of the patrols and the Corporation had lost one of their newest and finest ships. A serious gap was left in Trinity House's ability to fulfill its obligations. *Irene's* loss, tragic though it was, had been easily absorbed by the recommissioning of *Mermaid*. *Alert's* loss was less easily rectified, as she had been a very able ship.

The only solution was for *Argus* to take her place and for the Admiralty to supply a trawler then building under their requisition orders. Accordingly several of the Elder Brethren began inspecting ships on the stocks. In May they went to the Selby yard of Cochrane and Sons to view a vessel for which plans had been drawn up by "Admiralty experts" and delivery of which was expected in two months. The Brethren decided this vessel was not for them, for the necessary alterations would have been considerable, including removal of the forecastle, fitting of a larger mast and windlass and provision of a boat deck abaft a reconstructed bridge. But later that month Captain Marshall discovered what he was looking for in H.M. Trawler *Jeria*, then building at Yarmouth. Compared with the Selby vessels she was larger, with a "very considerable sheer", the forecastle could remain and beneath it there was sufficient room for a large windlass, and "as all fittings are already in place . . . the least possible alterations will be carried out to render her of use as a lighthouse tender, should the Admiralty agree to hand her over".

For once the Admiralty had little choice. At the end of May *Argus* had left Yarmouth for Dover and her position there was clearly dependent upon a replacement arriving quickly at Yarmouth. The launch *Ariel* was no substitute and was given over almost constantly to pilotage work. For a while *Satellite* covered from Harwich, but it was agreed that Trinity House should have *Jeria*.

The second *Alert*, seen off Cowes four years before her loss. With the fourth *Argus* she was the most powerful lifting vessel of her time.

Beken of Cowes

It was not long, though, before *Argus's* people were echoing the discontent of *Alert's*. On 21st June, 1917, the crew refused "to sweep for moorings of certain buoys laid for naval purposes".

Captain Golding, Elder Brother, hurried to Dover where he met the naval captain in charge of Drifter Patrols. This officer informed him that a buoy forming part of a barrage had been sunk by the enemy and it was essential that it was recovered. The area had been "carefully swept" and *Argus* was "requested" to grapple for the buoy with her own anchor. This the crew refused to do "in spite of the remonstrances of the R.N.R. Commander (the liaison officer) on the plea that it was quite possible to disturb . . . a mine . . . missed by . . . a minesweeper, as in the case of *Alert*; furthermore that when mines were brought to the surface on a former occasion they were promised that no more grappling should be done".

Golding went on to say that "they had not refused other work, in fact they have carried out all other duties as usual". The navy feared that the "example" of *Argus* would disaffect the fishermen employed on the drifters. This was countered by Golding who explained the terms under which the Trinity Seamen were engaged and pointed out that these made no mention of deliberately risking life in any way other than the normal business of the Lighthouse Service.

These terms, he said, had never been formally superseded. The only solution he could see was the invocation of the Defence of the Realm Act, a draconian measure which seemed over-hard, or, alternatively, to man *Argus* with naval ratings under the direction of Trinity House Officers. The naval officer did not think the Admiral commanding would entertain the latter suggestion.

Golding next boarded *Argus*, anchored in the harbour. Captain McCarthy had command of her at the time and he and the officers explained that they had not refused any duty, but that with the refusal of the ratings his hands were tied. He was most unwilling to exacerbate a delicate situation. The engineers also explained that they were in a similar position and had only abandoned the engine room when the firemen and stokers refused duty.

Golding mustered the crew and heard what they had to say. He clearly sympathised with the men, for in grappling a vessel drags her anchor beneath her, whilst a sweeper cuts loose mines at the end of a sweep wire. The crew's spokesman explained "that the dragging the anchor under the bottom to grapple for moorings *gave them no chance to escape* in the event of a mine being hooked and in doing this they ran much greater risks than the ordinary mine-sweepers". With some justice they did not see why their duties had to assume the character of a forlorn hope, and it is probable that this orderly strike saved *Argus* from eventually sharing *Alert's* fate. Eventually matters were settled when the naval authorities undertook to sweep the affected area more thoroughly and the method of grappling was altered to sweeping with a wire and grapnel. Golding finally called on Admiral Bacon, who was "much pleased" with the conclusion and "spoke in very complimentary terms of the work done by the Corporation".

Argus resumed her work, but the navy had not forgiven her for insubordination. Working with the Belgian coast patrol, she was proceeding along the Flemish coast with three monitors, *Erebus*, *Terror*, and *General Roberts*, six destroyers and an escort of minesweepers and coastal motor boats. *Argus* was astern of *General Roberts*, whose maximum speed was about six knots, when a signal was received that enemy torpedo boats were at sea and word was passed to clear secondary armament. Lacking anything but a pair of rifles, Chief Officer Barber loaded these up and awaited the action. The Germans failed to appear, and *Argus's* officers expected some acknowledgement of their gallantry. To their surprise the following day the Dunkirk Daily Dispositions merely stated the lateness of the patrol's return was due to the dilatory progress of *Argus*. At this time she was capable of twice the speed of the *General Roberts*!

Later in the war she was commanded by Yeates. It was while *Argus* was moored to the South Goodwin buoy with a gas line connected to the reservoirs that 2nd Officer Helsdon, supervising the recharging of the buoy, suddenly heard an ominous "scraping" on the buoy mooring chain and sang out to the ship in alarm. Yeates ordered the gas shut off and Helsdon disconnected the pipe and threw the ship's mooring rope off the Buoy. *Argus* began to fall back in the tide while Helsdon flung himself into the jolly-boat, also alongside the buoy. The boat drifted down tide while her occupants held their breath. Then her coxswain saw the cause of the alarm, a mine floating just ahead of *Argus*, and shouted to the ship. Yeates had the helm flung over and the mine passed close down the ship's side and no more than six feet from her boat. Grabbing a rifle from the chartroom rack, Yeates ran aft and drew a bead on the mine, hoping to sink it. Instead he hit one of the horns and the mine exploded. "It

The third *Vestal* as an old lady in semi-retirement as Cowes tender preparing for the Coronation Fleet Review of 1937. *Trinity House*

shook the old *Argus* and the Engineer, one of *Alert's* survivors . . . came running out of the engine room". The naval liaison officer remonstrated with Yeates but he was unrepentant.

The effects of a mine exploding while pumping oil gas on the tender's decks are too ghastly to contemplate. An accident, without the added force of high explosive, had occurred aboard *Ready* at Cardiff on the forenoon of 1st March, 1915. A gasholder was being lifted on board when, from no apparent cause, it blew apart.

> "The force of the explosion was very great . . . considerable damage was done to the . . . store and surrounding houses. The six men working at the crane were blown in all directions . . . none . . . seriously injured, beyond shock and bruises with the exception of Evans, the winchman, who may unfortunately lose the sight of one eye."

Argus suffered in a similar manner when at Blackwall moorings on 21st May, 1918. While a gasholder in the hold was being filled the union blew off, venting gas into the hold. Mr Mander, the carpenter, immediately shut off the pump and seizing the hose pressed its end against the steel casing to reduce the flow of gas. Unfortunately his action was too late. There was a flash and a serious fire began which gutted several stores and the apprentices' halfdeck. The fire was contained and overcome by the ship's crew ''in a most praiseworthy effort''. Mander was badly hurt and four other men less seriously affected.

The trials of *Jeria* took place on 24th October, 1917, when she sailed from Yarmouth with Elder Brethren on board. Escorted by two naval launches, she effected a changeover of South Scroby buoys. ''The moorings were badly sanded and the windlass and bow rollers were subjected to great and unusual strain in endeavouring to recover them . . . ''

Jeria carried no apprentices until after the war, when they were required to relinquish their accommodation when the ship carried lightsmen. Twelve seamen lived in a messdeck, four firemen in another, while the Bosun, Carpenter, Cook and Steward lived in cabins. The tween decks were fitted out as stores over the chain hold. A tunnel from the hold to the stokehold was fitted out as a buoy lamp room. Her chartroom, bridge, boat deck and master's cabin were described as ''excellent''. The side houses to starboard were fitted as pantries, to port ''three up to date WC's.'' Aft the only change was the fitting of towing bitts and wire compressors. An enlarged galley range was added but ''the space for officers and engineers has been altered as little as possible and while distinctly small is snug . . . ''

The former steam yacht *Miranda* seen in her new guise as *Patricia*, the principal yacht of the Corporation, at slow speed about 1925.   *Trinity House*

Although lacking a fresh water delivery pump, the former trawler was considered by the Brethren "as good for the work of the Corporation as any in the Service". That their knowledge of this was limited is borne out by the comments of her crew who, to a man, considered the ship unhandy, uncomfortable and cramped. Nevertheless *Jeria* remained operating from Yarmouth until *Argus* returned from Dover.

Towards the end of the war *Argus* played an important, though un-trumpeted, part in the raids on Zeebrugge and Ostend on St George's Day, 1918. Several buoys were laid for the task force to rendezvous and home on. The old cruiser *Vindictive* and her consorts raided Zeebrugge where a submarine, packed with high explosive, was run in under the viaduct and blown up to block the canal and docks being used by German destroyers and U-boats. At Ostend the blockships were improperly scuttled and the raid was repeated on the night of 9/10th May, the *Vindictive* being run right into the port. *Argus's* task had been coolly performed and the very inclusion of her in such an operation was a compliment in itself.

Tender officers were not solely employed around the United Kingdom. After secondment to the Imperial Lighthouse Service Mr C. K. Kendall-Carpenter joined Mr N. W. Pappineaux on special duty in the White Sea. Two merchant ships, the *Asiatic Prince* and *Wirral*, had been fitted up to lay buoys into White Sea ports for supply work to the British forces in Russia. The Trinity House officers acted as advisers.

Five years after the outbreak of the First World War, on 4th August, 1919, a Thames Water Pageant was held to celebrate the dawn of a peaceful new era. A procession of boats went from Tower Bridge to Chelsea and King George V led the procession in a Royal Barge manned by watermen. Exercising their prescriptive right, the Brethren preceeded the Royal Barge in *Ariel*.

As peacetime routine reasserted itself the loss of *Irene* as a committee ship was more acutely felt. In late December, 1918, Captain Golding visited Portland to view a number of armed yachts recently returned from the Mediterranean. He inspected several but none appeared suitable. In the end the armed yacht *Miranda* was purchased. She had been built by Thornycroft's at Southampton in 1908 for Lord Leith of Fyvie and grossed 793 tons. A twin-screw coal-burning steam ship with triple expansion engines and Scotch boilers, she was, at 17 knots, the fastest ship in the Corporation's service. To convert her a large saloon was removed from the foredeck to provide a buoy working area and a strengthened mast and derrick were fitted. She had an elegant figurehead, clipper bow and long, overhanging counter. In honour of Lady Patricia Ramsay, daughter of the then Master of Trinity House, Arthur Duke of Connaught and Strathearn, she was renamed *Patricia* (O.N. 128412) and entered service in 1920. He arrival at Blackwall released *Vestal*, which ship returned to Neyland. The old *Siren* at Neyland was sold in June, 1920, to Spanish buyers and

Mermaid, about whose stability problems we hear no more, was retained at Penzance.

By this time *Stella* and *Triton* had resumed their proper stations and in November, 1920, things were back to normal. *Patricia*, *Stella* and the new *Alert* were at Blackwall, *Argus* and *Ariel* at Yarmouth, *Satellite* at Harwich, *Warden* at Cowes, *Mermaid* at Penzance, *Vestal* at Neyland, *Ready* at Cardiff, and *Triton* at Holyhead.

The new *Alert* (O.N. 144273) was built at Admiralty expense as a replacement for her short lived predecessor. She was substantially similar, though a cruiser stern was substituted for a counter. She grossed 793 tons, with cabins for two Elder Brethen and a Superintendent. Her complement was a master, two mates, two engineers, two apprentices, a cook, steward, bosun, carpenter, 14 seamen, six firemen and additional accommodation for a buoy mechanic and lightsmen on passage to their stations. On her commissioning *Jeria* was returned to the Admiralty and the trawler's crew travelled to join *Alert*, under the command of Captain T. H. White. In parentheses, *Jeria's* mast and its second-hand crow's nest (obtained from some wreckage!) was removed and she was reconverted for fishing, being lost at sea in the 1930's. *Alert's* foredeck comprised two working gangways, each with a derrick, and her boat deck carried four boats. These were a 25 foot whaler and a steam launch to starboard. To port were stowed a 19 foot jolly boat and a 27 foot relief boat, known as the "hack

The first *Patricia* lying in the River Yare, seen from the foredeck. Note the barrel windlass and tiddly white chain.   *R. Dove*

110

The third *Alert* steaming seawards down the Thames with a bone in her teeth in the late 1930s. Her two gangways and heavy lifting gear can be clearly seen. *R. Dove*

boat'', which had a large capacity and, until the introduction of motor boats, did most of the tender's boat work. *Alert* was the only lighthouse tender built with incorporated oil gas tanks.

In the late 1930's under the command of Captain Guy Jarrett she carried out a salvage operation cited in modern seamanship manuals as an example of the holding power of anchors. The four-masted barque *Archibald Russell* was inwards for Ipswich with a cargo of grain when she ran aground off Landguard Point, Harwich. There was a south-easterly breeze and a slight swell at the time. *Alert* was in the vicinity and Jarrett laid out both of her anchors and secured his towing hawser to the barque. He then hove in on his cables and, using *Alert's* engines to assist, pulled the *Archibald Russell* clear with such force that she ran past the tender.

During the next few years lighthouse administration underwent some re-organisation. Cardiff declined as a district and became a sub-district. A new depot was built at Swansea and opened in 1925, when the Cardiff sub-depot was closed, as was that at Neyland. The new establishment at Swansea was situated at the head of King's Dock and, although limited by locks, was more central to

111

the work in the Bristol Channel. The Neyland tender *Vestal* had frequently had to steam east to deal with buoys on *Ready's* district and I find the following irresistible:

> "Buoy shifting was marvellous. The Chief Officer on the foredeck with about 8 hands lifted up the old buoy, unshackled it, put it back in the water and slacked it away to me (2nd Officer) in the after gangway, where with 2 hands and an apprentice, I had to pick it up, clean it off and stow it. There was no winch or capstan aft, so I had to manage with (rope) messengers along to the winch on foredeck, and you could only use that when the mate would let you.
>
> There were no gas buoys on the Neyland District, but two or three on the Cardiff District. One week the Superintendent said we would have to go up to Cardiff to move a gas buoy. So we spent two days . . . reeving off new guys, new topping lift and new three-fold purchase and off we went. The derrick (on the foreside of the foremast) was not fixed to the mast by gooseneck and socket, but the heel of the derrick was just rounded off and stepped in a wooden socket where the mast went through the deck.
>
> We lifted the buoy about six feet out of the water, then the heel of the derrick disintegrated and went out through the port bulwarks and the buoy dropped back in the water. Operation abandoned for the day whilst we shaped a new rounded heel on the bottom of the derrick again and re-rigged it to carry on next day."

Hoisting *Vestal's* boats was a similar palaver, considering she carried a brass funnelled steam launch, two whalers, two eight-oared gigs and a jolly boat. "The boat falls had to be led along the boat deck, through a fairlead in the teak cladding at the fore end down to the forward winch". In addition to this her bridge was "just the forward end of the boat deck with a chart house on it". It was impossible to see over buoys on the foredeck until, about 1935, *Vestal* went to Leith and a proper bridge was fitted.

In 1921 sea duty on the Neyland District was not over arduous. "We did not go to sea much. About six to ten days a month" mostly on lighthouse work, declares 2nd Officer R. Goodman with disarming candour. Perhaps this was a good thing, because *Vestal's* sea-keeping qualities were dubious.

> "Her hull was a fantastic shape. She had an after hold and this had to be kept full of sinkers and chains in order to keep the stern deep down so that the main deck was more or less horizontal. I think we used to draw 9 feet forward and 17 feet aft.
>
> In addition to this the fore end underwater part of the hull was like a knife—didn't begin to swell out till you got nearly back to the bridge, so we often used to get 'swell bound' instead of weatherbound. We'd be steaming along, blue sky, sun shining, no wind and just a long slow

With a working party completing cable work on an East Coast lightvessel, *Argus* is coming up to recover them in the late 1930s. The mainmast has been removed and the bridge raised; note also her unique crowsnest.   *R. Dove*

Atlantic swell, and suddenly she would bury her bow and swamp the whole damn ship. Sea down in our quarters (below amidships), sea down the engine room. It took a long time to run away through the wash ports and scuppers.''

Upon the opening of Swansea Depot *Vestal* became the District Tender and it was the following year that *Ready* was sold to Mr H. Pollard. The buoyage in the Bristol Channel was becoming more demanding and in 1929 *Vestal* went to Cowes, relieving *Warden*, which was sold in October, 1929. *Vestal's* duties at Cowes were not arduous, for she carried out inspection cruises on the west coast between 1931 and 1936. Perhaps the only traumatic event of her later career was a grounding in the Thames. Proceeding down river at high water, she turned inside the light beacon at Broadness which, at that state of the tide, appears to be in midstream. She had to be dug out at the next spring tide and the 2nd Officer responsible was dismissed. The remains of the channel may still be seen.

Her final appearances were in the Review lines at King George V's Silver Jubilee Fleet Review and in the Coronation Review of the Fleet held in 1937.

Vestal's replacement at Swansea was the new *Warden*, which with the *Beacon* and *Satellite* had replaced much of the older tonnage. In 1924 the

Harwich *Satellite* was replaced by the third ship of the same name. The last two years of the old ship's life seem to have been spent at Blackwall, for her replacement did not mean her scrapping. Accounts vary but it seems that in May, 1920, her original mast was removed and *Jeria's* fitted. Another account states that this occurred in June, 1924, leaving the ship without a foremast for two years, which seems impossible. In all probability she spent some time laid up or in use intermittently as the new ships commissioned. Another veteran was the old *Stella*. For some time she had been a liability and ended her days in ignominy. Her hull had become rotten, so rotten that only her port anchor was ever used, and that so gingerly that housing was an operation of the greatest delicacy to ensure that the flukes did not penetrate the plating. She was usually employed on estuary work, carrying out the relief of the Nore, Mouse and Girdler lightvessels and the Chapman and Maplin screw pile lighthouses. During the three weeks between reliefs she attended the river lights and all the oil gas buoys from the Ovens, off Tilbury, down to Sheerness bar and the Medway.

"She went to sea each week with four gas holders on deck, one each side abaft the engine room, and one each side of the fore (and only) hatch. When she lifted a gas buoy you hove the port forward gas holder over to the port side in the space you had made, then moved all the sinkers in the hold over to port until you had a very heavy list to port and the gunwhale was awash. Then, when you started to lift the gas buoy out of the water (with your derrick well amidships) she would come over to starboard until the starboard gunwhale was underwater. As the apron of the buoy came over

Three views of the first *Patricia*. On left is the after deck showing the secondary steering position, "Joey" the steam launch and two brass cannon from *Galatea*. Below is a view of the foredeck and on the opposite page is the Elder Brethren's dining saloon.   *All R. Dove*

the gunwhale and slid aboard a few inches, you set it down on the gun-whale whilst you hooked on a rope messenger from the port side and going forward to the windlass.

Then, holding your breath, you lifted the buoy again and hove on your messenger to get the buoy on the hatch, where you set it down hurriedly before it went anything towards port. She would certainly have capsized if the buoy had gone over to that side.

You never worked on the port side.''

Exaggeration? As 2nd Officer, Goodman carried out this evolution many times, for Captain Helsdon was usually assisting Captain A. C. Reynolds, Superintendent at Blackwall, and First Officer Smith commanded *Stella*. He should therefore be an impeccable witness. To have to shift all that lumber about must have been a labour that etched itself upon the memory with a fair degree of accuracy, and cranky ships were not unknown in the Corporation.

But worse was to come!

"One day, when we were somewhere down near Southend, there was a funny noise from just abaft the bridge and the funnel leaned forward. A liner passing close to us had made us roll and the plating around the base of the funnel had collapsed. It was only rust anyway, with layers of black paint on it. We propped the funnel up from the starboard side of the bridge with two boat griping spars, and returned to Blackwall.''

As a result of this episode *Stella* was forbidden to ''go below the Nore or Sheerness outer bar''.

Stella went to the breakers in February, 1927, and to replace her *Triton* was brought from Holyhead, where the new *Beacon* had been despatched on her commissioning in 1925.

The three new ships, *Beacon*, *Satellite* and *Warden*, were decidely ugly ducklings. The *Beacon* (O.N. 148607) and *Satellite* (O.N. 148517) were substantially identical vessels at 490 tons g.r.t. Their length between perpendiculars, and they were largely perpendicular, was 160 feet with a

moulded beam of 27.5 feet and a hold depth of 14.75 feet. Both ships were built by J. I. Thornycroft's at Southampton and shared one major fault: their fresh water deep tanks were not longitudinally subdivided and caused several serious lists. On one occasion *Satellite* lolled entering the narrow passage between Yarmouth piers, alarming a crowd of summer visitors! Eventually the effects of ''free surface'' were overcome by fitting the bulkheads. The ships carried two derricks on the foremast, one of steel and one of oak. The mainmasts were removed to fit guns at the beginning of the Second World War but replaced in 1951. They carried three boats, a cutter/lifeboat and jolly boat to starboard in radial davits and a new-fangled motor boat in luffing davits to port. This last was a great advantage over the former steam launches and carried more than the traditional hack boats. ''Great assistance (has been) derived from the use of the motor boat which advances matters considerably''. Later the lifeboats were increased to two and moved on to the quarters.

Warden was slightly larger at 172.5 feet between perpendiculars, with a beam of 31.5 feet and a depth of 15.5 feet. Her much larger gross tonnage of 828 tons was largely due to the extended boat deck and the closing in of her after maindeck. This was due to her specialised design, as she was intended for use on the west coast, shaped to cope with heavy swells and south-westerly gales. To this end she carried four boats: two 27 foot lifeboats, a 27 foot hack boat and 27 foot motor boat.

All three ships had triple expansion steam engines supplied by twin Scotch boilers. Their endurance was limited to about five days at sea by their coal

bunkers. They were incomparable sea ships, for all their ugly appearance, and in later years generated an affection only granted to happy ships. They were powerful buoy working vessels, though not fitted with towing winches, and relied on rope falls for their boats. As mentioned above *Warden* went to Swansea, *Satellite* to Harwich and *Beacon* to Holyhead. In the ten years since Goodman had joined the *Vestal* at Neyland all districts had acquired lighted buoys, and most of these were acetylene powered. All the old oil gas buoys were now located in the accessible inner reaches of the Thames estuary, though their shells were to go on for another fifty years after their final replacement as lighted buoys.

At the beginning of March, 1932, the elegant *Patricia* arrived at Harwich to join *Satellite* on the station. Commanded originally by Captain A. C. Reynolds, who went on to become Superintendent at Penzance and Blackwall, the *Patricia* passed under the command of Yeates in the late 1920's. Captain Yeates was a fine ship-handler, unafraid of unorthodox manoeuvres. He used *Patricia's* long, overhanging counter to put 2nd Officer Goodman on gas buoys and avoid the labour of lowering and recovering boats. Yeates would stem the tide, allowing *Patricia* to set down on to the buoy. At the 2nd Officer's signal he would ring full ahead and the propeller wash shoved the buoy clear with the junior mate hanging on to it. By 1935 Captain Guy Jarrett, as senior master, was in command.

Both *Mermaid* and *Triton* were unfit for further service by 1935, and in February *Reculver* and in March *Strathearn* were brought into commission. The

Opposite: In her dotage *Patricia* was renamed *Vestal*, and as such she is seen here in working rig in Harwich harbour about 1939.   *R. Dove*

Right: The figurehead of the first *Patricia*, now preserved at Yarmouth depot. The cannon in the background is a signal carronade fitted to lightvessels until about 1955.   *K. R. Thurlow*

117

Captain Williams, his officers and crew in the first *Patricia*. Apprentice Dove, squatting on the right, and Second Officer T. H. Catesby, seated behind him, both became Chief Superintendents.

two new ships were identical, both built on the Mersey by Cammell Laird's of Birkenhead. *Reculver's* trials took place on 12th December, 1934, and she reached 11.77 knots with her direct drive diesel engines. Her gross tonnage was 683.

Despite her motor propulsion her deck machinery was steam driven, and this necessitated the provision of a large donkey boiler. Neither she nor her sister was built for looks, despite the protestations of the Elder Brethren:

> "The tripod mast viewed fore and aft is by no means an unsightly erection but gives the impression that the vessel is one of considerable power, which no doubt accounts for the description given by the Dockyard personnel to the two vessels, namely 'pocket battleships'."

Clearly missing the point of acid Liverpudlian wit in the official report on acceptance trials, the Elder Brethren had acquired two innovative vessels. Certainly the new steel derricks and wire running gear provided considerable advantages, giving a safe working load of 12 tons which dealt adequately with the buoys then in use. But they had manoeuvring defects which were impossible to disguise. In Goodman's view their failure to stop when required was an unacceptable characteristic, although the experience he gained in handling ships that refused to go astern was, as we shall see, to stand him in good stead.

Strathearn's trials took place on 14th February, 1935, and the Elder Brethren were of the opinion that " . . . in the *Strathearn* and *Reculver* the

On *Patricia* in 1937. Left to right: An apprentice; First Officer E. Smith, lost when commanding *Argus*; Captain Guy Jarrett, the outgoing commanding officer; Captain Yeates, Superintendent, Cowes; Captain N. J. Williams, the incoming commanding officer; Second Officer Catesby, who later commanded the ship when renamed *Vestal*; an apprentice.

R. Dove

Corporation have acquired two vessels which reflect great credit on those responsible for the designs''.

Strathearn was sent to Harwich manned by *Satellite's* crew, while *Mermaid's* men travelled to join *Satellite* and steam her to Penzance where on 8th May the old, unstable and contentious *Mermaid* was sold to Sark Motorships of Guernsey, under whom she saw further service as an inter-island steamer.

Reculver was despatched to Great Yarmouth where she relieved *Argus*. In her turn *Argus* went to Blackwall where she replaced *Triton* on the London District. *Triton* went to the breakers in September. *Ariel* had for long been used mainly as a pilot cutter, and about this time she too was broken up.

The introduction of motorships into the ''Steam Vessel Service'' rendered the old cognomen ''Steam Vessel'' a misnomer, and after this period all Trinity House Lighthouse Tenders became Trinity House Vessels (T.H.V.s). Another minor alteration coming in at this time was the abandonment of man o' war style name on the stern only. From 1935 the practice was altered to conform with merchant ship custom and the name was borne on the bow.

In 1935 *Patricia* escorted King George V on his Silver Jubilee Review and in 1937 she did the same for the newly crowned King George VI. As already noted, the old *Vestal* was in the lines of inspected ships. But a year later the *Vestal* went to the breakers, leaving her name to the *Patricia*, for which it was required as the Corporation's principal yacht was about to be downgraded and renamed to make way for a newer, more modern and custom-built ship.

CHAPTER EIGHT

Dunkirk to D-Day

"Awkward as these waters would have been at any time,
navigation under such conditions as we experienced called for
qualities of superlative seamanship."
Dwight D. Eisenhower, Supreme Commander,
Allied Expeditionary Force Europe, 13th July, 1945

THE new *Patricia* was completed in 1938 by Smith's Dock, Middlesbrough, to a design by R. H. Kingdom, then Surveyor of Shipping to Trinity House. Kingdom had designed *Strathearn* and *Reculver* with twin-screw direct-drive diesels, and these frequently ran out of "starting air" when manoeuvring. This made them extremely unpopular with both deck and engineroom departments, the former blaming the latter for insufficient air, the latter blaming the former for excessive use of the engines! It was all most unsatisfactory, and Mr Kingdom was able to fit the new ship with bridge-controlled diesel-electric propulsion. Although initially expensive, it is ideal for vessels which are constantly manoeuvring. *Patricia's* installation comprised two 600 kw generators driving two propulsion motors. The machinery was made by English Electric and,

The new yacht *Patricia* on trials in 1938.   *Smiths Dock Company Limited*

although it earned *Patricia* the fulsome and somewhat inaccurate description of "Electric Yacht", it was not without teething problems. It was very economical, burning only six tons of gas oil per day at full speed, and gave 1330 i.h.p. The two main generators were specially built, one other being made for that aristocrat of London stores, Harrods.

Patricia's tonnage was an unprecedented 1,116.38 tons gross, with an initial net of 457.38. Loaded, she displaced 1,415 tons and had an endurance of 9,240 miles. However her major weakness was that she carried only 50 tons of fresh water.

Although she was intended to be 240 feet on the waterline, economics dictated a reduction in length so that she turned out 232 feet overall, 211 feet 6 inches between perpendiculars. Her beam was 35 feet 7 inches, her moulded depth 16 feet and her loaded draught 13 feet.

Patricia (O.N. 166352) has now been replaced by a new vessel incorporating accommodation for inspecting committees and the very lastest developments in buoy handling equipment, but for over forty years the Corporation's most famous vessel has played her part in both ceremonial and more mundane affairs. She was born to war and soon after commissioning she had her mainmast removed and her boat deck extended aft to form a gun platform. This was later turned into an elegant quarter deck which has enhanced the run of her sheer. A major reconditioning of her engines and ratings' accommodation was undertaken in the winter of 1966/67 altering her hold and bridge and increasing her fresh water capacity to 130 tons. As a consequence her gross tonnage was reduced to 1073.

Her complement of boats has also altered over a long life. When first commissioned she carried a motor launch, two rowing lifeboats and a fast committee launch on her boat deck and a rock boat (a light pulling boat) and a sailing gig on her foredeck, the last two being removed in the winter when *Patricia* went buoy working. Later the fast committee boat and rock boat changed places, after which the latter disappeared in favour of a second motor launch, both motor boats being then hoisted in gravity davits instead of the luffing davits fitted when new. The pulling lifeboats disappeared with the acceptance of liferafts and the two motor boats were finally supplemented by a high-speed inflatable, the foredeck being cleared of all boats.

Patricia retained manila hemp working gear throughout her life. It limited her lifting capacity so that she was unable to handle the largest class of buoys in service, but her derrick could be completely unrigged in a couple of hours and stowed unobtrusively away. Reassembly took four hours.

Commissioned on 5th February, 1938, she exceeded 14 knots on trials. For a brief period she was known as *Patricia II* until the old *Patricia* was taken out of service for alterations, becoming the fourth *Vestal*, stationed at East Cowes.

Thus at the outbreak of war the disposition of the tenders was Holyhead

The third *Alert* in her wartime guise, painted grey and with a gun aft, at Blackwall moorings about 1941. The mainmast has been removed and the ensign is worn from a funnel gaff.

Trinity House

Beacon, Swansea *Warden*, Penzance *Satellite*, Cowes *Vestal*, Blackwall *Alert*, Harwich *Strathearn*, *Patricia* and *Argus* and Yarmouth *Reculver*.

In 1939 the number of lightvessels was still large. The Yarmouth District consisted of the Corton, St Nicholas, Cockle, Smith's Knoll, Newarp, Haisbro', East Dudgeon, Inner Dowsing, Lynn Well, Humber, Warps and Swarte Bank. Under London and Harwich came the Nore, Mouse, Girdler, Edinboro', Mid Barrow and Barrow Deep, North, South and East Goodwins, Brake, Kentish Knock, Sunk, Shipwash, Outer Gabbard, Galloper, Cork, Varne and Longsand. East Cowes controlled the Royal Sovereign, Owers, Warner, Calshot Spit and Shambles. The Caskets, Alderney, Hanois and Sark lighthouses also came under Cowes. Penzance oversaw Bishop Rock, Wolf, Longships, Round Island, Godrevy and the Eddystone lighthouses and the Sevenstones lightvessel. Swansea Depot had five lightvessels; St Gowan, Helwick, Scarweather, Breaksea and English and Welsh Grounds; plus the two lighthouses at Lundy and those at Flatholm, South Bishop, Smalls and Skokholm. Holyhead serviced the Cardigan and Morecambe Bay lightvessels and the Skerries, St Tudwal's and Bardsey lighthouses.

In addition to the manned stations there were some unmanned offshore lights and the many shore lighthouses that came under the jurisdiction of the District Superintendents but presented no supply problem.

The outbreak of war was no more of a surprise to the men of Trinity House

The *Reculver*, which with her sister-ship *Strathearn* marked a change to diesel power, was among the first Trinity House vessels to be attacked from the air during the Second World War.

R. Dove

than to other sections of the British people, but the exposure of their stations left them vulnerable to attack. Employees of the Corporation did not regard themselves as combatants and one master of a steam vessel resigned the instant a gun was put on his ship. Risks were taken in the normal course of affairs in the tenders but they were taken for the general benefit of the service. When it came to war they were catapulted into an ill-prepared front line, paid for it in blood and received very little recognition for it.

The Admiralty decided that the tenders should be armed and during the first winter of the war all the ships had their mainmasts removed and gun platforms added to take 12-pounder HA/LA guns. A pair of DEMS gunners* augmented their complements.

On 9th January, 1940, T.H.V. *Reculver*, Captain W. Lees, was on relief duty on the Yarmouth District. The relieved crew of a lightvessel were still on the boat deck when a German aircraft attacked with machine guns and bombs. One boat was carried away. A bomb exploded on the boat deck, blast reaching the shaft tunnel. The boat deck was a shambles, 55 men were wounded and Mr George Purvis, 2nd Officer, was dead. The damage disabled the ship and she lay stopped until *Patricia* arrived to take her in tow.

Three weeks later the East Dudgeon lightvessel was bombed and machine gunned. Although in the event she did not sink, the crew were compelled to abandon her to save themselves. In appallingly cold weather they took to the

*Defensively Equipped Merchant Ship gunners were mainly "Hostilities Only" ratings trained by the Royal Navy or Royal Artillery personnel assigned to merchant vessels.

boat. They reached the Lincolnshire coast, but there the boat capsized in the breakers and six men were drowned. There was only one survivor. As a consequence of these two incidents guns were removed from the tenders and the legend "Lighthouse Service" was painted on the ships' sides in an attempt to buy immunity. Regrettably Luftwaffe pilots had other ideas and attacks continued. On 2nd June *Patricia* was shelled when working off Calais. She escaped damage but on 3rd July *Vestal* was less fortunate, sustaining slight damage and one seaman wounded when bombed and machine gunned off the Owers. On the 12th the newly repaired *Reculver* was attacked by an aircraft in the Harwich approaches, and six men were injured when, off the South Foreland, *Alert* was attacked from the air. By now the authorities had reversed their decision about defensive armament and the guns were reappearing. Six days later *Argus* succeeded in driving off an air attack with her own gun.

By this time France had fallen and the Superintendent at East Cowes, Captain Barber, received orders to discontinue the Channel Islands lighthouses and to evacuate "Lighthouse keepers and their families and anyone else who wished to come".

Barber had received an urgent signal from the islands at 03.00 on the 20th and transmitted it to Secretary Nicolle at Trinity House. *Vestal*, Captain J. C. McCarthy, was lying in Cowes Roads with the Shambles Relief on board but her departure was delayed and the lightsmen landed. At 13.00 on 21st *Vestal* proceeded to Portsmouth with a request for naval escort, which was refused. Barber and Nicolle both pressed for naval protection and failed. At her best speed *Vestal* steamed south alone.

The German occupation of the neighbouring Cherbourg peninsula had resulted in the Channel Islands lights being doused. On the afternoon of the 21st Sark, Hanois, Alderney and Caskets closed down, their keepers being withdrawn by boat where necessary. Attempts to run the oil to waste met with difficulties and it was left for the locals to use. The explosives for the fog signal at Hanois kept at Torteval and Fort Grey were also left.

Vestal arrived off Alderney shortly after midnight on Saturday. It was a bright, moonlit night but the island lay in ominous darkness. A boat was sent into Braye Harbour to round up the keepers, previously warned by telegram, and at the first glimmer of dawn Captain McCarthy took *Vestal* into the harbour. Here the keepers of Alderney and Caskets were embarked, together with their families, three Trinity House pensioners and several civilian refugees.

Captain McCarthy had been asked by Judge French not take civilians as this might start a panic, but his orders gave him a free hand and his inclination was to do everything possible to help. He stated he would take those on board by sailing time and at 06.05, having loaded the Guernsey mails, *Vestal* weighed and proceeded.

Three hours later she entered St Peter Port and embarked the keepers and their dependants from Sark and Hanois. There was "great confusion if not panic" at St Peter Port, where a barrier had been erected at the root of the pier. Here a crowd had gathered and it was only with the greatest difficulty that McCarthy and the local authorities contained the anxiety of these people. *Vestal* was a tiny ship, but she embarked 121 persons, 80 of whom had no connection with Trinity House. When her own compartment of 40 is added, the over-crowded state may be well imagined.

At 11.20, the Alderney mails embarked, she left the island. She discharged the mails at 14.10, then headed north for the English coast.

Vestal's crew demonstrated their ingenuity and openheartedness in feeding and accommodating their unusual complement. Preparations were made under the supervision of First Officer E. H. Harris for the possible abandoning of the ship and crude rafts constructed to hold the additional people. Unaccompanied men were accommodated in the lightsmens' large forward messdeck, married couples went into lights officers' or tender officers' messrooms, both of which were on the maindeck. Single young women "who kept together in groups" occupied officers' cabins, whilst in the two-berth stewards' cabin a crippled girl, an expectant mother in the last fortnight of her term and the Alderney District Nurse settled down. What had been the Elder Brethren's best after stateroom still had its double bed, and this amply accommodated six children, three each end, their mothers sleeping on deck beside them!

Shortly before midnight *Vestal* passed through the Spithead defences and anchored. Crew and refugees settled down for the night, officers and ratings dossing down where they could, in the galley and wheelhouse, on the engine top and in the radio room. All food was pooled and everyone fed, after a fashion.

Early the following morning, with Captain Barber on board, *Vestal* proceeded to Southampton. Here, with many protestations of gratitude, the refugees left before *Vestal* returned to Cowes and resumed her duties. By this period in her life she was largely relegated to towing duties and reliefs. The demands of war were to alter all that and decimate the carefully deployed tender fleet.

In August, 1940, though, there were signs of expansion. In anticipation of losses and profiting from the experience of the first war, the Board decided to acquire another vessel. Having the example of *Jeria*, they decided on a converted trawler. T.H.V. *Triton* (O.N. 168023), of 680 tons, was commissioned on 29th August, 1940. A deep-water trawler, she had been built by Cochrane's of Selby and was 189 feet 9 inches overall, 29 feet beam, with a depth of 15 feet 6 inches. Her coal-fired Scotch boiler operated at 218 psi to give 12.75 knots, but she was capable of 18. Basically intended as a lightvessel relief and towing ship, she was unable to lift buoys but carried large oil and water tanks.

She became the junior master's ship and was always unpopular, having poor accommodation and a forward bridge, and in heavy weather she behaved abominably. At mealtimes her motion was so violent that officers and steward wore boots in the saloon. Junior officers abandoned their cabins in bad weather and slept in the wardroom, and buckets were kept in the wheelhouse for the officer on watch and the quartermaster to vomit into. It was a frequent prank for old hands to throw an uncleaned cod on to the bridge wing occupied by a new officer after *Triton* had buried her bow! Ironically her original name had been *Queen of the Seas*.

The second *Patricia* soon after the outbreak of the Second World War, fitted with a gun and with "Lighthouse Service" painted on her side. *A. Thomas*

Triton (third of the name) was joined by the French lighthouse tenders *André Blondell* and *Georges de Joly*. These two ships had been brought to Plymouth by their crews after the fall of France. Recommissioned and manned by Trinity House, they became useful if eccentric additions to the fleet. Propelled by diesel-electric machinery and twin screws, they were small ships with no hatch and low freeboard. Only about 125 feet long, they were highly manoeuvrable with bridge control. Their lifting gear comprised a fixed jib crane with a 360° slew. *André Blondell* was sent to Cowes under the command of Captain George Sherman and *Georges de Joly* to Swansea under Captain John Meyrick.

As a result *Warden* left Swansea in March, 1941, for Penzance, where she relieved *Satellite* for service on the east coast until October, 1944. *Vestal*, being similarly relieved, moved round to the east coast where the action was getting warmer.

On 9th September, 1940, a near miss on *Strathearn* immobilised her port engine and on the 25th a fireman was killed aboard *Satellite* when, 2½ miles north of the Seven Stones, she was attacked by aircraft. On 10th October Dover Harbour was bombed and shelled when *Alert* was lying there.

Four days later real damage was done. T.H.V. *Reculver*, Captain J. J. Woolnough, hit a mine off the mouth of the Humber. The explosion injured five men. Attempts were made to get her into the Humber and beach her, but she foundered in fairly shallow water before this could be achieved. Woolnough was awarded an MBE, recognition that the Trinity Service was in the front line, and pleas were made by the tender masters for adequate escort. Their 12-pounder guns were inadequate against aircraft and as time passed these were augmented by additional machine guns and wire-carrying PAC rockets. The latter seemed as much a hindrance as a help. Entering Swansea locks in *Vestal*, 22-year-old Captain T. H. Catesby went to sound his whistle. In error he grasped the wrong lanyard and discharged his PAC rockets, to the delight of his crew!

In November *Strathearn* was straddled by a stick of bombs when eight miles off Orfordness, receiving no more than a shaking. In the Barrow Deep *Triton* opened up with her 12-pounder and Lewis guns and succeeded in driving off several fighter-bombers.

So far casualties had been light, but it was clear that the Corporation's stations were targets. Lighthouses, lightvessels and tenders had all been attacked by aircraft. The impartial mine had already accounted for *Reculver* and was now to do so for *Argus*. The ship that had avoided death throughout the First World War was sunk in the Thames Estuary on 12th November, 1940.

Captain "Big Eddie" Smith exploding mines from his bridge, 1940. He was lost when the *Argus* was mined in the Thames Estuary later that year.   *R. Dove*

The previous day *Argus* had been despatched from Blackwall bound for the Humber to attempt to salvage gear from the wreck of the *Reculver*. She was a very happy ship, almost entirely manned by Harwich men and under the command of Captain A. E. Smith, former First Officer of *Patricia* and known as "Big Eddie".

Argus had no escort and, it being the custom to anchor at night, at twilight on the evening of the 11th she brought up near the Mouse lightvessel. The skipper of the lightvessel requested his crew be withdrawn for the night as German aircraft had been dropping mines in the area for several nights and his men had had no rest. Captain Smith acceded to this request and the tender took the lightsmen aboard.

The following morning an easterly gale was blowing. *Argus*'s motor boat was defective (she was to have exchanged it at Harwich on her way north) and too high a sea was running to use the hack boat to replace the lightvessel's crew, so *Argus* lay at anchor until about 16.00, when the wind and sea abated and Smith ordered the ship under way. A few moments later the hack boat was lowered and the Mouse remanned, and 18-year-old quartermaster Archie Smith swung *Argus* on to course as the hack boat was recovered and secured. The crew drifted off the boat deck to take their tea and Captain Smith, having checked the course, went into the chartroom with the 2nd Officer to select another anchorage.

There was a sudden blinding flash. Quartermaster Smith was hurled into the corner of the wheelhouse where, dazed and semi-conscious, he reached instinctively for the wheel. It spun impotently in his hands. Eventually he stood up, a pain in his legs, staggered through what was left of the wheelhouse bulkhead and out on to the bridge wing. He was dazed and totally at a loss what to do. He stared aft. *Argus* was down to her boat deck. Below him most of his 34 shipmates were already dead, immobilised by broken legs and pelvises and finally drowned. Suddenly he was joined by another man. The 2nd Officer, in pilot jacket and leather half boots, took one look aft and dived overboard. Smith followed his example, finding the water bitterly cold. He never saw the 2nd Officer again. Around him wreckage and dead fish filled his head with irrelevant regrets that he could not fry up some of the latter. Eventually he clambered, with great difficulty, on to a carley float and lay half in the water, shivering with cold.

Luckily for Smith the master of the Mouse had seen *Argus* lifted bodily from the water and immediately signalled the news to the Nore. Soon a paddle steamer and a tug were on the way and the former, the *Royal Eagle*, converted into an anti-aircraft vessel, arrived on the scene in time to rescue Smith. Fortunately a naval surgeon was on board and Smith was dried out, his quartermaster's uniform confusing his rescuers. Having explained his identity, he was given a cabin and eventually landed at Chatham. The only survivor, Smith spent three months in hospital, his face cut, his kneecaps splintered and the ligaments torn.

The news of *Argus's* sinking desolated both the Service and Harwich. One mother lost two sons and a son-in-law, another woman her husband, brother and brother-in-law. A London mother mourned the loss of both her sons. The effect on the officers and men of *Patricia*, which arrived to lay a wreck buoy, was horrible. They "found it a very disturbing experience . . . gushes of bubbles were emerging, usually bringing up items of personal belongings, but we removed no bodies . . ."

Before leaving Penzance *Satellite* scored hits on German planes. Off Land's End she suffered slight damage but no casualties when machine gunned, and when in Penzance Dock she hit an aircraft engaged in strafing the port area.

December saw *Patricia*, Captain N. J. Williams, bombed and machine gunned by two aircraft off the Kentish Knock when towing No. 93 lightvessel. She was badly shaken, electrical circuits were damaged and the starboard shaft bearings shattered. The 3rd Engineer and one greaser were burned by battery acid, and one window of the Elder Brethren's dining saloon has never subsequently opened. *Patricia* steamed into Harwich at three knots.

By this time the war channels had been well established. Regularly swept by minesweepers, these channels extended up the east coast. Up to the time of the evacuation of the BEF from Dunkirk swept channels were maintained across the Straits of Dover. After the Dunkirk evacuation *Patricia* removed some of these buoys, the job being completed under shell fire from the shore. Captain

Hooking on in quiet weather. A view on board the fourth *Argus*.
R. Dove

Williams received an M.B.E. for the ship's services. *Argus* had been straddled from German batteries on Cap Gris Nez while employed on similar duty.

All this extra buoyage had to be established quickly, usually without the withdrawal of peacetime stations. There was a shortage of equipment, especially sinkers and dimming and aerial screens,* which had to be fitted to many buoys. German aircraft frequently shot up buoys by way of additional sport, and this necessitated constant repairs. Later ladders, first aid equipment, flares and food were put on buoys for ditched aircrews.

In the early months of the war extra lightvessels were laid, an additional Barrow, East and West Oaze, and East and West Swin, all at five-mile intervals in the swept channels, but the persistent attacks of aircraft resulted in many being left unmanned, only their daymarks as guides. Later in the war they were withdrawn and moored in Sea Reach and the crews, ostensibly mine-watching, replaced and relieved regularly by *Triton*. Only the Nore seems to have been armed, for on 8th November, 1940, she drove off a German fighter.

Harwich was assuming its old role of a naval base and as early as 15th September, 1939, the main depot of Blackwall was transferred there. In June, 1940, however, after the fall of France and with the increased threat of invasion, it was transferred back to Blackwall just as the London Blitz started, and Blackwall was damaged. Harwich again became, and has remained ever since, the principal depot.

Early in 1941 tragedy struck again. On the evening of 7th January the officers of *Patricia* and *Strathearn* were making arrangements for a party. Those of *Strathearn* showed an uncharacteristic lack of enthusiasm, except for the 2nd Engineer. The following day *Strathearn* hit a mine when in the Wallet. Fifteen men were killed, including the master, Captain R. S. Raven, the First, Chief Engineer and 3rd Engineer Officers. The two latter, together with several ratings on board, had been survivors from the mined *Reculver*. A boat was lowered from the sinking ship and 2nd Engineer Porter, the senior officer, took charge. They landed at a remote spot near Chevaux de Frise Point, Essex, and eventually returned to Harwich. Porter had a long argument with Trinity House over the expenses incurred!

The loss of *Strathearn* seriously affected the Corporation's ability to carry out its obligations efficiently. From January to April, 1941, *Alert* was the only ship capable of full buoy servicing on the entire east coast. Shifting her base to Great Yarmouth, she covered the area from the Tyne to Dungeness, coaling weekly, her officers driven mad by paperwork! Urgent arrangements were made to acquire another ship. In the meantime requests for naval escort were re-doubled, with some success. In February *Alert* was attacked off the Norfolk coast and returned fire. Able Seaman H. W. G. Wildney was killed. *Triton* was luckier when again attacked in the Thames Estuary, her escort driving off two planes.

---

*Modifications fitted to buoy lanterns to reduce their visible intensity and to restrict their vertical diffusion, thus rendering them less visible from the air.

Caught in a bombing raid on Plymouth on the night of 20th/21st March, 1941, *Georges de Joly* was slightly damaged by near misses and several incendiaries were thrown overboard from the ship. Winchman Frank Davies was killed. More fortunate was Captain Sherman of *André Blondell*. Leaving Cowes, the tender was attacked by a large bomber and the pitched battle that ensued was fought in full view of people on the Cowes promenade. Sherman fired his PAC rockets in an attempt to drive off the plane, and *André Blondell's* two Hotchkiss machine guns opened fire as the bomber made passes over the ship. Exposed on the upper bridge, above his cemented wheelhouse, Sherman escaped unscathed, losing a button off his reefer jacket to a shell!

The former French lighthouse tender *Georges de Joly* in Holyhead during the Second World War.
E. C. Scott

George Sherman also had the unique distinction of receiving German air cover when working on a French gas buoy. Operating from Dover under cover of night, he ran into snags and at daylight the buoy was still on deck. The ship's French name was in large brass letters on both bows but the Trinity ensign was blackened by exhaust fumes. At first light a British plane was overhead, but within minutes he had been driven off by a German aircraft whose pilot, totally misreading the situation, circled the ship giving victory rolls as the crew lowered the buoy back into the water. The German plane finally flew off towards France, Sherman and his ship's company beating a hasty retreat in the opposite direction.

With the Allied occupation of Iceland that followed the German invasion of Denmark a convoy was assembled with equipment to set up a naval base at Hvalfjordur, near Reykjavik. T.H.V. *Patricia*, Captain N. J. Williams, was loaded with gas buoys and despatched to the rendezvous, and with several merchant ships loaded with building materials, boom-defence and cable ships, and an escort of two Flower-class corvettes, she sailed with a Halifax bound convoy, separating to proceed to Iceland. The voyage was made in heavy weather at about 4½ knots, the best speed of the boom-defence vessels. In Icelandic waters she spent a week laying buoys before making the return passage, also accompanied by heavy weather. *Patricia* passed through a heavy air attack when off Aberdeen.

The laying of acoustic mines on the east coast prompted the authorities to transfer *Patricia*, a noisy ship and a potential victim, to the west coast. She made a north-about passage to Holyhead and Captain Goodman and his crew relinquished *Beacon* to Captain Williams and settled down with the nearly new "electric yacht". Shortly after this rearrangement acoustic mines were being laid in the Irish Sea. Goodman soon found that he had an army of Gremlins to contend with in addition to the enemy. Whilst astern of the Morecambe Bay lightvessel fuelling her the whole ship shook "as if in an earthquake". A blockage in the lubrication system had melted the bearings in the port main diesel and *Patricia* had to limp round at six knots for two months until arrangements were made for laying up at Holyhead whilst the engine was reconditioned.

A watercolour by an unknown artist of the *Georges de Joly* in heavy weather. The picture, now in the author's collection, was commissioned by Captain J. Meyrick, the vessel's wartime master.

Later Goodman had the propulsion motors jam full astern when reversing off his mooring buoy at Holyhead. Only by letting go both anchors was *Patricia* prevented from committing *seppuku* on the rocks at Soldier's Point. They jammed ahead on another occasion when lowering a boat off the Skerries, and there was a further incident of total failure in the entrance to Milford Haven.

But if *André Blondell* had the distinction of receiving German air cover, to *Patricia* belonged the dubious honour of compelling a British aircraft to ditch. Twenty miles north of Fishguard Captain Goodman spotted a plane approaching low and rang "action stations". The crew raced to their guns and trained them on the "enemy", which Goodman now recognised as an Anson trainer. He prevented the guns' crews from opening fire, but the silent guns followed the plane round, a circumstance which so alarmed the pilot that he waggled his wings in friendship. However, he was too low and half a mile astern of *Patricia* hit the water. A rough sea was running at the time but *Patricia* turned and lowered a boat to pick the aircrew up. The pilot bore no ill-will, and later named his new-born daughter after the ship.

The Trinity flagship sustained one further attack while at Holyhead. On 9th April, the day after the loss of *Strathearn*, a stick of bombs from a lone raider straddled the ship, but no serious damage was done.

A replacement for the *Strathearn* had been found in the form of the R.R.S. *Discovery II* (O.N. 161322). Loaned by the Ministry of War Transport, she was overhauled in William Gray's Hartlepool yard prior to entering the Corporation's service. She was a twin-screw steamship, with reciprocating engine and two Scotch boilers and a gross tonnage of 1036 tons. When recommissioned on 1st April, she still had sledges and husky harnesses in her after hold. Built in 1929 by Ferguson Brothers, of Port Glasgow, she was 233 feet 7 inches overall, with a speed of 13 knots, though 11 was more normal. Fitted with Asdic and a smaller derrick than was normally used in the Service, she presented certain difficulties to Captain Woolnough and his crew. However she was ideally suited to the purposes of pleasure on which her officers were hell-bent when opportunity arose. A large piano graced her roomy and well furnished wardroom. This instrument "contributed indirectly, but in no small measure, to the defloration of a considerable number of WRNS on the east coast".

"*Disco 2's*" service was almost entirely on the east coast where most of the tenders were now concentrated, though one voyage was made to Iceland to overhaul the buoys at Hvalfjordur. She was the first to operate on the Tyne Command and rotated this duty with the old *Vestal*, now minus figurehead and bowsprit, and *Beacon*. A small buoy store had been established at North Shields and the duty tender operated under the Flag Officer, Newcastle, tending the routeing buoys between the Humber and the Farne Islands from the summer of 1941 until D-Day. No Trinity ship now moved without escort. On these northern patrols this was usually an armed trawler or whale catcher, further south an armed drifter. The latter were frequently so slow that the tenders towed them!

Further south pleasure steamers like the *Royal Daffodil* had been converted to flak ships and acted as escort, whilst occasionally a Norwegian destroyer or an ex-American destroyer-escort were available. A close relationship existed between the volunteer branches of the Royal Navy and the Trinity House Service which contrasted with the more unbending patronising of the First World War, for the east coast of England was an unhealthy place to be in 1941. Between May and November *Satellite* was attacked six times by Dornier Do.17's or Junkers Ju. 88's, *Beacon* thrice, once in an air raid on Harwich, and *André Blondell* twice within a week in the eastern Channel. On 17th January, 1942, *Triton* was steaming in convoy in the Barrow Deep when an aircraft attacked her with bombs, but it was driven off by fire from *Triton* and an escorting destroyer. Again in April *Discovery II* and her escort beat off a night attack.

Three men were wounded by flying splinters when *Alert* was servicing the N.W. Goodwin buoy on 19th December, 1942. Attacking at low level from the ESE, three Focke-Wulf 190s machine-gunned the tender as the buoy was hanging from the derrick. The falls were shot through and the buoy crashed over the side. *Alert* opened up with her Oerlikons, but the Focke-Wulf's remained in the area until the tardy arrival of British fighters, which downed two and forced the third to flee.

A year later, on 22nd September, 1942, *Alert* was working on No. 7 Dover Straits buoy when batteries on the French coast commenced shelling her. Work was completed, the anchor weighed and at 16.10 she made off at full speed, taking evasive action. Twenty rounds were fired, all near misses, but one *DEMS* gunner received facial injuries from shell splinters and one seaman sprained his ankle jumping from the hatch into cover.

March and May of 1943 saw *André Blondell* attacked off Eastbourne by bombers returning from a daylight raid. *Vestal* was shelled off Dungeness while on passage to the C1 buoy and again on her return. Her Marlin machine gun position was disabled, her radio aerial destroyed, hand steering disabled and several men wounded by splinters.

André Blondell was attacked when at Plymouth during a raid on the city, but the time for reprisal was approaching. Volunteers were being canvassed early in 1944 and it became apparent that the Trinity House ships were going to play a tiny but vital part in Operation Overlord, the invasion of Europe.

The great accumulation of ships, aircraft, munitions and *materiel* that took place in southern England during the spring of 1944 preparatory to Overlord was an epochal event. Its story has been told elsewhere, the graphic details of "The Longest Day" concentrating on military and naval exploits. The part played by Trinity House has been largely ignored, a fact which rankled among those who took part.

The gradual assembly of ships in the Solent included six Trinity House Lighthouse Tenders anchored in Cowes Roads. These were *Patricia*, Captain Goodman, *Warden*, Captain Le Good, *Georges de Joly*, Captain Meyrick, *Alert*, Captain White, *André Blondell*, Captain Sherman and *Discovery II*, Captain Woolnough. In the Medina River Captain Barber's Cowes Depot had assumed a new importance. Tiers of Thames lighters, twenty in all, were moored in the river, loaded with gas buoys, fully charged in readiness. Three small tugs were under the direction of 2nd Officer Carstens whose job was to supervise the supply of buoys to the tenders when required.

The six ships lay in unaccustomed idleness, their crews watching the number of vessels, large and small, steadily grow. From time to time, when enemy aircraft were overhead, fast motor launches roared up and down laying smoke screens. All knew they were to attempt the breaching of Hitler's Atlantic Wall; shore leave was stopped and an atmosphere of impending events in the air. The Chief Superintendent, Captain Guy Jarrett, boarded each of the ships in turn to address their crews. His speech was brief and to the point: "I can promise you days of great boredom and days of great excitement, other than that I can promise you nothing".

The ships were fully loaded with their maximum capacity of buoys and at the end of May the six commanding officers and Captain Barber crossed to Portsmouth for a briefing.

The Admiralty's requirements were that Trinity House establish seventy-three lighted buoys across the Channel on a scheduled programme that interlocked with the initial movements of the invasion forces. This could not be interrupted by weather or any other circumstance, making a considerable demand on the professionalism of the Trinity seamen.

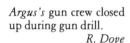

Argus's gun crew closed up during gun drill.
R. Dove

The preparatory programme had, by this time, come to its end. The site for the invasion was chosen, the swept lanes and allocation of buoys to those lanes had been decided, but difficulties had arisen in the transportation of all the assorted hardware, since the fighting services claimed priority. This had been overcome by the Admiralty ordering several LCT's on passage to Cowes to stop at Harwich *en route* and load buoys, sinkers, chains, lanterns, etc.

The job on which the six masters were to be briefed, on that May morning, was the precise timing and nature of the operation as a whole. Astonishingly at this late date Barber met with objections from the naval staff officers to his being fully briefed, with particular regard to the exact locality of the landing areas. Barber stated he already knew the date of the assault and the senior operations officer confirmed that this information had been passed to Trinity House personnel with Admiralty approval. All this secrecy seems a little ludicrous in the light of events in London, when secret documents giving these details blew out of an office window into the street. Fortunately the chairman, Admiral Little, saw the irony of the situation and solved it in Nelsonian fashion. He asked Barber what the latter thought of this development. Barber said if the Admiralty wanted the buoys laid in certain positions he must be able to direct his ships to those positions, and given this information he would undoubtedly be able to tell the Admiral the landing beaches. The Admiral smiled broadly and instructed his staff officers to cut off the title of the disputed chart and give it to the Superintendent. The tender captains chuckled at this and at the red faces of the staff officers.

The task of the ships was to lay an initial line of buoys to the various beaches for the primary assault immediately after the channels had been swept, and thereafter to expand the buoyage as the swept channels increased for the passage of the second and subsequent waves of troops and armaments. This would be a snow-balling operation, since it would greatly increase as more French ports were cleared. Moving in directly behind the minesweepers, the Trinity House tenders would be among the first ships to appear off Occupied Europe.

Five of the ships were to be used, with *Patricia* in reserve in case of losses, but when Admiral Little wanted a further eight buoys laid in the first wave Goodman volunteered *Patricia*. So it was all six tenders that waited for the order to proceed.

The suspense occasioned by the bad weather at the beginning of July only rendered the task of the tenders and minesweepers more difficult. Eisenhower's final "Okay, we'll go!" released the pent up energies of that vast armada, and late on the evening of 5th June, 1944, *André Blondell* and *Georges de Joly* left Cowes in company with the first minesweepers. Their task was to mark the first swept channels with small dan buoys. Within hours the remaining tenders were under way, following *Alert* in line ahead.

Five miles south of the Nab Tower *Alert* laid the "Zulu" buoy. The sea was

A painting by Rowland Langmaid of the "Juno" lightvessel, with *Warden* and warships, in June, 1944. The painting is in the possession of the Marine Society.   *Tony Othen*

rough and the topmark became bent. From this position the ships fanned out, laying their buoys to the very beaches of France, steaming in the wake of the gallant minesweepers to Utah, Omaha, Gold, Juno and Sword.

As soon as their decks were cleared they steamed back to Cowes to load from Carsten's lighters and return, for as the beach-heads were established and the mulberry harbours constructed more and more buoys were laid. In addition, the enormous amount of traffic, including vessels often inexpertly handled in the strong Channel tides, resulted in collision damage to the various seamarks. In the four months following the invasion collisions totalled 350 and at worst averaged 7.5 per day. The maintenance and augmentation of the established channels was essential if the allied armies were to be supplied. The harbours established at Arromanches in the east and in the western American sector were marked by two old lightvessels, that in the west named "Kansas", that off Arromanches "Juno". These were established by *Discovery II* and *Alert*, both of these ships being employed close inshore.

On 15th June, *Patricia*, *André Blondell* and *Alert* were all in Arromanches. *Patricia* and *Alert* were due to cross the Channel for more buoys the following day as soon as the duty sweepers had made their morning run over the port approaches. *Patricia* had some gear to pass over to *André Blondell* and signalled *Alert* to pass ahead of her the following morning. Captain White complied and a few minutes later *Patricia* steamed out of Arromanches in the wake of *Alert*. The sea was calm and blue. Captain Goodman paced his bridge, watching *Alert* ahead of him. Suddenly, at 08.10, Goodman saw the sea astern of *Alert* heave and the concussion of a terrific explosion rolled towards him.

Clouds of steam gushed from *Alert* as someone on her bridge morsed a warning to *Patricia*. Within minutes *Alert's* boats were being lowered, as were *Patricia's*. Shortly afterwards an Admiralty tug arrived to take the stricken ship in tow, but it was too late. She sank quickly, though without casualties, disappearing at 9.40. Her crew were picked up by *Patricia*, which returned to Arromanches, leaving for Cowes the following day. All aboard *Patricia* felt they had had a lucky escape, for had she been in position astern of *Alert* the mine would have exploded beneath her.

She did not escape unscathed, for on 18th July a mine exploded four cables astern of her near No 6 Baie de la Seine buoy, badly shaking the ship. A few days later, with the Deputy Master and a number of Elder Brethren embarked, she was returning from an inspection of the French beaches when she ran into an LCT at full speed just after midnight. Neither ship was lit. The starboard side of the LCT was badly gashed, and *Patricia's* stem was damaged necessitating docking at Southampton for six days whilst repairs were made. *Vestal* had a similar collision off Arromanches, when her beautiful bow was ripped apart. It was replaced by an unsightly raked stem.

As the allied forces moved eastward the tenders followed, laying more buoys to mark more swept channels and to mark the wrecks that littered the seabed whilst continuing with the maintenance of those already established.

Early in 1945 *Patricia* was out with five large sweepers buoying a channel across to Boulogne. Returning to Dover through the eastern entrance, Goodman stopped engines as he passed into the crowded anchorage beyond. Just inside the breakwater a flotilla of assault craft loaded with troops waited. *Patricia* swung towards them. "Starboard", ordered Captain Goodman. "She is hard a-starboard, sir", answered a puzzled quartermaster.

"I looked quickly at the revolution indicators and saw that only the port motor stopped; the starboard motor was still going full ahead. I put the port engine full ahead again so as to steer properly and jumped to the telephone and when the engineer answered I said 'Stop both engines quick'. Answer: 'I can't hear what you say, sir'. Me shouting louder, 'Stop both engines!' Answer, 'Can't hear what you say, sir.' Me louder still: 'STOP THE BLOODY ENGINES!'

Same reply.

By now I had to give my full attention to the steering as we were tearing through Dover Harbour, full of ships, at full speed. After a number of hair-raising misses I decided that I'd either hit a ship or a breakwater, so I turned for the beach and ran ashore, still at full speed.

By good fortune it (the bottom) was quite soft and the tide was low. We floated off on the rising tide and hauled off to a buoy."

This was the culmination of a number of incidents, and much to Captain Goodman's relief someone at last took notice of his complaints. Amazement was expressed by omniscient "experts", who always appear at such moments, that the ship had been approved for service. After modifications to the main wiring, ordinary bridge telegraphs were fitted in addition to her engine controllers (which were considered very advanced for the time) specifically for such an emergency manoeuvre.

The victorious progress of the allied armies kept the buoy laying tenders busy. In addition to the routine reliefs of manned offshore stations new channels were still being laid, those into the Scheldt while fighting was still in progress on Walcheren. So many casualties were occurring to buoys that other methods of repair had to be considered other than the despatching of a tender. A solution was found in the utilisation of high-speed shallow-draught motor launches. These naval craft, based at Harwich, were able to speed from the Essex coast over the minefields with a Trinity House 2nd Officer and a couple of seamen on board. They replaced damaged lanterns, relit extinguished buoys and carried out minor repairs.

Patricia was in company with a force of two squadrons of fleet mine-sweepers escorted by six destroyers engaged in buoying a channel to Heligoland and the work was almost completed when a signal was received: hostilities would end at noon. The task force returned to England in the worst gale ever experienced by Captain Goodman.

Before Goodman left *Patricia* to become Superintendent at Penzance he commanded her as escort to King George VI in H.M.S. *Vanguard* when the king proceeded to South Africa in 1947. *Patricia* led the new and already obsolescent battleship clear of pilotage waters. It was a mute and significant comment on naval power. The Corporation's little yacht, a bloodied and worthy veteran, preceeding the mighty anachronism of the world's best-looking battleship.

As the war ended, rolling across the plains of North Germany, its noise receded from the Narrow Seas. The last Trinity House tender to be attacked by the enemy was *Vestal* on 26th July, 1944. At 17.50 guns at Gris Nez opened up on the old yacht and her escort. The shells landed abeam and astern of her and she escaped unscathed.

But it was not only the ships that had suffered damage. Yarmouth Depot was damaged in 1941 in a severe air raid on the town. T.H.V. *Alert* was alongside and her crew attempted to help, acting as a refuge and casualty shelter and assisting in firefighting until the ship became endangered and had to be shifted. Nevertheless 24 hours later the depot was operational. Several light-houses were also damaged, mainly by machine gunning. At St Catherine's, Isle of Wight, incendiary bombs fired the buildings and incinerated all the keepers.

Trinity House itself was similarly damaged in 1940 and many treasures were lost.

But to the Wolf Rock belongs the oddest distinction of the war. During the last months of hostilities a hunted U-boat was in the vicinity. Manoeuvring to avoid a closing ring of anti-submarine ships, it ran into the isolated pinnacle of rock and was compelled to surface and surrender.

In the period following VE Day repossession of the Channel Island lighthouses took place. Captain Barber with Captain Glasson, Elder Brother, took passage in H.M.S. *Lynx*. The destroyer's 4-inch guns covered the landing at Caskets, where thirty German soldiers awaited *Lynx's* boat. They surrendered and were taken on to Guernsey, where the rest of the destroyer flotilla was anchored off St Peter Port.

The Trinity House party were taken to Torteval, amused that they had German officers as outriders ahead in case of landmines. From Guernsey they went on to Alderney, a vast concreted bunker of an island, a mute and moody sepulchre for thousands of forced labourers from the "lesser races". That atmosphere prevails to this day.

The third *Satellite* working at the Wolf Rock lighthouse in the 1950s.   *Trinity House*

CHAPTER NINE

Keepers of the Sea

" . . . the North Sea . . . will come as a surprise. The waves
are steep, short, aggressive; the currents are strong and navigation
becomes tricky . . . For trouble on the North Sea is about the
worst to be got anywhere."
Captain Jan de Hartog, *A Sailor's Life*

IN THE aftermath of war the situation facing the lighthouse authorities was
complex. The coastal waters of Europe were littered with minefields, the ports
that were open operated under enormous difficulties. Buoys were not available
to meet the demands of the continuing work of minesweeping and marking
wreck and obstructions. Trinity House is the authority responsible for dispersing wrecks in the coastal waters of England and Wales, but the detritus of
war was too much for the resources of the Corporation, depleted as they were. In
the immediate post-war years and until 1958 the Admiralty acted as agents for
the work of wreck dispersal.

Their lordships were also called upon to assist in more immediate matters.
In March and April of 1946 H.M.S. *Wizard* carried out the reliefs of the
Eddystone and other Cornish lighthouses because no tender was available. To
ameliorate this the Admiralty loaned Trinity House two boom-defence vessels.
In January, 1946, *Barndale* was sent to Harwich and *Barmouth* to East Cowes.
Identical vessels of 750 tons, they were 179 feet long, drew 13 feet 2 inches aft at
960 tons displacement. Their designed speed was 11.75 knots, but 9.75 was
more usual. They were far from ideal. The one boat was launched by a derrick
which could not be topped. Buoywork was restricted to one side and rendered
somewhat uncontrollable by the guys leading aft to the stern winch. At sea they
resembled half-tide rocks. One master remembered *Barmouth* as "a single screw
with bulwarks"! However, they did not long remain in service, *Barndale* being
returned to the Admiralty on 12th August, 1947, and *Barmouth* on 11th April,
1949.

By the latter date the final ship of a new class had been commissioned and
the tender fleet settled down to a peacetime routine.

But in 1946 a new ship was urgently wanted. On March 9th the two French
ships were returned (in 1980 *Georges de Joly* underwent a major overhaul and
remains in service with the French lighthouse service), and it was to bridge this
gap that the "Bar" vessels were supplied, though these were of little value.

However, the Admiralty had cancelled building of one of their Bullfinch class cable ships designated H.M.S. *Bullseye* and arrangements were concluded to launch her as T.H.V. *Alert*. The ceremony was carried out at Swan Hunter's Wallsend yard on 20th November, 1945. *Alert* (O.N. 180855) commissioned on 20th April, 1946. She was the biggest tender ever, grossing 1527 tons (572 net) with a loaded displacement of 2223 tons. She was 244 feet overall, with a beam of 36 feet 4 inches, she drew 15 feet 9 inches loaded and had 140 tons of iron ballast concreted into her bottom. Propelled by twin screws driven by triple expansion engines, she had two Babcock and Wilcox watertube boilers giving her a working pressure of 220 psi and 1487 ihp. On trials she did 13.37 knots. Although like *Patricia* she was only fitted with a single derrick, this 57 foot spar was the most efficient in the Service, and her large capacity of twelve gas buoys made her a useful vessel. She retained her luffing davits and rope boat falls until her scrapping at Burntisland in 1970.

Under the command of J. J. Woolnough she remained on the Harwich station until 1954, when she was fitted with a large flying bridge and transferred to Swansea, remaining there until her sale.

Her commissioning initiated a new building programme under the then Surveyor of Shipping, Captain Twinberrow R.N. (Retd.). Twinberrow accepted a certain amount of Admiralty advice, particularly on the question of buoy laying capacities, which had been considered inadequate during the D-Day operations (Were those thwarted naval staff officers having their revenge?). The result was the three steam vessels of the *Ready* class. These were substantially

Opposite: The third *Beacon* in 1948 before the fitting of a mainmast. Her generally smart appearance is noteworthy, and so is the oak derrick.
Trinity House

Right: The fourth *Alert* as Swansea tender in 1967, alongside her depot. *Author*

similar vessels, *Vestal* and *Argus* grossing 1918 tons and *Ready* 1920, and costing about £225,000 each.

Vestal (O.N. 181728) was launched from the Bristol yard of Charles Hill and Son and commissioned as Swansea tender on 18th September, 1947, under Captain Alec Batte. *Ready* (O.N. 181735) was launched "in a flurry of snowflakes" in February at Blyth, but it was 25th October, 1947, before she commissioned. Her departure from Blyth attracted much local notice as she was the first "non-warlike" vessel built there for some years. Curiously the local paper referred to her as "the new Trinity Steam Yacht". Under the command of Captain H. W. T. Owen, she proceeded to Harwich where she remained based for the next thirty years. Despite her long life she was outlived by her original namesake. Anxious to revive an old Trinity name, the Corporation persuaded the owners of the sailing barge *Ready* to relinquish their title to that name. The owners agreed and as *Mirosa* the spritsail barge is still to be seen on the Essex coast.

The introduction of these ships necessitated the paying off of the old *Vestal* (ex *Patricia*, ex *Miranda*). This elegant old ship belonged to a byegone age. In November, 1946, she was in Blyth undergoing repairs but it was found that her boilers were beyond economical overhaul. She was condemned to lay forlornly alongside for some months awaiting disposal. Captain Batte and his crew left for the new *Vestal* and after their departure Blyth Town Council considered utilising her as an accommodation ship for homeless families. At the end of the year she was acquired by the Crown Agents and appears to have been used as a lighthouse tender in the Persian Gulf, but in 1949 she returned to Grimsby for scrapping, being joined at the breakers' yard by *Discovery II.* The research ship had been loaned to the Commissioners for Irish Lights after the war and then returned to the Antarctic until 1954.

The final new steamer, the *Argus* (O.N. 181821), was launched at the Port Glasgow yard of Messrs Ferguson Bros. on 17th June, 1947, and commissioned on 24th January the following year. The three ships were 266 feet overall, 253.5 feet between perpendiculars, with a beam of 40 feet. The hulls had a moulded depth of 17.4 feet and at a loaded draught of 13 feet 6 inches, they displaced some 2,400 tons.

The Admiralty influence was apparent in their long flush-decked hulls, and they became well known for their sea-keeping qualities. Their two three-furnace Scotch boilers produced 220 psi feeding the two triple expansion engines which developed 1928 ihp. Capable of 13.5 knots, they had a full speed endurance of 4,188 miles with bunkers of 308 tons of oil. They carried 344 tons fresh water, plus 48 tons of gas oil for lightvessels. Their capacious holds and steam deck machinery made them able consorts of *Alert.*

Their greatest weakness was the fact that their wheelhouses were only one deck above their upper deck and fully rigged buoys obscured visibility. All buoys had to be stripped down immediately they were lifted aboard, something *Alert's* crew never had to do. At first this mattered little, the masters conning from the flying bridges a deck higher, but as time went on and more and more electronic gear was crammed into the wheelhouse, all requiring monitoring whilst manoeuvring, this became an annoyance. From an annoyance it became a positive danger that seriously affected navigation in the congested waters of the North Sea and English Channel.

They also had a poor towing facility. *Alert* had no special winch for towing, being fitted with large bitts and a wire in the forward hold which was man-handled through the officers' accommodation to the after deck. The *Ready* class had towing winches but they were only for hauling and veering. If any weight came on them they had a habit of shattering the cast drive wheel. Under tow, when shortening in, some classes of lightvessel sheered heavily. If this happened at the wrong moment the disintegration of the drive wheel and consequent running off of five-inch wire at high speed made the tender crews most proficient at diving for cover. It happened several times.

These vessels were built without mainmasts, but these were fitted to all tenders in 1951 to comply with new regulations regarding navigation lights. *Patricia's* was replaced a few feet further forward than had originally been fitted (it had been removed during the war) and this improved the look of the ship. Another modification to *Ready* and her sisters was the raising of their funnels to keep smoke off their decks. In the case of *Ready* her engine room vents were also raised. In 1960 the three steamships and *Patricia* had their motor launches slung in gravity davits.

Although only the second of the name, *Ready* was the last steamship to be run in the now misnamed "Steam Vessel Service". Flying a paying off pendant, she entered Harwich for the last time under Commander P. Fairplay at noon on 11th October, 1977.

Vestal and *Argus* were fifth of the name. *Argus* under Captain J. Meyrick, manned by the former crew of *Barmouth*, went to Holyhead, so that by 1949 all the new ships were on station.

In the post-war years up to 1949 the tenders were continually shifting about. In 1947, for instance, *Triton* was at Swansea where the inspecting Elder Brethren found the ship's side scuttles "daubed with paint", which circumstance brought the disapprobation of the committee on the ship's company. The ship's officers hit back complaining "of excessive heat and poor ventilation in their mess. This complaint is well founded; the mess is close to the boiler uptakes and is very hot indeed".

Triton, Captain Bennet, had an even unhappier experience in Swansea. Leaving the old Corporation Drydock stern first into the River Tawe, she failed to respond to her telegraphs and ran on to the opposite bank where, at low water, immaculately painted, she lay on her beam ends.

The fourth *Alert's* boat deck with duty seaboat swung out, in the Irish Sea in 1969. A drawing made by the author.

The third *Triton* fuelling the ill-fated No. 90 lightvessel at the South Goodwin station in 1954. *Triton's* trawler ancestry is easily seen in this view. *Skyfotos*

The 1950's were peaceful years, and the tenders plodded about their duties with unhurried efficiency. Their larger size formed a reason for the introduction of 3rd Officers, converted to Junior 2nd Officers in April, 1960. The duties of the ships remained the same; the servicing of the ever-increasing number of buoys, with fortnightly reliefs of half the crew of every lightvessel and monthly reliefs of offshore lighthouse keepers. Prior to 1938 lightsmen had done two months on station and one ashore, when they laboured in their district depots. After this the depots were employing their own full-time staff, and the routine was altered to one month on and a fortnight off. Lightvessel masters worked a month about, the rest of the crew as above, a few men always being ashore. No working was carried out in the shore period except the occasional manning of a lightvessel under tow. By 1975 with the phased introduction of helicopter reliefs for all offshore personnel the entire crews were rotated monthly.

Each district had its own buoy servicing programme, and lightvessels were towed to and from station as required for overhauls. All the above reliefs were attended to by the ship and her boats, as was the replenishment of offshore stations. The skill and expertise of the Corporation's boats' crews deserves more publicity than it receives. Perhaps because of its routine nature it lacks glamour, but the jumping of buoys in gale force winds to relight them is commonplace, as is the lowering and recovery of the boats.

Occasionally duties of an invidious nature are undertaken. Officers who are technically employed as navigators may find themselves acting as bailiffs, evicting a lighthouse keeper from a dwelling he is no longer entitled to occupy; as mountaineers scaling a cliff because urgently required stores cannot be got ashore any other way; as delivery men manoeuvring heavy and awkward items of equipment up the spiral staircase of a lighthouse while outside the rising wind warns them of possible trouble in getting their boat out of a dangerous landing. Just as incongruously, they may find themselves in full dress at a Fleet Review.

The constant contrast caused by the unpredictable nature of the sea is an element that dominates the work of all lighthouse tenders on whatever coast they work. Operations in the congested waters of the Narrow Seas have their own characteristics. The duty of marking wrecks often brings a tender fresh on the scene of recent incidents. From the misfortunes of others they occasionally profit. Minor salvage is often carried out because the Trinity ship is in the vicinity, and these services are usually rendered gratuitously. Many yachtsmen have been assisted, from the foolish who is given a drum of diesel to the unfortunate who is boarded in a sinking condition and brought safe into port. Occasionally a bigger casualty occurs, sometimes with financial gain to the crew. Trinity House invariably waives the owners' claim but the ship's company involved may net a modestly proportioned fish.

Satellite, Captain C. Horne, stood by the prolonged and much publicised sinking of the *Flying Enterprise*. *Stella*, Commander T. M. P. Tarrant, attended the polluting bulk of the *Torrey Canyon*; *Mermaid*, Commander J. M. Barnes, the *Eleni V*; *Winston Churchill*, Commander G. Roberts, the *Christos Bitas*. But it is not always standing by that is to be done. Sometimes an active role, that of salvor, has to be undertaken.

One such salvage was that of the 10,000 ton "Liberty" ship *Nymfea* by T.H.V. *Vestal*, then under Commander T. M. P. Tarrant. Just after midnight on 15th July, 1965, ten miles south east of Beachy Head, *Nymfea* was in collision in dense fog with the Liberian tanker *Francesca*. *Vestal*, then based at Harwich, was making passage for the Channel Islands to service the buoys on the Plateau des Minquiers. She too had run into fog and was proceeding at a slow speed. At 00.55 she monitored a Mayday relay signal from Niton Radio and Commander Tarrant altered course for the damaged ships.

At 02.00 she located a lifeboat with fourteen men in it and these were taken on board. Some were suffering from injuries sustained when the lifeboat they were launching capsized. *Vestal's* crew hoisted the lifeboat on the foredeck. Immediate language difficulties were experienced, but first aid treatment was administered. During this operation Tarrant's main preoccupation was with other ships which swept past at full speed, disregarding the fog and the danger of the damaged ships in their tracks. A second boat was located from *Francesca* and this was hoisted but left over the side as the occupants requested they be returned to their own ship. The two vessels had now been located and *Vestal* closed with them to identify which was which. At one cable distant they found *Francesca* and returned her boat and men, then they closed *Nymfea*, which was repeatedly calling for help. 2nd Officer Fiander was sent over in one of the tender's boats and found the Greek ship had a lifeboat lowered and filling with men, who transferred themselves to Fiander's launch as soon as he came alongside. Fiander returned to *Vestal* to disencumber himself of survivors, and it was 02.30 before he was able to get aboard *Nymfea* and assess the damage. He found her port side opened up to the sea in Nos. 4 and 5 holds. The gash made by *Francesca* extended from the deck to below the waterline, and she had left

The fifth *Vestal*, the first of a final class of steamships, seen with a lightvessel under tow about 1950. Known as the "whispering giants," this class of vessel proved powerful and comfortable and were great favourites with their crews. *Skyfotos*

her anchor in the Greek ship's side. *Nymfea* was already down by the stern and water was filling the engine room. Complying with his orders, Fiander offered the Greek captain *Vestal's* services to tow under a Lloyd's Open Agreement. This no cure—no pay contract is legally binding even when made by word of mouth, and Captain Fouskas accepted the offer. Fiander and two of *Vestal's* seamen stayed aboard *Nymfea* with Captain Fouskas, his Chief Officer and 3rd Engineer.

It was still foggy but daylight had begun to break as *Vestal* was manoeuvred under *Nymfea's* high bow. On the tender Mr P. F. Howard, the First Officer, with his bosun and able seamen, got a six-inch manila hawser across and, once secure, *Vestal* slowly got under way. A messenger was then passed across to the *Nymfea*, together with oxy-acetylene cutting gear. *Nymfea's* port anchor was "hung off" in its hawse pipe and the cable cut and brought forward through a panama lead where, after great exertions, it was shackled on to *Vestal's* five-inch towing wire. Finally both wire and cable were paid out, 75 fathoms of cable acting as a spring on the 600 feet of wire. *Vestal* then recovered her boat and slipped the manila rope.

Whilst the final stages of this operation were in progress there were two further arrivals on the scene. At about 05.00 the Eastbourne lifeboat came alongside *Vestal* to remove *Nymfea's* crew, who were at first reluctant to leave the comfort of *Vestal* for another boat but were eventually persuaded that they would be landed much quicker by lifeboat. The second arrival was unexpected. At 05.15 the German salvage tug *Hermes* appeared and, in accordance with the complexities of maritime law, offered his services to Commander Tarrant. Referring to Fouskas, Tarrant agreed to accept the services of the tug's pumps, although *Hermes's* master pressed to expedite the tow. This was tried briefly, but it put too much pressure on the *Nymfea's* damaged bulkheads and was quickly terminated. By this time *Vestal* was making down Channel for the shelter of the Isle of Wight and on board *Nymfea* all oil tank valves were shut, the vent pipes plugged and the inner end of the port anchor cable disconnected in the locker in case it was necessary to slip the tow in the event of the Liberty ship sinking.

By noon the three ships were six miles south of Shoreham and radio traffic was dense. The Portsmouth and Southampton port authorities gave permission for Commander Tarrant to take *Nymfea* through Spithead into the eastern Solent, but it was guarded permission, hedged with reminders that he alone was responsible if anything went wrong and the commercial traffic to Southampton or the naval movements in and out of Portsmouth were disrupted. Tarrant's legal position was one of total responsibility, able to fantasise on the possibility of making money but personally liable if disaster struck.

Fortunately the weather held, and despite pressure from *Hermes's* captain to beach *Nymfea* on the Hampshire coast Tarrant and *Vestal* pressed on. At

16.40 off the Nab pilots were embarked, one for *Nymfea* and one for *Hermes*, as pilotage was compulsory. *Vestal* was exempt, but *Nymfea's* pilot was carried on *Vestal's* bridge where he was available for consultation.

As *Vestal* moved up the Solent looking, in her master's words, "like a puppy pulling an elephant", other interested parties came off in boats. It is not part of this history to digress into the various interests of port representatives, *Hermes's* owners' agent and the officials of the Salvage Association except to say that they put Commander Tarrant under enormous pressure to accept various pieces of advice which operated in their clients' interests.

Tarrant had already decided to ground *Nymfea* on the Ryde Middle Sand, over which *Vestal* could pass but upon which the deeply trimmed *Nymfea* would settle. This at least satisfied the port authorities, who wanted the ship out of their fairways. Shortly after 20.00 the screech of cable through a windlass band-brake told that *Nymfea* had taken the bottom. *Vestal* anchored immediately, still connected to the tow.

Vestal and her people had now been working for twenty hours. *Nymfea* was aground but not yet salved. After making a visit to his "prize" Tarrant gave orders that dispelled any thought of rest for his crew. At 01.00 the tow was disconnected and Mr Fiander and a small working party of seamen from *Vestal* succeeded in resecuring the inner end of *Nymfea's* port cable, a particularly difficult job carried out in the confined space of her cable locker in total darkness with the men reaching a state of exhaustion. Shortly afterwards *Vestal* reanchored and her crew turned in. Six hours later, at 08.00 on 16th July, Mr Fiander was sent off again to *Nymfea* and *Vestal* weighed. There followed an intensely busy two hours. Manoeuvring under her bow, Tarrant had *Nymfea's* port anchor lowered to *Vestal's* deck, then steamed ahead to recover the loose end of her cable, to which he reshackled the anchor. This was then lowered to the sea bed.

Nymfea was now safely anchored, and there followed a number of meetings between the interested parties. The outcome of this was that Commander Tarrant subcontracted the salvage of *Nymfea* to the firm of Risdon Beazley, and at 23.00 that night *Vestal* resumed her passage to the Plateau des Minquiers.

The conduct of *Vestal* speaks for itself. Commander Tarrant had little sleep in two days, yet he had performed a not inconsiderable feat of seamanship. Of his officers and crew the Commander wrote in his official report:

> "Finally I wish to place on record that the standard of work expected from a ship's company in this Service was abundantly maintained during this whole operation. All the officers and crew worked willingly and well to assist the survivors in the first place and the casualty later. I have nothing but praise for any of them and in particular the three Deck Officers who were a great support to me at all times."

It was all over bar the shouting. For the repairs Risdon Beazley's were awarded £13,000, *Hermes's* owners received £10,000 and *Vestal* £5,000.

The imbalance between *Vestal's* apportionment and that of *Hermes* was justified on the grounds that the tug existed solely to salvage ships and therefore her owners should receive due recompense to maintain that service. Since Trinity House were not a commercial company they waived all claim to an owner's share, levying a small charge for fuel expended against *Vestal's* award. This effectively released the ship to Commander Tarrant and his crew for the duration of the salvage.

The second *Ready*, which served for thirty years from Harwich.   *Trinity House*

A similar arrangement was made in the case of T.H.V. *Patricia*, Commander E. V. Parry, when, in the early hours of 6th February, 1974, she intercepted a distress call from the roll on/roll off vessel *Leila* aground on the South Middle Haisbro bank. *Patricia* closed the casualty at 04.00 and with the concurrence of *Leila's* master, Captain Manfred Wietfeldt, a boat was sent over with *Patricia's* First Officer, Mr R. M. Woodman. His report showed *Leila* had sustained bottom damage and all her machinery cooling intakes were blocked with sand. She was immobilised and a dead ship, and it was agreed that *Patricia* should attempt to tow her into deeper water and anchor her pending the arrival of a salvage tug. This was accomplished, but no tow was forthcoming and a new arrangement was concluded (on the no cure—no pay basis) of a tow to the Humber. *Patricia* was unable to connect her towing wire because there was insufficient power, including manpower, to heave it across to *Leila* and the tow was undertaken with twin six-inch polypropylene ropes. The light south-

151

westerly breeze veered and freshened during the day and by evening both ships were pitching into a north-westerly gale. With a foul tide off the Docking Bank they made no headway. Aboard *Leila* the next morning the crew saw the low coast of Lincolnshire with relief, for she was freezing cold and they were subsisting on iced milk. Off Spurn Head the tow parted. *Leila* was anchored and *Patricia* anchored close ahead. It was agreed to wait for the flood tide to assist them into the Humber but *Leila* could now not recover her anchor. Fresh tow-ropes were run down from *Patricia* to *Leila* and another rope from *Patricia's* forward capstans up *Leila's* hawse pipe to her anchor cable, which was stoppered off and disconnected. At slack water this was slipped and *Leila* fell back on the tow ropes while *Patricia* manoeuvred to recover *Leila's* anchor at her gangway. In the gusting wind, with the *Leila* sheering about astern, the line to the anchor parted. However, the frayed end of the polypropylene rope floated and was spotted by Coxswain Thurlow on *Patricia's* foredeck. *Patricia* was manoeuvred ahead and a grapnel thrown over the rope. A few minutes later *Leila's* anchor rose dripping over *Patricia's* rail. *Patricia* struggled into the Humber and off Immingham handed the *Leila* over to tugs. Woodman returned to his ship at 17.30 on the 7th, having seen *Leila* safely berthed in Immingham.

Patricia's salvage of *Leila* was in sharp contrast to her task in 1952. In that year the Royal Yacht *Victoria & Albert* (the third ship to bear the name) was judged unfit for sea and *Britannia* was not then completed, so Prince Philip, Duke of Edinburgh, took passage in *Patricia* bound for Helsinki and the 1952 Olympic Games. She was escorted by the cruiser H.M.S. *Swiftsure*.

By the end of the 1950's the older steamers were showing signs of age and in 1958 plans were approved for the construction of three diesel-electric motor vessels. Substantially identical ships, the *Mermaid* class were all built by J. Samuel White's at Cowes. First to enter service on 8th September, 1959, was T.H.V. *Mermaid*, 1425 gross tons, 455 net. She and her sisters have an overall length of 221 feet, and a beam of 38 feet. Their English Electric propulsion gives 1450 shp at 228 rpm.

Under the command of Captain Eric Moat, *Mermaid* (O.N. 300985) proceeded to Great Yarmouth where she relieved the old *Warden* on 22nd September. *Siren* (O.N. 301080) was the next of the class to commission. She had a slightly longer foredeck than *Mermaid*, did 13.56 knots on trials (against *Mermaid's* 13.71) and remained at Cowes to relieve the old *Beacon* in February, 1960, under the command of K. Carstens. In April *Beacon* was sold for scrap.

Next to complete was *Stella* (O.N. 302778), slower at 13.45 knots, which under Commander C. C. Parsons proceeded to Penzance at the beginning of October, 1961. *Satellite* was sold in November and was destined to become a pirate radio ship but eventually scrapped.

By 1960 *Triton*, never built to Trinity House's specifications, was also showing signs of wear. Much of her construction had been skimped due to wartime conditions, and by this period her boat deck leaked and her boiler, which had already had £3,000 spent on it, was in a similar condition. "Extreme care" had to be exercised when raising steam and this, combined with a general concern over her condition, suitability and sea-keeping qualities, led to the recommendation that she be replaced by a new vessel.

Accordingly a modified *Mermaid*-class tender was ordered from White's and on 16th October, 1962, T.H.V. *Winston Churchill* was commissioned as the Cowes District Lighthouse Tender, displacing *Siren*, which was removed to Harwich by the crew of *Triton*. On 24th January, 1963, the Belgian tug *Martine Letzer* towed the old "Mechanical Plank" to Messrs Van Heyghen Freres of Ghent for breaking.

During her life *Triton*, like the ex-yacht *Vestal* before her, had been a light-vessel tender and little else. The fact that she was commissioned as a stopgap measure and lingered on until her useful life was over was no fault of hers. She too had had her glorious moments. Coal-fired to the last, she featured in the film "Yangtze Incident" masquerading as the smoky Chinese steamer *Kianglang Liberator* in whose pall H.M.S. *Amethyst* took cover during part of her escape down the Orwell, on which river the film was made.

The lightvessel had changed very little in outward appearance in the pre-war years. Internally radio beacon equipment was becoming common and since the war radar responder beacons, or Racons, along with other devices, have been fitted. These include position and tide monitoring instruments. Further, the

The second *Patricia* at the Silver Jubilee Review of the Fleet in 1977, with the Royal Yacht *Britannia* and H.M.S. *Ark Royal* in the background. *Ambrose Greenway*

lightvessel itself has been replaced on some stations by Lanbys, Large Navigational Buoys. These 40 foot diameter dishes support light towers and are electronically controlled and monitored generating stations, the power from which operates xenon discharge optics and whining fog horns.

The most tedious operation formerly undertaken by the tenders had been the changing of four-arm moorings. These were designed to restrict the swinging area of the lightvessel to increase its accurate location in its charted position. The first of these was laid at the Tongue station in 1892. By 1894 the Sunk, Shipwash, North Goodwin and Haisbro' were secured to this type of mooring, which had the bonus of being capable of bearing a telephone cable up its central arm, at least in theory. When telephones were replaced by radio telephony the lightvessels reverted to single moorings until 1940, when a second attempt was made to introduce the four-arm type.

The principal disadvantage was the time taken to do this work and the occupation of two tenders. Each of the four arms was clenched at Blackwall and carefully loaded under the supervision of the Chief Officer. The total 780 fathoms of heavy cable had to be exactly right for laying, all shackles bow out from the proposed centre. Anchors or mushrooms were then loaded, together with a plentiful supply of spare shackles and swivels. Good weather was now required and once set fair, a second tender was directed to assist. The function of the second ship was to look after the lightvessel and recover her existing moorings, an exacting task in itself. When the lightvessel had been re-anchored 2½ cables from her station the laying tender arrived with the first 210-fathom ground arm and anchor over her bow, all hands on deck and her portable forge glowing redly, shackle pins steadily warming in it. One thirty-fathom bridle was ready at the foredeck gangway; one end buoyed, the other led to the bow for clenching. The laying tender lowered the first anchor in position at slack water, then as the tide made she veered away, backing astern down-tide. If the cable had been incorrectly stowed great difficulties would be encountered, for as the inner end of the first 210-fathom arm came on deck the inner end of the other should be joined to it. At this join a four-arm swivel was fitted, and to this was clenched the end of the thirty-fathom bridle which, buoyed, was passed overboard as the tender continued to veer down tide. The second anchor was clenched on and stopped off with rope. This was cut away and the anchor dropped.

While this was in progress the assisting vessel approached and recovered the thirty-fathom bridle and hove it in until she had the four-arm swivel on deck. The laying vessel now approached her, went alongside and took the centre from the assisting ship. Six hours had now elapsed and the tide was again slack. One of the 150-fathom side arms was now veered out and laid while the tide remained weak. A rest was then taken, meals eaten and final preparations made. On the next slack water the second side arm was laid.

The final stage was tensioning the mooring so that all was taut but the lightvessel could lift the centre at low water springs to examine it. This was done by the laying vessel grappling for the down-tide arm and running back to the anchor, which was lifted, then lowered back on to the seabed on a bight of wire. The moorings were then ready and the lightvessel brought up to them.

This long and tedious job was not carried out in the relative calm of harbour approaches but in the open sea. Before the days of oxy-acetylene gear, mistakes had to be cold-chiselled or sawn out, and the time taken to rectify them might cost the ship's company a tide or their good weather. The Chief Mate was therefore particularly on his mettle on such occasions. On the one hand he might earn a rebuke from the master, on the other the crew might make his life rather difficult if they missed a meal or a watch ashore!

Though much simpler, Lanby moorings are still attended in a similar fashion, while lightvessel moorings present fewer problems these days due to the fact that all of these craft lie to single-arm moorings.

A rare but absorbing job formerly undertaken by the tenders was beacon building. It took many forms, but the most dramatic was that undertaken on drying banks by grounding the ship over the desired position. The pile was hoisted outboard and, by means of the derrick and tackles, pulled vertical. It was then sunk into the bank by sending a man inside the tube at low water when all was high and dry. Armed with a bucket on a line and the galley shovel, the unfortunate seaman dug bucket-full after bucket-full, his mates hoisting each load out and relieving each other at the task until the pile was sufficiently embedded in the sand to mollify the civil engineers. The illustration on page 97 shows *Triton* engaged in this work, building the North West Shingles beacon in the 1930's, when commanded by First Officer S. T. Cope.

Buoy-work remains the predominant task of the tenders. The classes of buoys vary from small blind buoys to high focal plane buoys, some weighing in excess of 11 tonnes without moorings. Hoisting them inboard is a task requiring a high degree of professional skill on the part of all concerned. From the master on the bridge, holding the ship in a tideway while the hands get the gear over, to the two young seamen sliding down the ship's side to hook in the hoisting purchase, every member of the tender's crew forms a part of a team on whose co-ordinated teamwork depends the success of the job. Until the mooring chain has been disconnected from the buoy and shackled down on deck the ship is virtually anchored by her derrick head. Should she sheer in the tide at this point the consequences could be serious, if not fatal, on a deck criss-crossed by wires, ropes and chain. Techniques vary according to circumstances such as depth of water, strength and relative direction of wind and tide, characteristics of individual ships and so on. Sometimes the tender lies to the buoy mooring, sometimes, particularly in areas where the tide runs strongly, the vessel is anchored with the buoy on the quarter. Cable is veered away and the ship given a powerful sheer across the tide to bring her up alongside the buoy. This method is utilised in narrow channels where it may be desirable to pull the vessel back into deeper water.

Boarding buoys is not only undertaken alongside. After periods of very severe weather a few buoys may be extinguished. This also arises from careless navigation by other ships, making insufficient allowance for the tide and knocking a buoy hard enough to put out its light. Relighting is done by a junior mate and a seaman from a motor launch and it is a boast made, not without pride, that this job is undertaken in any weather, gales notwithstanding.

Another task undertaken regularly is the removal or establishing of light-vessels from or to their stations and the towage of them to and from base ports and dry docks. When changing over on station the ship occupying the post is ordered to hoist her anchor and allowed to drift away from her position. Meanwhile the tender, hovering close, boats down, with the new lightvessel in

The Second Officer and a seaman carry out a routine check on the South Varne buoy.
K. R. Thurlow

tow, shortens her towing gear and manoeuvres into the postion. The tow is slipped and the new lightvessel anchors on station. The tender then rounds to and picks up the old lightvessel, towing her away on completion of the transfer of the lightship's crew by her motor boats.

But lightvessel work is not necessarily routine. Lightships occasionally break adrift due to cable failure, usually at a swivel. In February, 1936, No. 56 on the Morecambe Bay station and in March, 1948, No. 80 on the Sevenstones, for instance, succumbed to this fate. The North Goodwin and Owers frequently fouled their own anchors, and in September 1949, the *Cairo City* under tow by the tug *Masterman* fouled and holed the Cross Sand. As late as 1977 the West German coaster *Eberstein* holed the Newarp. Even when under tow lightvessels are not immune from collision. In the crowded waters of the Narrow Seas careless watchkeeping occurs and there is often nothing the tender officers can do to avert a "Last minute situation". Under tow of *Vestal*, No. 83 lightvessel was sunk by a Polish fishing vessel, whilst a German freighter ran into No. 1 lightvessel being towed by *Patricia*.

Natural disasters also have their effect. The great tidal and storm surge of January, 1953, that caused such widespread flooding on the east coast of England found the Trinity House seamen rowing about among the chimney pots of Harwich rescuing anything from old ladies to cats. Reports came in that the Saltscar lightfloat off Redcar had capsized and *Vestal* proceeded in the teeth of the north-westerly gale that was still blowing. She found the light float keel uppermost, but the weather was foul and she took shelter in Hartlepool. On 9th February *Ready* laid a temporary buoy as a substitute, then joined her sister in an attempt to right the float. Manoeuvring either side of the hull, they attempted to parbuckle it upright. They failed, trying again on the 10th and 14th, with no better luck. Bad weather still lashed the North Sea and on the 15th a further parting of the wires was followed by the sinking of the float, much, it may readily be conjectured, to everyone's relief.

In November, 1954, the worst peacetime disaster since the Cockle explosion of 1909 occurred with the loss of No. 90 lightvessel on the South Goodwin station. At about midnight on the night of 26th/27th November at the height of a severe southerly gale No. 90 parted her moorings and drove north for 6.5 miles before grounding on her beam ends in the Kellet Gut. The seven-man crew were all lost, the only survivor being Ronald Murton, a Ministry of Agriculture and Fisheries officer.

The reason for the failure has never been established. On the 12th the lightvessel's master, Mr H. T. Skipp, reported the pin of the 150-fathom shackle a little slack. This is a common occurence and *Patricia* arrived to deal with it. However the weather was very bad and the lightvessel crew hardened it up with blow lamps and a maul. Skipp was satisfied, for he reported to the Chief Superintendent at Harwich that "trusting us amateur smithy's have made a good job of the clench, in our own interest . . ."

Skipp was a conscientious man who on 17th November assured the Superintendent of his diligence: "having served for 20 years on the East Goodwin I realise only too well the importance of 'Cable Drill' and having a sound cable and in my estimation you should and will be acquainted at all times of any irregularities concerning cable . . . "

Was there some defect that was worrying Skipp? If so he never specified it. Or was he touched by premonition?

When the cable parted it was not immediately known that anything was wrong, for the motion of the lightvessel had been so violent. Whatever happened, or at whatever point Skipp and his men realised they were rolling in the trough of the sea, it was already too late, for the lightvessel would have been driving over the Goodwins. Why no distress signals were sent remains a mystery.

The alarm was raised by Mr Tilsey, of Deal Coastguard, who informed Harwich that the lightvessel was off station at 01.15. Shortly afterwards permission was sought to launch lifeboats and at 02.30 the Ramsgate boat left harbour, followed by the Dover boat at 02.50. It was 07.30 before the beach-launched Walmer boat was away. Meanwhile at 05.20 T.H.V. *Vestal*, Captain R. N. Thompson, left Harwich.

A lull in the wind about 07.00 allowed an American helicopter to pass over the wreck. None of the lifeboats had got near the lightvessel and several passes were made overhead before Murton was spotted clinging to the rails in his pyjamas.

A little before he was winched to safety Murton had been able to talk to seaman Porter, who said that Skipp and Fog Signal Driver Viney were trapped with him. This conversation was held through a damaged port hole and gave relatives ashore a false hope. At 10.30 *Vestal* arrived and attempted to land a party on the sands at low water, but a high sea was still running and the boats were in great danger. A second attempt in the afternoon also failed.

Patricia left Harwich at 10.15 with a temporary buoy and at dawn on the 28th she relieved *Vestal*. Also arriving on the scene was the naval diving tender, H.M.S. *Romola*.

Patricia's First Officer, Mr Parsons, joined Lt. Cdr. Brooks, R.N., and his divers in a search of the wreck. Most of the compartments were already filled with sand and nothing, not even bodies, was ever found.

Whilst this search was being made *Patricia*, Captain J. R. Meyrick, laid a buoy in place of the missing lightvessel to keep shipping off the South Sand Head of the Goodwins. *Vestal*, having returned to Harwich, was by 16.15 that afternoon towing No. 65 lightvessel, hurriedly prepared for sea and manned at dead short notice, past the Cork. At dawn on the 29th a further search of the wreck was made but nothing came of it. Skipp, Lanham, Philpott, Viney, Cox, Lynn and Porter were victims of the terrible Goodwins. By noon *Vestal* had established the lightvessel and withdrawn the buoy.

The wreck of the South Goodwin lightvessel on the Goodwin Sands in 1954.   *Skyfotos*

The weather that caused the disaster was extraordinary. The wind had been from the SSW, force 10 to 11, and caused a 10-12 foot swell in the shelter of Dover Harbour. At midnight on the 26th the tide had been running north at its maximum velocity, so that a combination of extreme natural forces had been at the root of the trouble. Whatever the cause, nothing more could be done and No. 90 rapidly disappeared in the sands.

The new lightvessel was laid with commendable speed and Captain Meyrick and the *Patricia's* crew earned themselves a commendation for laying the emergency buoy in the apalling conditions of the 27th. Mr Parsons had demonstrated a bulldog tenacity in the hopeless task of searching the wreck and was awarded an M.B.E.

The loss of the South Goodwin was national headline news. Only a few days later the English and Welsh Grounds lightvessel in the Bristol Channel also broke adrift, but her crew let go a spare anchor and she brought up before grounding.

An unpublicised yet dramatic incident occured on 16th February, 1961. T.H.V. *Mermaid*, Commander P. C. V. Inman, was on general sea duty when a message was received that the Haisbro lightvessel had been holed by the s.s. *Marshall*. Inman advised the master to take certain action and broadcast a mayday. *Mermaid's* course was altered and she increased speed. The *Marshall*

The third *Mermaid* in the Channel in January, 1979, with a high focal plane buoy on her foredeck. Smaller than their predecessors, the ships of this class were less seaworthy vessels.

Ambrose Greenway

and the m.v. *Ordinance* were standing by, as was the RFA *Wave Chief*. On the lightvessel her crew had hove their cable in short and stowed it to port, giving the vessel a list. Following Inman's instructions, all fresh water was pumped out and the forepeak was filled, while the panelling masking the hole aft was stripped out.

As she sped towards the casualty *Mermaid's* crew, under the direction of First Officer D. Evans, were busy preparing a collision mat and fenders and rigging an emergency buoy. As soon as she arrived on the scene *Mermaid* ran alongside the lightvessel and clapped the collision mat over the hold. Immediately the influx of water was reduced and finally overcome. *Mermaid* removed the lightvessel from station and laid the buoy before towing the ship south. On the 18th *Ready* arrived from Harwich with a spare lightvessel as a replacement.

Lightvessels are extremely vulnerable to collision damage since they can take no avoiding action. The list of incidents in which they have been involved is too long to enumerate, but the above serves as a good example. Weather occasionally forces them off station, particularly when their holding ground is poor or the cable liable to foul, as at the North Goodwin. Bottom wreckage can strain a cable, as occurred on 12th November, 1961, with No. 13 on the East Goodwin station. Dragging north, she fouled the St Margaret's Bay/La Panne No. 6 telephone cable. When *Vestal* sorted out the mess it was found that a link of her cable had straightened when fouled by an old aeroplane propeller, an ancient anchor and ninety fathoms of cable.

This list of incidents serves to illustrate the seamanship of the tender crews. These are not rehearsed exercises but improvised solutions to problems that may be basically similar but are always different in detail. A combination of planning, quick thinking and brute strength are qualities often required of these ships' companies.

Navigating amongst the dangerous banks and rocks of our coasts, masters of lighthouse tenders are apt to come face to face with misfortune and disaster many times. Because of constantly plying their trade in the Narrow Seas their fund of experience is constantly growing, as is that of their officers and crews. It is frequently used for the benefit of others.

On fire in the Dover Straits, the coaster *Eleanora H* was calling for assistance early on 16th October, 1974. T.H.V. *Patricia*, Commander P. C. V. Inman, arrived on the scene shortly after 01.00 together with several other ships. One, the British coaster *Frendo Spirit*, was already alongside and Inman despatched his First Officer, Mr T. A. Catesby, and a party of men to assist. Two launches were sent over with firefighting equipment and for ten hours Catesby and his party fought the blaze in the coaster's accommodation until, with additional assistance from other ships, the fire was brought under control. Two of the German ship's crew had already died and the remaining three were insufficient to tackle the blaze. The coaster with her undamaged cargo of sugar was finally towed into Dover by a tug from Gravesend.

Shortly after midnight on 27th February, 1976, T.H.V. *Siren*, Mr. R. M. Woodman, First Officer Commanding, was towing No. 20 lightvessel for the Tyne. Off Hartlepool a mayday was received and *Siren* diverted, shortening her tow to manoeuvre through a cluster of fishing boats to where the minehunter H.M.S. *Brereton* was badly holed. Also on the scene was the port auxiliary craft *Kinloss* and some other ships, including the Danish fishing vessel *Cyrano*, which had collided with *Brereton*. First Officer Milkins was sent over with a working party, collison timber and a pump, and the hole crudely repaired by Carpenter B. J. Dale. A U.S. helicopter arrived to lower sandbags into one of *Siren's* launches, and these were incorporated into the repair work. *Brereton* reached Hartlepool safely, as did *Cyrano*.

Less fortunate was Mr B. J. Collingwood, First Officer Commanding T.H.V. *Mermaid*, in October, 1972. Sent to survey the wreck of the Belgian trawler *Amelie Mathilde*, which had sunk off the Lincolnshire coast, the tender narrowly avoided a similar fate. Using sonar, *Mermaid* searched for the wreck in the early afternoon of the 24th. The boats were then sent off to carry out sweeps in deteriorating weather until dark. During the night *Mermaid* marked the clear side of the wreck herself, and at 07.45 the following morning the search resumed. At 08.50 one boat reported a peak sounding, and an hour later the foul area had been established and *Mermaid* circled the area with her sonar. Meanwhile the boats established a least depth over the wreck which gave Collingwood ample water to sweep *Mermaid* over the top with chains, to calculate an accurate "least depth". This manoeuvre is standard practice to determine how much water exists over a wreck before it is declared a danger to navigation and buoyed as such.

At 11.50 *Mermaid* lay stopped at right angles to the tide, her hands at the sweep chains. Forward and aft officers leaned outboard to see if, at the depth set, the chains fouled or swept clear. At 12.03 the engine room reported flooding. No contact had been felt, and the cause was thought to be a fractured pipe. Pumps were started, and a few minutes later a hole was discovered. Collingwood anchored and took precautionary action in case of abandonment. In the meantime the Chief Engineer, Mr J. Bray, reported the pumps were holding and the water would not reach *Mermaid's* propulsion motors, which were unprotected by a double bottom. At this news *Mermaid* was got under way and headed for the Humber. Great exertions were performed by 4th Engineer Penney to stem the inflow of water, which was coming from a small hole in a most inaccessible part of the engine room bilge. With all available pumps at work, arrangements were made for an emergency docking and at 20.30 that evening *Mermaid* was drydocked at Hull.

A six-inch diameter hole was found in her bottom, probably from a trawl boom, for no obstruction above the hull of the trawler was found the following day when *Patricia* arrived to complete the survey and lay two gas buoys on it.

This example demonstrates the extreme dangers of wreck locating and marking. At one period Trinity House seamen dispersed wrecks, but this work is usually contracted out today. Seamen divers used to be borne on the ships' books, but the 2s. 6d. (12½ p) that was allowed them has long been overtaken by more lucrative opportunities in the North Sea.

Wreck blowing had its humorous moments. A 2nd Officer landed at Sheringham from *Warden* to clear the beach of holidaymakers. His task was to blow the wreck of a Dornier aircraft just offshore which was a constant obstruction to fishermen. Enough tonite "to do the job thoroughly" was lowered and the resulting explosion showered the beach with debris. *Warden's* party beat a hasty and embarrassed retreat!

By far the most disastrous incident to occur in recent years was the "pile-up" of ships in the Dover Straits in early 1971. On the morning of Monday,

11th January, the Peruvian cargo ship *Paracas* collided with the tanker *Texaco Caribbean* and the latter blew in two. She sank close west of the Varne Bank, slap-bang in the middle of the outward-bound traffic lane, and immediately constituted a serious danger to navigation in the overcrowded Straits.

At Harwich T.H.V.'s *Siren* and *Ready* were mustering their crews when the depot telex machine began clattering in a perturbing series of messages. By 09.30 *Siren*, Commander A. Burnell, had loaded two wreck buoys and was proceeding from Harwich at her best speed. At 16.30 she anchored close to the reported position of the wreck and, despite failing daylight, both motor boats were lowered in an attempt to locate the wreck. A fresh south-easterly breeze hampered work but by darkness, although nothing positive had been found, surface detritus indicated that *Siren's* position placed her with the wreckage between her and the long tongue of the Varne. No prudent master, Burnell thought, would run between *Siren* and the Varne, particularly as North Foreland Radio was transmitting a constant stream of navigational warnings. *Siren* was therefore anchored exhibiting wreck marking signals to warn ships to pass to the west of her, away from the Varne Bank and into clearer water.

At 18.30 *Siren* had loaded another wreck buoy from *Vestal*, herself on passage to Cowes. Aboard *Siren* the anchor watches were set and the hands warned to get plenty of rest, since the following day was likely to be a long one. All went well and the officers and seamen were grabbing hasty breakfasts by 07.15. By 08.00, having briefed his two 2nd Officers, Burnell watched the men getting gear into the boats, and five minutes later they were both launched, operating on the extremes of visibility, which was under a mile.

Some time while this activity was taking place in the last hour of darkness the German cargo liner *Brandenberg* ran over the dangerous wreck at full speed, opened her bottom and sank immediately with tragic loss of life. Those who escaped were swept rapidly away from *Siren* and her boats by the tide. A confused situation now existed. Nobody at the time was possessed of the full facts. In some disastrously ironic way *Siren* had been unable to warn off *Brandenburg*, which had ignored her signals. She had acted more like her mythical namesake to the unfortunate Germans. Fishing boats down-tide of *Siren* began to rescue survivors and recover bodies and, intercepting radio traffic, Burnell began to sense something had gone wrong. After three hours his boats had completed a preliminary survey of the wreckage and by 11.15 two buoys had been laid. By noon *Siren* was manoeuvring round other patches of turbulence (unlike *Mermaid*, *Siren* had no sonar) and at 12.38 anchored close to the position now being reported as the last position of *Brandenburg*. The boats were sent off again but found nothing. Returning to the previous area he had been examining, Burnell soon discovered the *Brandenburg*, and this was confirmed when divers arrived from the cable ship *Dame Caroline Haslett*. Further investigations revealed the second part of the *Texaco Caribbean*, and

this was marked by dan buoy before darkness. Adjusting his position slightly, Commander Burnell marked the wrecks as he had the night before.

During the succeeding days *Siren* was joined by other tenders bringing hurriedly prepared wreck buoys to attempt to fence off the area. Despite copious navigation warnings and the provision of these buoys, ships were still coming perilously close to the wrecks and the dangers of further, as yet undetected, wreckage were paramount in the minds of Burnell (whose ship was in a hazardous position and compelled to remain there), the Superintendent at Harwich and the Elder Brethren in London. On 13th *Mermaid* was directed to proceed to the area "with all speed" for sonar operations.

Meanwhile *Siren* had been joined by H.M.S. *Lowestoft*, and the picture was now becoming clearer by courtesy of the frigate's anti-submarine sonar. The location of the three wrecks (the two parts of the tanker, and the *Brandenburg*) being established, by the morning of the 14th Commander Burnell was able to signal Harwich the position of four more buoys he proposed laying. *Patricia* joined *Siren*, and the Dutch rig *Orca* now arrived with a diving team to operate on behalf of the owners and insurers of *Brandenburg*. If this concentration of vessels was not enough, ships were still "passing to eastward of (*Siren*) dangerously close to wreckage despite warnings".

By 15.30 on the 14th the periphery of the dangerous area had been marked by six buoys in a diamond pattern. They were all green wreck buoys, the internationally recognised danger signal under the Lateral System of Buoyage.

On the 15th *Patricia* returned to Harwich and a salvage team began work on the wrecks. On passage back from Cowes *Vestal* fitted two radar reflectors on two buoys, *Siren* and *Mermaid* having expended their stock. On the evening of the 15th *Ready* arrived to do the same. That night *Siren* anchored at the up-Channel apex of the diamond with wreck-marking signals hoisted. Ships still tore down-Channel perilously close to the area, and the navigation warnings, signals and buoys had no apparent effect.

On the 16th the Folkestone Salvage Company had positively identified all wreckage and undertaken the dispersal agency on behalf of Trinity House.

During the days following the disaster Harwich Depot had been working flat out. Apart from the provision of the wreck buoys, No. 6 lightvessel had been painted green from trucks to waterline and modified to show a green light and wreck lights from a specially constructed yard. On 14th *Patricia* had laid her on station at the up-Channel apex of the buoys and *Siren* was relieved, returning to Harwich, while *Patricia* patrolled the area constantly warning ships off. *Mermaid* also left the area on the 15th. At the end of January *Siren* moved the lightvessel slightly, but her master continued to report ships passing terrifyingly close, and he and his crew were frequently at collision stations in anticipation of being sunk themselves.

Winston Churchill, as originally built, tied up to the new Royal Sovereign lighthouse about 1970, pumping oil and water to the tower. *BICC Limited*

It was now decided that an older lightvessel be prepared to relieve No. 6. All through February the men on No. 6 flashed warnings, fired signal rockets and maroons at rogue ships. On the 10th a Russian freighter actually penetrated the area, but crash stopped at the last moment. Other ships passed right through the area, some being stopped inside the complex of buoys. Late on the evening of the 27th what observers felt was inevitable occurred. Ignoring the lightvessel's warnings, the Greek cargo ship *Niki* entered the complex, struck the wreckage and sank. Ten bodies, including that of a woman, were recovered. The following morning *Vestal* was locating her broken hull.

It became apparent that news of this massive obstruction in the Channel was not getting through to ships leaving continental ports and that the standards of watch keeping were poor. Alarm signals, radio navigation warnings, wreck buoys and additional lightvessels were just not enough. Trinity House exerted itself and the old lightvessel was laid, not as a substitute for No. 6 but as an additional seamark. Extra buoys were added to the complex, almost sealing it off and a high-speed inflatable craft was loaned by the R.N.L.I., kept on No. 6 lightvessel and manned by volunteer seamen from the tenders. It says much for the Corporation's Service that these lightvessels were converted, painted and manned in so short a time. Visits were made to the scene by the Elder Brethren, various legal representatives and senior officials of the French lighthouse service. A special trip was made by *Ready* with the press corps.

The whole incident raised far-reaching questions. When the matter was debated in Parliament only twelve Members attended, but the buoyage authorities acted with more speed. Liaison between the European members of the International Association of Lighthouse Authorities (I.A.L.A.) improved and in 1977 the I.A.L.A. system of buoyage was introduced to European waters. It combined the Lateral and Cardinal systems of buoyage and was designed to remove the ambiguities that existed between countries, particularly in the matter of wrecks. Mr Striven's contentious wreck buoy has now disappeared.

The wrecks off Folkestone have now all been dispersed to a least depth of 70 feet at the lowest astronomical tide. Today there are no extra lightvessels or buoys in the area. Nevertheless, the episode was one more demonstration of the urgent need for international co-operation and control of shipping beyond the hard interests of trade so that pollution and environmental destruction should not be the inevitable cost of progress.

The 1970's were to be a period of great change in the Trinity House Service. The numbers of tenders were progressively reduced and the two-crew system of double manning introduced over a period of several years. In February, 1970, cracks were discovered in the boilers of T.H.V. *Alert*, Commander R. Dove. They were considered too expensive to repair and she left drydock on one boiler bound for Harwich to de-store. T.H.V. *Vestal* had been sent to escort her south from the Tyne, but this was more than *Alert's* engineers could stand. With the old ship's swan song singing in their ears they increased speed and left *Vestal* astern!

The loss of *Alert* initiated a period in which the various districts were re-organised. The dispositions of the tenders also underwent a number of changes. In 1973 the depots at Holyhead, Penzance and Great Yarmouth were down-graded to buoy depots and the coast was divided into East and West Coast Districts, meeting at the Isle of Wight. The tenders were regrouped. In 1966/7 *Patricia* had undergone a massive overhaul at her builder's yard, Smith's Dock, on the River Tees. Her ratings' accommodation had been modernised and expanded, her engines reconditioned and her bridge modified. She lost her lightsmen's accommodation but continued to be based at Harwich and used for inspection cruises every summer by the Elder Brethren.

Exploration and prospecting for oil and gas fields in the North Sea in the 1960's doubled the buoy stations north of Orfordness almost overnight. Well heads, rigs built and building, production platforms jutting with their strange utilitarian silhouettes from the turbulent grey wastes, all required marking. *Mermaid* bore the brunt of this phenomenal expansion and the Yarmouth buoy yard remains busy with the constant repair and preparations for many of these stations still in use.

Argus was laid up in Swansea and sold on 5th April, 1974, for £74,650 and the West Coast was then served by T.H.V.'s *Stella* and *Winston Churchill*,

Winston Churchill and *Mermaid* in the English Channel in 1979. *Mermaid* is unmodified, while *Winston Churchill* has been converted for helicopter operations.   *Ambrose Greenway*

based on the Swansea Depot. The transfer of the latter vessel left Cowes without a tender but intact for lighthouse administration. *Ready*, *Patricia*, *Siren* and *Mermaid* were based on Harwich, with the latter ship still substantially covering her old parish north of Orfordness. Following *Argus*, *Vestal* was sold for scrap for £35,869 on 24th July, 1975, having been laid up in Harwich for some time. On 16th May, 1978, the full transition to double manning having taken place, the tug *Ionia* arrived in Harwich to take T.H.V. *Ready* to Messrs Thomas Ward's shipbreaking yard on the Thames. She fetched a mere £29,402, and lay for a long time beside the river that had seen the first Trinity House steamer a century and a half earlier. She was the last steam vessel in service, the last to give credence to the now misnamed Steam Vessel Service of Trinity House.

One of her last tasks was the laying of the first I.A.L.A. buoy at the Sandgate station, not far from the site of the *Texaco Caribbean/Brandenburg/Niki* wrecks. The ceremony had an international flavour. *Patricia* accommodated a host of international observers and flew the flag of Captain M. B. Wingate, Deputy Master, and the two Trinity House tenders were accompanied by buoy tenders from the European countries that initiated the I.A.L.A. system in its first phase. From Dunkerque came the French *Emile Allard*, from Den Helder the impressive Dutch tender *Breveertien*, from Ostend the little *Zeearend*. It was a jolly occasion. In Dover the crews entertained one another, a precedent enjoyed by *Patricia* in 1973 when the German buoy tender *Walter Körte* visited

Under the author's command, *Winston Churchill* works with helicopter G-BATC off Lundy Island. *R. R. Roberts*

With the ship's company at the rail, Elder Brethren on the quarterdeck and Deputy Master's flag at the main, *Patricia* dips her ensign to H.M. The Queen and the Prince of Wales off Cowes in 1980.   *Flag Officer, Royal Yachts, Crown Copyright*

Dover and again in 1974 when *Patricia* visited Germany. Ironically *Patricia* secured at Heligoland where the once-British lighthouse is still in use.

In January, 1977, the South Coast District was expanded, though without a tender. But three years later T.H.V. *Stella* was transferred to Cowes and the Service settled into its current state.

One of the profoundest changes to be effected during this period and that which made reduction of the tender fleet possible was the phased introduction of helicopters. Initially intended to carry out the personnel reliefs of all Trinity House's offshore states, the helicopters took some years to become fully operational owing to the necessity of constructing helipads at some of the world's most isolated spots. It took an immense amount of labour to accomplish much of this, which was the major reason for the 1970's being a period of flux. The inelegant flat platforms that have appeared on lighthouses are in accord with the pragmatic principles of the age we live in. There is, however, an incongruity about them that argues with the aesthetic used by the towers' builders ever since Smeaton based his Eddystone on the bole of an oak tree.

The helicopter has relieved the tender crews of much tedious labour. It has also enabled the lightsman or keeper to be home quickly, and no-one deserves that more than he. But it is sad that the once familiar cry of "Boat away!" is less frequently heard off the wild and beautiful skerries and stacks of these sea-girt islands. It has been replaced by the air-rending clatter of the speedy "chopper" that sends the guillemots and razorbills in clouds from the cliffs. To the keeper the approaching helicopter is a symbol of release, a triumph of science over discomfort and delay. To the seamen on the tenders it was at first an intrusive

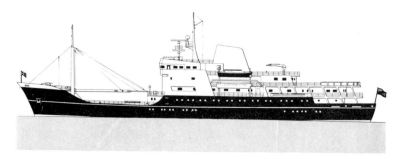

The third
Patricia.

threat to their traditional skills. A decade after the introduction of airborne reliefs of offshore stations the tender crews operate regular 'Vertreps', the vertical replenishment of lighthouses by under-slinging loads beneath the Bolkow M 105D helicopters on permanent charter from Management Aviation Ltd. To accomplish this all the *Mermaid* class ships have been fitted with flight decks over their sterns, and this new skill enables vast quantities of stores, building materials, oil and fresh water to be delivered rapidly in weather that would once have made delivery by boat nothing short of suicidal. Just as the motor boat extended the capability of the ship by ousting the pulling boat, so the helicopter has made commonplace what would once have been considered impossible. The gutting and automating of the Eddystone lighthouse was carried out entirely by this method.

In May, 1982, the old *Patricia*, after 44 years in service, was sold to German buyers and left Harwich under the alien hands of a "run crew". It was a sad moment for the handful of former crew members who lined the quay to watch her leave.

Her replacement entered service a month later. Known while building at Robb Caledon's Leith yard as Ship 530, she was named at a ceremony in the Thames as T.H.V. *Patricia* by the Countess Mountbatten of Burma in the presence of H.R.H. the Duke of Edinburgh, Master of Trinity House.

At 2,541 grt the third *Patricia* is the largest lighthouse tender ever built for the Corporation of Trinity House. She is 284 feet long, with a beam of 45 feet and draft of 14.6 feet. Her maximum speed is 14 knots, current being provided to her electric propulsion motors by six Ruston diesel generators. Her twin screws and bow-thruster are computer controlled when manoeuvring, automatically producing the correct thrust for the desired vector selected by joystick control on her bridge.

She is equipped with a battery of the latest navigational and communications systems, has a helicopter capability and a revolutionary buoy handling foredeck. Her 20-tonne SWL Speedcrane is capable of handling buoys of the largest class, while she has traditional towing gear. Her accommodation includes a spacious suite of rooms for Board members on their tours of inspection, and individual cabins for her crew.

The sophistication of a modern lighthouse tender is a far cry from the sloop of Mr Widgeon or Mr Poulter's yacht, yet the cause they serve remains substantially the same. But a ship can be no better than the men who man her. It remains to be seen to what degree they have altered over the years.

The third *Patricia* employing her "Speedcrane" at Harwich shortly after commissioning, 1982.
Trinity House

CHAPTER TEN

The Men

> "No matter how good the ship, its performance on the exacting Trinity House tasks depends on the skill of its commander, officers and ratings."
>
> Lloyd's List, 25th January, 1975

STEVENSON, on his visit to the Eddystone, summed up the qualities of the tender's crew as distinct from the qualities of the tender. The new vessel was fast, handy and well constructed. Its ancient and rather foolish crew were, in the observant eyes of the Scotsman, bordering on the incompetent.

The management of the cutter *Eddystone* was in sharp contrast to the work of the energetic Striven in *Antelope* and amply demonstrates that performance and efficiency go hand in hand with seamanship and ability.

Little can be discovered about the early conditions of employment in the sailing yachts. The men were theoretically free of the press gangs, some 200 exemptions being issued to Trinity House during the Napoleonic Wars for the men engaged in the buoyage service. Anxious naval captains were frequently given to unscrupulous behaviour when manning their ships. One of the reasons why Trinity House so rapidly manned the blockships at a time when the ten frigates were laid up for lack of men was that service aboard them was press-free.

In the balance sheets appended to Cotton's memoir to the Earl of Liverpool the amount paid out for the maintenance of lights, buoyage and beaconage is small: "Salaries and contingent expenses" being £5,765 15s. 11d. in 1805 rising to £8,644 1s. in 1815. These amounts included "salaries paid to Members of the Corporation filling offices requiring constant attendance, amounting to £1,090 per annum." Whether this included those of agents, crews and keepers is doubtful when the revenues are analysed. The gross takings for buoyage and beaconage in 1805 were some £6,426, to which must be added those for the lights which were some £48,000. However, the net takings on lighthouses and lightvessels were £22,729, so many running expenses were deducted at source. It is therefore likely that all agents' fees and the wages of those contracted by the agents were not included in the "salaries and contingent expenses", but that the upkeep of the London Yacht Establishment was. Mr Widgeon and Mr Poulter doubtless had their salaries included in the £1,090 annually disbursed, and these were probably in line with the agents' salaries of £30 per annum.

That there was an additional, presumably optional, payment is revealed by the Warden's minutes for 3rd January, 1805. Gratuities were paid to Mr John Poulter, Master of the Yacht, 30 guineas; Richard Govey, Mate, 20 guineas; John Stout, Steward, 15 guineas; William Stout, 2nd Mate, 10 guineas; and Isaac Pearson, Acting 2nd Mate, 5 guineas.

This is contemporary with Stevenson's note on the *Eddystone*.

"The Captain of the tender has 3 shillings per day, each of his men 2 shillings and 6 pence, and they find themselves in everything both at sea and on shore. The tender is well found in cordage and tackle, but has no bedding or conveniences of any kind in the cabin but what is found by the crew, and, as may be expected, this is as little as possible."

The manning of tenders at outports seems to have been at a minimal level, whether on the empirical Plymouth system or the more rational Ramsgate one. Striven's use of the lightsmen themselves started a precedent that died hard, although his cutter had a small standing staff of which he was commander.

The complement of the London Yachts was larger and permanent. They were heavy craft to handle and the act of buoy servicing is labour intensive. Their crews were probably in the region of 30 men. Their remuneration was probably no more than a few shillings a week at the end of the French wars. Certainly the end of that conflict marked the beginning of wholesale unemployment, during which wages remained low until Lord Liverpool's government fell. Nevertheless, employment in the Trinity Yachts was prestigious enough amongst the waterfront population of the Great Wen.

The 1836 Act and the introduction of steamers coincided with better social conditions and the beginning of a slow but steady rise in the prosperity of the labouring classes. By 1858 proper salary scales were laid down. A seaman earned £3 2s. 8d., a fireman £3 17s. per month; the coal trimmers the same as seamen, the cooks £3 13s. 8d. and the steward and carpenter £4 19s. There was then no bosun and the two petty officers were better off than the 2nd Mate, whose salary was £4. The mate received £6 and the master £12.

To attract the exponents of the new technology a first engineer earned the same as a master, a 2nd engineer the same as the mate. However, these rates included one shilling and six pence per day victualling which, for some reason, was paid to engineers only, the rest of the crew being victualled by Trinity House. Mr Jones, First Engineer of *Irene*, received 6s. 6d. per day plus his victualling whilst Mr Emerson, of *Argus*, received slightly less in victualling which presumably indicated less time at sea. At this time the master of the mysterious *Tortoise* received only £4 10s. per month and his seamen £2 15s., which suggests a distinct lack of parity with the new-fangled steamers.

By comparison the master of a lightvessel had £5 per month, plus £20 per annum house rent allowance. There were auxiliary staff attached to the tenders.

Weekend tender keepers were paid £2. 17s. 2d. per month and may have been retired seamen. They were allowed 1s. 6d. victualling a day. At Blackwall the old wooden wall *Africa* had no strutting post captain upon her deck but a grimy coal hulk keeper paid at £3 2s. 9d. a month! In the depots other essential staff laboured. A steam crane engineer received £3 17s., the lordly first blacksmith £8. 6s. 8d., his staff descending in strict precedence to 4 shillings a day for the 5th blacksmith.

Trinity House's catering was not of a very high standard, for in October, 1881, *Siren's* crew petitioned the Board to be allowed to victual themselves and a week or so later sanction was obtained from the Board of Trade for victualling payments to be made to all tender crews. Masters were allowed 3s. 9d. per day, mates and engineers 2s. 3d. and seamen 1s. 9d. This figure included beer and spirits allowance, which in 1891 amounted to three gallons a week for seamen. Self catering persisted until January, 1970.

By 1890 an incremental pay scale had been introduced. The master of a tender was paid £200 per annum on appointment, rising in ten years to £300. The First Engineer, having become a fairly common breed, rose from £144 to £162 over the same period. Mates were paid from £90 to £180, 2nd Mates £50

The foredeck is prepared as a tender approaches a wreck buoy, 1935.   *R. Dove*

rising to £82 and 2nd Engineers £124 rising to £132. The larger tenders now carried a 3rd Engineer at a flat rate of £102 per year.

Apprentices had also been taken on, being paid £18 4s. over a four-year period. It was never very popular except with boys intending to stay in the Corporation's Service, since the Board of Trade did not recognise time in light-house tenders as reckonable for foreign-going certificates.

The carpenter remained the senior rating on £66 18s. rising to £72 18s., while cooks, winch drivers, steam launchmen and coxswains received around £50 a year, senior fireman £55, seamen and coal-trimmers £43. Modest life assurance was provided for all personnel after probation. The ratings were also entitled to 2s. 6d. per month good-conduct money.

Life aboard tenders at this time was not particularly strenuous. They were run man o'war fashion at a pace today's management experts would consider ruinously lethargic. Uniform was provided by the Corporation and had to be worn for church if the vessel was at sea on Sunday. Seamen wore serge blouses and caps. The officers wore reefer jackets on weekdays, frock coats on Sundays and for ceremonial duties. Leather belts were worn, and though application was made to wear swords, like the Brethren, this was refused. The sword was still the hall mark of the "gentleman" and the tender officers, whatever apotheosis the Brethren had passed through in their careers, remained unequivocally of the "mariners". The frock coat was last worn in 1932, even by engineers in the engine room, and must have been quite a contrast with today's ubiquitously decomposing boilersuit!

The braid worn by officers derived from that of the Elder Brethren, which is developed from the decorated full cuff of the 18th century. The Elder Brethren wear the broad band of cuff lace below which three buttons and vestigial lace button holes complete the insignia. Originally the Superintendents wore only two bands, the tender masters one, below which were three plain buttons. Mates wore a similar pattern with thinner braid, 2nd Mates the buttons only. First Engineers wore a single gold stripe, 2nd's nothing at all. The early Service button depicted a paddle steamer surrounded by a garter bearing the words "Trinity Steam Service" and this was later replaced by the Corporation's arms and motto. Officers wore small-crowned caps with a cap badge of the Trinity lion and dagger, Superintendents and Masters having lace on their peaks. In 1907 an apprentice was fitted out with seven uniforms: two suits of canvas ducks, a blue guernsey and blue serge trousers, a bum-freezer jacket and trousers for Sundays, a pilot jacket and trousers for bridge watchkeeping and a great coat. For headgear, being neither fish nor fowl, he had both an officer's cap and a seaman's round hat plus a red wool night-cap! It was the Mate's duty to inspect the apprentices and keep them well kitted.

Percival Yeates joined in 1895. His first trip on *Irene* involved the towing of a lightvessel to Holyhead in bad weather. On their return they stopped at

Cowes, Yeates's home. He arranged for his brother to row out a hamper of food but *Irene* was under way when the laden dinghy appeared. Yeates rushed to the bridge to remonstrate with the captain, "Chuffer" Browne. "I don't remember what he said but I soon came off the bridge and we did not stop".

Later, aboard the paddle yacht *Vestal*, Yeates was on the bridge when buoy working. Captain Reading was shouting to the mate on the foredeck, who was having difficulty hearing above the clatter of the steam winch. "I went up alongside him and shouted too. You can imagine what happened, the crew and Mr Phillips, the Chief Officer, were laughing somewhat. The Captain told me to shut up and get off. I said 'I was trying to help you, sir'. That made him laugh, too, but I had a pretty good talking to—but it was kindly talk . . . ''

Another apprentice aboard *Argus* in 1908 at Yarmouth remembers a subterfuge of a crew under sailing orders. A cancellation of sailing delayed the ship a tide and the time thus gained could be put to good use. The night watch of a seaman and apprentice, having called the crew, repaired to the captain's house. Knocking at the door, the boy would look up at the bedroom window

M. J. Davison, Superintendent at Holyhead from 1879 to 1915.
Trinity House

where a respectably shrouded Mrs Captain would appear. Hidden under a tree in the garden the seaman would shake the trunk for all he was worth. "Morning ma'am", said the innocent face of the boy.

"Good morning, what's the weather?" The rustling of a high wind in foliage prompted the reply, "Fresh nor'easter, ma'am", lied the lad. Turning to consult her husband Mrs Captain would presently reply "Cancel steam!" and the deceitful duo would return triumphant to the ship, later greeting their commander with wide eyes and an explanation of a sudden moderation!

The larger ships had a full permanent crew, but up to 1914 the smaller *Warden* class carried only a skeleton, or standing, crew. Off-duty lightsmen made up the sea staff when buoy work was done, and this was always a source of irritation. In July, 1872, men of the London District lightvessels refused to sail on *Vestal*, stating they had done a hard day's work and would not go until the following morning. They were all on board *Vestal* except one who had resigned. A seaman from *Billow* had been substituted and the Blackwall superintendent, Captain E. W. Jones, urgently required instructions from London.

Mr. Johnson, Bosun of the second
Warden.   *R. Dove*

Again in September, 1906, the crew of the Dee lightvessel complained to the Brethren "re amount of work at Depot, complaining of long hours and difficulty of getting a day off during stay ashore; the complaint was respectfully made and moderate in tone, and, if true, deserves consideration". It was unquestionably true and the writer's incredulity is a little ingenuous.

This requirement for off-duty lightsmen "always to remain ready to render service in navigating the Tender, or in executing such duty ashore or afloat as shall attach to the District", was relaxed after 1918 to shore service in the Depot, except when a lightvessel had to be towed. By this time, due largely to the war, the tenders were always fully manned.

The uniform was also altered after the war. Straight cuff braid was worn and the buttons dispensed with. Superintendents wore four bands, masters three, mates two, with two-and-a-half after five years' seniority. 2nd mates wore a single stripe. When the third officer was introduced the 2nd officers had two and the 1st officers two and a half irrespective of seniority. Engineer officers wore similar braid with purple cloth backing. In 1960 because of titular embarrassment over the Captain of *Patricia* relative to the Elder Brethren all masters of tenders were officially designated "Commander". Later the

Lightsmen of the Shipwash lightvessel, 1900. The requirements for lightsmen to supplement the tender crews at outports went on until after the First World War.   *A. Gosling*

Second Officer and Coxswain prepare to lower the hack boat on board *Argus*. Note the turk's heads on the davit.   *R. Dove*

Corporation's crest was added to the officers' cuff lace. Warrants were also issued to all officers giving them statutory authority to implement the powers delegated to them through Trinity House under successive Charters and Acts of Parliament.

Prior to 1850 merchant shipping companies had not been obliged to have their officers formally qualified. The better class of passenger company took a leaf out of the navy's book and had their navigators examined by Trinity House. However in 1850 official and statutory certification was introduced by the Board of Trade, with which tender officers found they were unable to comply, and special arrangements were made by which they were certificated by a combination of examination by Trinity House in matters relating to the lighthouse service and by the Board of Trade in navigation.

No guarantee of a berth as 2nd mate on completion of his indentures was given to the apprentice. He could leave for the merchant service and reapply when a vacancy occurred or remain in the ships as a "retained apprentice" on a wage (in the 1930's) of £10 monthly, working as a seaman until a 2nd mate's berth fell vacant.

The restrictions on sea time and the Second World War destroyed the apprenticeship system. Since the 1920's an increasing number of officers had been recruited from the merchant navy, and after 1945 this practice became

general. In addition to Board of Trade certificates all tender officers take examinations in coastal pilotage at Trinity House, continuing a tradition of what must be one of the oldest professional examinations and leading directly back to Sir Thomas Spert, Master of the king's most powerful warship.

The 1902 Regulations, in which the term "officer" displaced the more traditional "mate", enumerate the syllabuses: A 2nd Officer was expected to understand the Uniform system of buoyage, Rule of the Road at Sea, local bye-laws of his District, the characters of all the lights, names of all the channels, reaches, headlands, shoals and dangers, the fairway courses, distances, depths and seamarks, and the lighthouse landings; a First Officer all the above on a more detailed level plus the anchorages on the District; while a Master had further to amplify the above and extend it to the whole coast. Knowledge of the tides was essential, and today the examination remains substantially the same. Officers attend Trinity House in a time honoured manner to demonstate that technology, having improved their conditions, has not materially affected their working environment. They, like their forbears Widgeon and Poulter, still use the old vocabulary that has the magic of incantation, Swatch and Gatway, Flat and Oaze, Spit, Tail and Voe, Stack, Skerry and Gore.

But to err is human and occasionally internal enquiries are held with all the formality of courts-martial. In September, 1904, *Siren*, entering Milford Haven bound for Neyland, struck the battleship *Triumph* at moorings off Weare Point. The officer commanding her was disrated. Another officer responsible for grounding the first *Patricia* was dismissed.

Opposite: Landing stores for Bardsey lighthouse from the *Beacon.*

Right: Seamanship at its most superb: moored head and stern, one of *Siren's* motor boats pumps oil and water to the Caskets lighthouse.
M. P. Lee

Of the ratings the carpenter was traditionally the senior, and he had charge of the deck in the absence of the officers. He was a highly valued member of the ships' company, combining all the talents of furniture maker, shipwright and blacksmith. The bosun, introduced in the 1920's, supervises the seamen, and the watchkeeping routine aboard lighthouse tenders is heavily dependent upon good quartermasters. Whilst the introduction of helicopters has reduced reliance upon boats, coxswains still have to be intimate with the tricky navigation round the isolated rock lighthouses.

Some degree of promotion through the hawse pipe was available. Mr Roskruge started as a lightvessel seaman and rose to become First Officer commanding *Ready* and Cardiff agent. In 1904 Coxswain Moss was promoted 2nd Mate of *Vestal*, but men were more frequently years in the same rank. The steward of *Vestal* in 1913 asked "if after 31 years' satisfactory service he could have an increase of pay".

By 1917 the war had increased food prices to such an extent that the ratings became disaffected. A meeting was held in November at Blackwall when they confronted Board members. The general mood seems to have been one of dissatisfaction grown out of the work of the Dover Patrol. Victualling in ports where the men were not known, soaring prices and the high wages paid to the wharf staff and workshop mechanics combined to unsettle the men.

There were other complaints, too, about uniform clothing and delays in its supply. In 1913 Mr Smith, carpenter of *Vestal*, couched his request in just that tone of reasonable deference that failed to conceal a waspish irritation.

"Smith . . . prays he may be supplied with an ordinary coat instead of the small round jacket now supplied, he complains of a serious hiatus between his coat and trousers when stooping, the Committee think this request reasonable."

The Service became a father and son affair, generations succeeding each other so that incidents like the loss of *Argus* hit families badly. The men were a hard-bitten lot. Conditions in the mess deck fo'c's'les were often foul and the food was not insipiring. Coal-fired steamships were notoriously dirty, and when coaling was carried out weekly it was not surprising that the air between decks was rank.

The ability of the crews of the tenders to deal with any eventuality that occurred, or occurs, in the course of their duties is the foundation of their professional worth. Much improvisation is the essence of their work and that

Seaman Rignal, lost with the *Argus* in 1940.   *R. Dove*

stimulation, missing increasingly from deep-water shipping, is still to be found in abundance aboard these ships. To some it is more than a living; one retired Superintendent quietly accomplished two solo Atlantic crossings. Though not a glamorous calling, it is one of the last strongholds of true seamanship, for the sea remains the same demanding taskmaster as ever.

On 11th January, 1940, T.H.V. *Vestal* was landing stores at the Eddystone. The weather was fresh but the boat lay at the landing when her stern anchor dragged. Within minutes the boat broached and was dashed against the rocks. 2nd Officer Gibbs and seamen Reynolds, Hammersley, Stephens, Wyatt and Trenoweth were drowned. It was wartime and the incident passed almost unnoticed, like the whole story of these ships. In October, 1676, the newly elected Master of Trinity House, Samuel Pepys, wrote to his brother "Why should we deny ourselves the credit and reputation justly due to us by omitting to publish it to the world . . . "

As long as Britain relies on the carriage of goods in ships off her coasts men will have to attend the seamarks that indicate the safe water of fairways. That "walle of England" has become a highway of trade, and where there is trade there is also toleration. So must the seas be kept safe "and then is England kepte by Goddes hande."

Selected Bibliography

Archives, Court Minutes, Committee Findings, Manuscript Notes, Returns etc, etc in the possession of Trinity House, London.

The Trinity House from Within, Captain Golding, Private publication.

The Trinity House of Deptford Strond, C. R. B. Barrett, Limited edition, Lawrence and Bullen, London, 1893.

The World's Lighthouses before 1820, D. Alan Stevenson, Oxford University Press, 1959.

English Lighthouse Tours of Robert Stevenson, Ed. D. Alan Stevenson, Thomas Nelson.

Memoir on the Origin and Incorporation of the Trinity House of Deptford Strond. Joseph Cotton, 1818.

The Floating Republic, Dobree and Manwaring, Pelican Books, 1937.

Trinity House, Commander Hilary Mead, Sampson Low.

A History of Yachting in Pictures, Peter Heaton, Tom Stacey Ltd, London, 1972.

Royal Yachts, Paymaster Commander G. M. Gavin R.N., Rich and Cowan, London, 1932.

Life on a Lightship, Arthur O. Cooke, Henry Froude, Hodder and Stoughton.

Yachting, Badminton Library, article by R. T. Pritchett, Longmans Green and Co.

The second *Warden* as Swansea tender in the 1930s.

E. C. Scott

Appendix

ENGLISH LIGHTHOUSE TENDERS 1724-1982

Name	Tonnage	Dates in service	Remarks
Trinity Sloop	—	1742-c1770	
Trinity Yacht	—	c1770-1788	
Trinity Yacht	100	1788-1828	John Poulter's yacht
Buoy Yacht	—	c1780-1828	
Argus(?)	100	1791-1827	
Zadora	c120	1828-1838	
Vigilant	30.5	1819-c1850	Littlehampton based
Betsey	38.5	1818-1842	Based Littlehampton and Blackwall
Wells Tender	60	c1789-1827	Name possibly *Dudgeon*
Dudgeon	62	1827-c1856	
Yarmouth Tender	60	1785-1820	
Yarmouth Survey Tender	20	c1785-1820	
Diligent	60	1820-1839	
Trinity Buoy Yacht	94	1821-1856	Stationed at Great Yarmouth
Eliza	51	1833-1856	
Yarmouth	60	1826-	
Antelope	—	c1790-1839	
Lyra	67	1839-1865	
Sunk	61	1826-	All above rigged as cutters
Charon	—	1827-1853	Schooner, possibly steam engined in later life.
Eddystone	—	? -1811	Cutter
Eddystone	36	1811-1846	Cutter
Scilly	47	1827-1834	Cutter
Billow	—	c1834-c1872	
Diligent	50	1845	Possibly pilot cutter
Tortoise	—	1840-1858	
Wolf	92	1862-1883	Converted to lightvessel sold 1898. Originally schooner rigged.
Solva	—	c1860-1875	Steam Tug
Satellite	67	1840-1865	Cutter
Mermaid	76	1865-1897	Sold 1902 Schooner rigged and last sailing tender.
Triton	105	1865-1902	Sister to *Mermaid* converted to steam.

STEAM TENDERS

Vestal	173	1835-1853	Steam Paddle Schooner
Beacon	112	1837-1862	Steam Paddle Schooner

Argus	158	1840-1858	Steam Paddle Schooner
Irene	271	1852-1881	Steam Paddle Schooner
Vestal	343	1855-1900	Steam Paddle Schooner
Argus	331	1856-1910	Steam paddle converted to screw steamer
Beacon	262	1862-1890	Steam Paddle Schooner
Galatea	507	1868-1890	Steam Paddle Schooner
Alert	144	1869-1913	Screw steamer
Arrow	192	1869-1884	Specially built for lighthouse con-
Hercules	191	1870-1893	struction work in Far East.
Stella	176	1875-1927	
Siren	421	1878-1921	
Ready	119	1883-1926	
Warden	246	1884-1930	
Satellite	242	1886-1926	
Irene	543	1890-1915	Lost by mine
Mermaid	293	1897-1935	
Vestal	576	1898-1938	
Triton	234	1901-1935	
Argus	653	1909-1940	Lost by mine
Alert	700	1911-1917	Lost by mine
Jeria	—	1917-1921	Converted trawler
Alert	793	1920-1944	Lost by mine
Patricia	793	1920-1947	Ex Yacht *Miranda* later renamed *Vestal* (1938)
Satellite	491	1924-1961	
Beacon	490	1925-1960	
Warden	828	1929-1959	
Strathearn	683	1935-1941	Lost by mine First diesel ship
Reculver	683	1935-1940	Lost by mine, Diesel ship
Patricia	1116 (1072)	1938-1982	Diesel-electric yacht
Triton	680	1940-1963	Converted Trawler
André Blondell	481	1940-1946	Taken over by T.H. after Fall of
Georges de Joly	481	1940-1946	France.
Discovery II	1036	1940-1947	Loaned by Min of War Transport, then to Irish Lights, returned to use as a research vessel until 1954
Barmouth	750	1946-1949	Loaned by Admiralty as replace-
Barndale	750	1946-1947	ment for French vessels
Alert	1527	1946-1970	Building as H.M.S. *Bullseye*, taken over on stocks.
Vestal	1918	1947-1975	
Ready	1920	1947-1977	Last steam ship in service
Argus	1918	1948-1974	
Mermaid	1425	1959 onwards	Diesel-electric ''class'' ship
Siren	1425	1960 onwards	
Stella	1425	1961 onwards	
Winston Churchill	1430	1964 onwards	
Patricia	2541	1982 onwards	

General Index

Illustrations in bold type

INDEX OF SHIPS

INDEX

WARSHIPS & ROYAL YACHTS

OTHER VESSELS